LINDLEY J. STILES
Professor of Education in Interdisciplinary Studies
Northwestern University
ADVISORY EDITOR TO DODD, MEAD & COMPANY

CLINICAL EXPERIENCES IN TEACHING

FOP THE STUDENT TEACHER OR INTERN

CLINICAL EXPERIENCES IN TEACHING FOR THE STUDENT TEACHER OR INTERN

EDGAR M. TANRUTHER

INDIANA STATE UNIVERSITY

DODD, MEAD & COMPANY

NEW YORK   1970

Sixth Printing

Library of Congress Catalog Card Number: 67-16217
Printed in the United States of America

EDITOR'S INTRODUCTION

Learning to teach requires practice—with professional help. Student teaching and various forms of internships are the ways in which systematic practice under clinical conditions has been provided to those preparing to teach in elementary and secondary schools. Whatever the formal arrangements for supervised practice, experts in teacher education and experienced teachers in the field consider two kinds of assistance to be indispensable. One is the personal, first-hand guidance that is provided by supervisory personnel in schools and colleges; the other is the independent scholarship that is made possible by the availability of good professional literature.

The professional supervisor and the textbook are interdependent in helping the student teacher or intern to develop skill in teaching. College supervisors and supervising teachers in elementary and secondary schools find their work made more effective by the use of a good textbook to guide and reinforce first-hand instruction. The student in preparation benefits from access to a reference that reaches beyond the local situation. A need of both supervisor and prospective teacher is for a synthesis of professional knowledge drawn from both the successful experience of good teachers and carefully planned research.

This book is unique in its approach, content, and usefulness. It deals with the practical problems that confront beginning teachers—and it treats each in realistic terms that are easily understandable to the novice. Those in charge of programs to prepare teachers, in the various subject fields and at differing levels, as well as prospective teachers themselves, will find a double use for the wealth of material incorporated. The book will serve both as a textbook and reference guide to provide basic and comprehensive understanding of the various components of teaching and the techniques of perfecting professional skills.

v

A special strength of this book is the instruction it provides to the student teacher or intern in the many details, procedures, and relationships that are not commonly treated in textbooks of this type. The author has drawn on his own vast experience as a director of student teaching and internships and on that of supervisors and classroom teachers who have served in such programs, as well as the ideas of thousands of students-in-preparation. The suggestions offered have been verified in practice in a variety of situations, in different types of schools—urban, suburban, town, and rural—throughout the United States.

Dr. Edgar M. Tanruther has long been recognized as an expert in his field. His efforts to focus attention on practical ways to improve the clinical experiences of prospective teachers have won support on a broad scale and he stands out among those who have dedicated their professional careers to leadership in this area of teacher education.

LINDLEY J. STILES

PREFACE

Each year large numbers of prospective teachers are involved in clinical situations in schools as student teachers or interns. The internship is being introduced in an increasing number of teacher education institutions with the result that some individuals participate in both student teaching and the internship. This book is directed to the student teacher or intern preparing to teach in an elementary or secondary school. In the preparation of this volume, the author was aware that the student teacher or intern will usually have completed, or be enrolled in, courses in psychology or methods of teaching and that he is a very busy person while working in an elementary or secondary school. The purpose of this book is to provide pertinent, concise, and helpful information. It is much more complete than a handbook might be and yet not so comprehensive and detailed as to be difficult to use.

Although written primarily for the prospective teacher as he works in a school situation, much that is included will be useful to those most directly responsible for his guidance—the supervising teacher and the college supervisor. The first year teacher will also find the volume of value to him.

This book focuses upon the roles and responsibilities of the prospective teacher through the period which begins with his thoughts about plans for student teaching or the internship and ends with his establishment in the profession of teaching—usually the first or second year as a full-fledged teacher. Part I is intended to help the student prepare for profitable clinical experiences and deals with the resources which the novice may utilize in his preparation for teaching—getting acquainted with the situation, understanding roles and relationships, and working as a member of a team. Continuing opportunities for growth, both in and out of the classroom, are considered in Part II.

Part III is written to aid the prospective teacher in obtaining a suitable position, in planning for the first year, in developing increasing competency, and in strengthening the teaching profession.

The attention of the prospective teacher is directed to the importance of working toward self-improvement while also being assisted by others. He is encouraged to aid the pupils he teaches in acquiring a similar attitude about their development. Quotations by student teachers and interns, examples, illustrations, and lists of specific suggestions appear throughout the book to make it practical and to help him accomplish this goal. The summary at the end of each chapter provides a concise review to assist the reader in making content useful. In addition to numerous helpful references cited throughout the book, lists of "Useful References" at the ends of chapters are included to help the reader extend his thinking beyond this volume. They are for the most part taken from recent publications, and they represent the best thinking in professional education and other fields. A list of references selected to aid the supervising teacher and college supervisor appears in the Appendix.

This book has been made possible through the assistance of many people. The author is indebted to the student teachers, supervising teachers, college supervisors, and other teacher educators with whom he has been privileged to work over a period of years. From them has come the inspiration to work toward improved programs for the preparation of teachers.

Lindley J. Stiles, advisory editor to Dodd, Mead & Company, made helpful suggestions for the improvement of the outline for the book and important contributions to the development of the manuscript. Dr. William E. Engbretson, Dean of the School of Education, Indiana State University, when the manuscript was prepared, gave support and encouragement to the author. Gratitude is expressed to others who were colleagues at Indiana State University when the outline for the book was developed. The following persons read and criticized the outline: Dr. Harriet Darrow, Mr. Joe Hal Miller, Dr. R. Duane Peterson, Dr. Donald

M. Sharpe, and Dr. Otto J. Shipla. Mr. Russell P. McDougal, Director of Audio-Visual Education, read and made helpful suggestions for the portions of Chapter 7 dealing with audio-visual aids. Mrs. Mitchell Thomas read the manuscript and assisted with the mechanical aspects of its preparation. Thanks are also expressed to others who read the outline and made suggestions for its improvement. They include Dr. William A. Bennie, Coordinator of Professional Laboratory Experiences, University of Texas; Dr. Robert Hayes, Dean of Teachers College, Marshall University; Dr. George Hollister, Professor of Education, University of Wyoming; Dr. Alfred C. Moon, Executive Secretary, The Association for Student Teaching; Dr. Alex F. Perrodin, Professor of Education, University of Georgia; and Dr. Graham Pogue, Director of Student Teaching, Ball State University. Dr. Don Davies, Executive Secretary of the National Commission on Teacher Education and Professional Standards, made helpful suggestions relating to internships.

Appreciation is expressed to authors, editors, and publishers for the use of materials and excerpts from their publications. Acknowledgment of such permissions is made at appropriate places throughout the book.

Most of all, the author is indebted to his wife, Evelyn, who has been a constant source of encouragement to him in this project. She has not only tolerated neglect while the manuscript was in preparation but has read it in its entirety and has made numerous helpful suggestions.

EDGAR M. TANRUTHER

CONTENTS

Development; WORKING FOR AN IMPROVED PROFESSION OF
TEACHING. MAINTAINING CONDITIONS FOR WHOLESOME
PERSONAL LIVING: Maintaining Good Physical and Mental
Health; Managing Personal Finances; Living as a Person
and with a Sense of Well-Being. SUMMARY. USEFUL
REFERENCES.

TERMINOLOGY

To clarify meanings, the following standardization of terminology to identify different aspects of the teacher's preparation is employed throughout this book.

Teacher Education Program. The total college program required for prospective teachers, including courses in general education, subject fields to be taught, and the professional sequence.

Professional Sequence. The portion of the collegiate program of preparation for teaching that includes the professional (education or pedagogical) courses and requirements. Included are two areas of study: (1) study in formal courses in such education fields as history, philosophy, and sociology of education, as well as educational psychology; (2) methods and clinical experiences in teaching.

Clinical Experiences. Supervised experiences provided prospective teachers, including observation of pupils and schools, participation in educational programs, and clinical practice.

Clinical Practice. A period of student teaching or internship in which the prospective teacher is given opportunities to practice under supervision the various processes and responsibilities of teaching. Ideally opportunities are provided to analyze and evaluate teaching performance and to develop teaching skill through conceptualizing teaching.

Student teaching is a period of supervised induction into teaching, scheduled usually during the fourth year of college study as a part of a bachelor's degree program. Organizational arrangements vary from assigning the student to help instruct a class in an elementary or secondary school for one hour a day for an academic year or for a half-day at a time for a semester, to full-time daily instruction for a period of six to eighteen weeks.

The full-time pattern, now widely used, is frequently called the "block semester" since it necessitates blocking off and integrating a semester of college courses to make possible full-time student teaching.

Internship is a period of full-time, supervised clinical practice, lasting not less than a semester and frequently for a year, that may be an alternative or subsequent requirement to student teaching. The internship usually differs from student teaching in the rate of assumption and range of teaching responsibilities. Such clinical practice usually carries with it an official appointment to the faculty of a school system for which a salary is paid. An intern license to teach is usually required. Typically, the school system providing intern stations assumes joint responsibility with the preparing institution for organizing internship programs, for offering a seminar concurrently with the clinical practice, and for providing supervision for interns.

Clinical Station.   The classroom situation to which a student teacher or intern is assigned for supervised clinical practice through an arrangement between a preparing institution and a school system.

College Supervisor.   A faculty member of a teacher education institution who assumes responsibility for the clinical practice of student teachers or interns in particular subject fields of the secondary school or for the elementary school level. It is inclusive of a variety of titles in general use, including "Student Teaching Supervisor," "Intern Supervisor," or "Intern Consultant," as well as "Consultant to Supervising Teachers" and "Team Teaching Consultant." A person holding such an assignment usually is a specialist in a subject field and/or level of school instruction who frequently teaches methods courses as well as supervising the clinical practice of prospective teachers.

Supervising Teacher.   A teacher in an elementary or secondary school in charge of the clinical station. Responsibility for the day-by-day supervision of the work of the student teacher or intern is assumed by this person. An older title for the person performing this type of function was "Critic Teacher." In programs that provide for the prospective teacher to become a member of an instructional team, the "Team Leader" usually assumes this responsibility.

Laboratory School. A school maintained and controlled by a teacher education institution to provide clinical experiences for prospective teachers and research and innovation to improve schools.

Coordinator of Clinical Experience. The teacher education staff member who organizes and coordinates the institution's total program of clinical experiences. Another commonly used title for this position is "Director (or Coordinator) of Student Teaching." Such an individual is responsible for negotiating with school systems for clinical stations, for admitting and assigning students to clinical practice, and for leadership in evaluating and improving the program.

PART ONE
PREPARATION AND RESOURCES FOR CLINICAL PARTICIPATION

CHAPTER ONE
PLANNING FOR TEACHING

Most prospective teachers anticipate their clinical preparation with eagerness and enthusiasm and, no doubt, with some apprehension. Such feelings are natural. They reflect the desire to succeed as well as a realistic evaluation of the complexities of successful teaching.

Achieving professional competence as a teacher requires help —even for the most capable and most promising candidates for teaching. Clinical practice under supervision is designed to supply the various kinds of assistance needed. This chapter provides an overview of clinical practice as it is offered in most institutions and includes suggestions to help the student prepare for profitable and successful experiences in learning to teach.

THE VALUE OF CLINICAL EXPERIENCE

Clinical experience is an essential part of the preparation for every profession. Until professional preparation was made a part of the college or professional school curriculum, the apprenticeship was the primary means of preparing for a profession. When the various professions established scientific and scholarly institutions, they retained clinical practice as a required final phase of preparation.

Over the past century, as programs to prepare teachers for elementary and secondary schools have been lengthened and formalized, controversy about how teachers should be educated has increased. The conflict has centered on the amount of professional preparation, as opposed to specialization in the liberal arts and subject fields, that should be included in college programs. Throughout the debate, however, support for the clinical experience has remained strong from both critics and supporters of the professional phase of teacher education programs.

The best testimony to the value of clinical experience comes from teachers themselves. Beginning teachers typically rate this part of their preparation as more valuable than any other—including liberal arts courses and those in fields of specialization. Similarly, teachers of long experience attest that first-hand supervised observation, participation, and practice in teaching are essential to the development of professional teachers. Furthermore, in selecting teachers school administrators give a high priority to the level of success achieved during clinical experience.

The importance of clinical experience to the prospective teacher has been emphasized recently by Dr. James Bryant Conant, former President of Harvard University, after a two-year study of teacher education.

As we have seen, the one indisputably essential element in professional education is practice teaching. . . . The state should provide financial assistance to local boards to insure high-quality practice teaching as part of the preparation of teachers enrolled in either private or public institutions.[1]

Other authorities on teacher education have stressed the fact that the more real clinical experience is, the greater its value. Typical of their views is the following statement by two distinguished leaders in the field of teacher education, Professors Stratemeyer and Lindsey, of Teachers College, Columbia University:

Future generations of America's children will be guided in their school experiences by college students currently preparing to teach. The quality of the educational opportunity available to these children will depend to a large degree upon the kind of teachers our colleges prepare now. While many factors contribute to the development of skillful and artistic teachers, few are more important than the firsthand contacts with children and youth in school and community situations which are provided by teacher education programs.[2]

[1] James Bryant Conant, *The Education of American Teachers* (New York: McGraw-Hill Book Company, Inc., 1963), pp. 142, 211.
[2] Florence B. Stratemeyer, and Margaret Lindsey, *Working With Student*

TYPES OF CLINICAL EXPERIENCE

Student teaching (see "Terminology") has for years been the most common pattern of clinical experience for prospective teachers. Recently, however, the internship has become more prominent, particularly in those institutions that offer Master of Arts in Teaching programs. Some institutions offer, and some require, both types. When both are required, student teaching precedes the internship.

Student Teaching

Wide variation prevails among teacher education institutions as to the characteristics of student teaching programs. A few colleges and universities offer such preparation in on-campus laboratory schools, the original facilities for most clinical experience. However, a growing concern for reality in the clinical situation, as well as expanding enrollments of prospective teachers, have led to increasing use of off-campus schools—both public and nonpublic—as settings for first-hand experience for prospective teachers.

The amount and distribution of time devoted to student teaching also varies from institution to institution. One significant trend in recent years is toward assigning student teachers for full-time work in schools for extended periods, e.g., all day for six or more weeks. Such arrangements permit concentration on learning how to teach. Engaging in clinical experience for an hour a day or for a half-day, while devoting the remaining time to other college courses, is an older pattern for student teaching that still prevails in some institutions.

Cooperative arrangements between preparing institutions and local school systems range from informal, year-to-year agreements to legal, long-standing contracts that specify the responsibilities of the partners in teacher education. Supervising teachers

Teachers (New York: Bureau of Publications, Teachers College, Columbia University, 1958), p. v.

(see "Terminology") may or may not be compensated for their assistance by released time, money, or perquisites such as the waiver of tuition fees. When an honorarium is provided by the college or university, it most likely represents only a token of appreciation rather than adequate payment for services rendered. The honorarium varies for different institutions; thus, a supervising teacher may receive different stipends from two or more preparing institutions for almost identical supervisory assistance to student teachers.

Other differences that prevail with respect to arrangements for student teaching relate to amount of supervision, division of supervisory responsibilities between college supervisors and supervising teachers, amount of credit awarded, and required experiences.

Such divergent practices may well be confusing to both student teachers and those responsible for student teaching programs. However, most leaders in teacher education oppose standardization of requirements for clinical practice because of differences that prevail in philosophy, size, type, and location of institutions, as well as the availability of resources in local schools.

Internship

Efforts to improve and extend the clinical experiences of prospective teachers have resulted in the development of the internship in many institutions. Originally, the internship was viewed as a post-student teaching opportunity. Its primary purpose was to orient the beginning teacher to a full-time teaching assignment. Early programs were often initiated by school systems and were viewed as a part of the beginner's probationary period. More recently, the internship has been developed by teacher education institutions as an alternative to student teaching. The key objectives have been to place greater emphasis on the apprenticeship aspects of teacher education, to give clinical experiences more reality, and to help the prospective teacher conceptualize teaching.

The operation of internship programs requires close cooperation among colleges and school systems and the state educational agency. The placement of an intern in an assignment requires long-range planning, since the school system must provide a clinical station and college officials must match the intern with the assignment. School systems have shown increasing willingness to participate in internship programs, despite the amount of extra work involved, because of the already demonstrated value of such plans in the preparation of good teachers. Most state departments of public instruction, whose responsibility it is to lead in the improvement of teacher education and to license teachers, support the establishment of internship programs. Some help to coordinate intern assignments made by different colleges. A few states, including California, Michigan, New York, Oregon, and Wisconsin, issue temporary teaching certificates to interns.

Advantages claimed for the internship over more traditional programs of clinical experience have been summarized by McCuskey.

For the learner they provide:

1. A longer period of time in which to achieve scholarly and practical competence
2. Recognition of his status as a learner during initial periods of practice
3. Increased opportunities to integrate theory and practice under the guidance of both theoreticians and practitioners
4. Increased opportunities for participation in professional responsibility outside the classroom
5. Opportunity to participate in the life of the community
6. Financial assistance during the professional period

The potential advantages of these internship plans to schools and colleges include:

1. Built-in avenues of cooperation for preparation and follow-up
2. Time for planning and evaluation in the basic load
3. Addition of research specialists to staffs
4. Up-grading of staff through participation in research and in two-way consultation and participation in both institutions.[3]

[3] Dorothy McCuskey, "Internships," Association for Student Teaching, *Teacher Education and the Public Schools,* Fortieth Yearbook (Cedar Falls, Iowa: The Association, 1961), p. 92.

OPPORTUNITIES FOR LEARNING IN
CLINICAL PRACTICE

During the academic part of the preparation the prospective teacher is primarily a student and, as such, can assume a more or less passive role. Even aggressive individuals and highly creative persons find limitations to the leadership and responsibilities that students can assume in the academic life on campus. The teacher, in contrast, must give active direction to the learning of pupils. Planning, making decisions, evaluating, counseling—all are daily activities of those who instruct.

During his clinical practice the prospective teacher has a unique and challenging opportunity to lead a double life. At the same time he is both a college student learning from others and a teacher responsible for teaching others. This dualism is characteristic of the life of a scholar-teacher. Hence, the student entering into clinical practice is beginning a type of behavior that will be characteristic of his professional career.

Prospective teachers who sense the vital interrelationships between learning and teaching will find in clinical practice new experiences which will help them to learn and to apply knowledge. Observation of supervisors, as well as of other teachers and professors, takes on greater meaning when one anticipates moving in and out of the teacher role. The chance to test one's readiness to teach under the watchful and sympathetic eye of the college supervisor or supervising teacher helps to build confidence. Availability of advice, even after full-time teaching has been undertaken, helps to eliminate weaknesses and to generate creative ways to solve the daily problems that confront every teacher. In short, supervised clinical experiences can set the pattern for professional performance that continues to accent both scholarship and teaching.

Bridge from Theory to Practice

Whether the clinical experience is provided by a program of student teaching or by internship, or both, the purpose is the same—to provide a bridge from theory to practice. Of necessity, preparation for teaching prior to the clinical experience is academic in nature—in general education courses, in subject fields or areas of specialization, and in professional courses. Success of the student during this period of scholarly development is vital to later success in teaching. Good academic scholarship, however, is no guarantee that instructional competence will result. It remains for the program of clinical experience to help the scholar become a teacher. Many scholars, as every college student is well aware, have never crossed the bridge to successful teaching. Yet with proper help in a program of clinical experience most could have done so.

Clinical experience, as Dr. Conant and others have observed, is the test of all that has gone before. It gives the prospective teacher the opportunity to synthesize all he has learned and to translate it into professional skill. Effectiveness in the clinical program will be increased if the student sees the whole of his preparation as a sequence of different but related educational emphases. His clinical experiences should be a part of, not something apart from, the total program of preparation for teaching.

Skill in Teaching

Few prospective teachers, whether they are college seniors or graduate students, approach casually the assignment of learning to teach. All have observed teachers and teaching throughout elementary and secondary school and college. Whatever their reactions to individual teachers may have been, they are not likely to have been convinced that teaching is easy. Some teacher candidates, no doubt, will have developed a yearning to try their own skill, to experiment with different teaching procedures—to do a better job than some teachers they have observed. Others may be apprehensive, even doubtful, about their ability to cope with a complicated classroom situation.

One should not expect his first efforts in teaching to match the skill of good teachers he has known. This point should be remembered, especially by the individual who may be working in an inner-city "slum" school or with underprivileged pupils. In such situations the skill of even superior experienced teachers is tested.

Skill in teaching develops slowly and often painfully, as it does in any other complex undertaking. "Practice" may not make one a "perfect" teacher, but certainly one cannot hope to achieve competency in teaching without considerable practice. Practice and experimentation with a variety of methods and with the guidance of a capable and experienced teacher can help one develop teaching skill.

Understanding Children and Youth

A professional person needs an understanding of those he serves. Close association with pupils over an extended period of time provides opportunities for child study. One can observe the range of abilities that is found in every classroom. Such differences become significant as background for studying individual personalities. Knowledge of the socioeconomic status of pupils can help the prospective teacher to understand them better. A study of cumulative records brings to light pertinent information about the history, performance, problems, and accomplishments of each individual, as well as significant characteristics of the classroom group. Home visits and other contacts with parents help one to understand family background and its influence upon individual behavior and achievement.

For the capable observer, opportunities abound to learn how individual differences are identified and ways to provide for such traits in a program of classroom instruction. The teacher can find ways to help the well-adjusted pupils and to make special provision for pupils who have difficulty in adjusting to classroom living. The alert teacher will take advantage of every situation, formal and informal, to increase his understanding of students as a basis for providing appropriate professional service.

Knowledge of Schools

Day-to-day work in a school makes it possible to learn how a specific school is organized, how it functions, and how it is related to the total school district.

The prospective teacher can understand all schools better by discovering how the one in which he works is organized. He can learn, for example, how the elementary, junior high, and senior high schools are organized and how these three units are integrated. He can discover how the central office is staffed and how its staff members work with the principal and teachers in a specific building.

The student teacher or intern can learn much about school policies by observing how they are formulated and carried out. He has opportunity to observe how newly employed teachers are oriented and how their unique contributions are utilized to improve teaching and learning in the school. He can study school policies on such aspects of teachers' welfare as absences, sick leave, and retirement. He can gain some understanding of school policy with regard to admission, retention, acceleration, and promotion of students. Understanding school policy relating to in-service education of teachers can be helpful in formulation of plans for professional growth. The prospective teacher will also find it useful to learn how unwritten policies gain acceptance and come to influence the operation of schools.

Professional Objective

Most people who have pursued a teacher education program throughout a college career probably believe that they will enjoy teaching and be successful in the classroom. However, neither they nor those who may have turned to teaching late in their college program can be certain of their interest or success in teaching until they have spent time in the classroom with pupils. One young woman expressed her genuine interest in teaching after spending several weeks in the classroom as a student teacher when she wrote, "I am discovering that I love teaching as much as I loved going to school."

Working as a student teacher or intern will help the individual to determine whether teaching requires more or less hard work than he had imagined. One capable intern was surprised to discover that much more out-of-school time was required to prepare for teaching classes than he had anticipated. Another, who had worried about his ability to maintain good classroom behavior, discovered that as a result of learning a great deal about each individual in his group and of thorough daily and long-range planning he had very little trouble with discipline. In commenting on his experience in student teaching one individual said, "You get a different outlook on the role of the teacher when you are teaching on your own than when you are just reading about teachers and their work."

PREPARATION FOR CLINICAL ASSIGNMENTS

Everything the prospective teacher studies in college may be thought of as preparation for the clinical assignment and, ultimately, for teaching. Nevertheless, specific steps taken just prior to his entry into clinical practice will increase his chances for a good beginning.

Scholastic Background

The good teacher possesses a breadth of knowledge in many fields, is well informed in his field of specialization, and is skilled in the art of teaching. A teacher needs to help pupils to discover relationships in the subject-matter presented to them; he cannot succeed in doing so unless he understands these relationships himself.

During college years the student has been enrolled in numerous courses, has taken work in various departments, and has been taught by many different instructors. The important task of bringing together the knowledge acquired, of understanding relationships between fields of knowledge, and of achieving integration in his own thinking can only be done by the student himself. Through introspection and, where possible, by conferring with the adviser, the coordinator of clinical experience, the college supervisor and the supervising teacher, the prospective teacher can assess his degree of adequacy in general education, in his field of specialization, and in his readiness for teaching.

Personal Orientation

In planning for work in a school, as for any new venture, the prospective teacher cannot anticipate in detail the experiences he will have or the many variables that will be part of his working environment. Fortunately, he can learn from the experiences of others about the kind of preparation that will prove helpful. The following suggestions for personal preparation for a clinical assignment have been obtained from individuals who met with success as student teachers or interns.

Time for the job. Success in any venture is largely dependent on how time is used. Success in teaching, particularly, requires wise and careful investments of personal time.

Every college student is familiar with the treadmill of academic life. Most of the scheduling is controlled by the class bell. Only out-of-class time is at the student's disposal. It thus comes as somewhat of a surprise to many who are preparing to teach in elementary and secondary schools that scheduling of time is even more pronounced at those levels of the school system—for both pupils and teachers. Every minute of the school day is scheduled. Thus, the teacher's study and preparation must take place after the "working day" is over. Furthermore, care must be exercised during the day to "stretch time" to provide for all of the responsibilities that the teacher must assume.

Meeting the time requirements of clinical practice is an individual problem. No prescribed schedule or formula will fit everyone. Some individuals will require more time than others for study, some will be taking courses that impose heavy time commitments, some will be working part-time, many will be involved in college activities, and others will be married and carrying family responsibilities.

Because of the importance of clinical experience and the need for time for the job, many teacher education institutions do not permit a student to work at a part-time job or to engage in other time-consuming activities while engaged in clinical practice. Whether or not the institution imposes restriction, the wise individual will pare his own schedule to allow sufficient time to make the most of the opportunities provided for learning to teach. He will recognize that a strong investment of time and energy during the period when the most help is available may make a difference throughout his professional career.

Self-examination. Probably no better time exists for self-examination than during preparation for a teaching assignment. The prospective teacher might well begin by making a list of personal strengths and weaknesses, taking care to be as objective as possible. A prospective teacher who did this included the following guidelines in her own self-analysis.

I believe there are a few personal qualities a teacher must possess or he won't be a constructive force in the education of children. These qualities are: self-control, poise, tact, a sense of humor, impartiality, consistency, friendliness, and a willingness to use recognition and praise.

Another prospective teacher wrote, "I feel that there is no excuse for a teacher's use of incorrect English. Also, I think a teacher should examine himself for any unpleasant mannerisms he might have."

The student might ask his college counselor or a respected faculty member to give his reactions to the list of traits the student believes he should possess. Perhaps later the supervising teacher will be willing to discuss the results of the self-evaluation. The evaluation forms which appear in Chapter 10 and Appendix A may be helpful in making such a self-appraisal.

Emotional maturity. Most people regard favorably a person who takes what comes in stride, is not easily upset, and can disagree with the opinions of another without disliking him. These are some of the qualities which characterize the emotionally mature individual.

Emotional maturity is essential for effective teaching. This is true because teaching, more than some other professions, involves continuous association with people. The teacher spends most of his day with pupils in the classroom. Throughout each day he works with his peers, with supervisory personnel, with administrators, and with custodians. He has a variety of contacts with parents, individually and in groups. Also, pupils tend to reflect their environment and they may acquire the kind of behavior displayed by the teacher; certainly, they are affected by it. These are good reasons for the prospective teacher to make every effort to become emotionally mature.

If one recognizes the limitations of personality tests and interprets test scores accordingly, such instruments can be useful for evaluation of emotional maturity. The *Minnesota Multiphasic Personality Inventory* (MMPI) [4] is a test of this type. At most teacher education institutions personality tests are administered, scored, and interpreted for the prospective teacher. Other sources of assistance include the student's adviser, the office of student personnel services, or a faculty member well-known to the student.

Health. In most states the applicant for a teaching certificate must pass a physical examination. In view of this fact, most college students preparing to teach are required to take a health examination prior to enrollment for clinical practice. The person who has not had a recent health check-up will want to do so before he begins his assignment. In one instance a prospective teacher who had just completed student teaching discovered through taking the physical examination required for teacher certification that he had a long-standing case of rheumatic fever. Though symptoms of this disease were present over an extended period he had not recognized them as such. Earlier examination, diagnosis, and treatment would have prevented discomfort and loss of time during his student teaching period and the first year of teaching.

It is advisable to consult with a physician about receiving immunization against communicable diseases that are sometimes prevalent in schools. The prospective teacher should do so well in advance of his application for a clinical assignment.

Some college students, unfortunately, become careless about

[4] Starke R. Hathaway and J. Charnley McKinley, *Minnesota Multiphasic Personality Inventory* (New York: Psychological Corporation).

maintaining good health habits. Preparation for teaching's rigorous demands on physical and nervous energy should include provision for a mode of living which emphasizes good diet and adequate rest, relaxation, and exercise.

Scope of interests. Children and youth profit from working with teachers who are creative, versatile, resourceful, and interesting. A wide range of interests and experiences contributes to the development of these traits. Some education students can look forward to work with pupils knowing that they already possess such qualities. Others, perhaps through lack of opportunity, have developed few interests and have had few experiences outside their home communities. Persons in the latter category will want to consider ways to extend their interests and experiences. Reading, discussion, participation in college or university activities, travel—all are examples of ways to increase one's scope. Not to be overlooked, also, are formal college courses outside one's field of specialization, such as art, music appreciation, speech, drama, philosophy, literature, history.

A young man who had done little traveling met this deficiency by helping to conduct a travel tour to Europe each summer. A young woman accomplished a similar purpose by working as a dining room hostess in the lodge of a national park each summer. Contacts with and understanding of people with different economic, social, educational, and vocational backgrounds can increase both personal satisfaction and effectiveness as a teacher.

Knowledge of current affairs. The useful and effective citizen is well informed in fields other than his speciality. He is alert to what is happening in his own community, his state, the nation, and the world. The teacher who wishes to be comfortable in personal relationships and competent as a member of the profession has a special responsibility here. His acquaintance with various fields of knowledge and his understanding of current social, economic, and political developments should be such as to make it possible for him to take advantage of every opportunity to stimulate and challenge the minds of his pupils. As a student and, later, as a teacher he should budget his time so that his daily or weekly schedule permits information-seeking through such media as newspapers, magazines, radio, and television.

THE TEACHER AND THE CHANGING SCENE

From the time the college student begins thinking of himself as a prospective teacher, and particularly as he actually undertakes clinical practice, the challenges and opportunities that confront all members of the teaching profession unfold as his own. He soon realizes the great extent to which those who teach are involved in all that influences the life of the community, state, nation, and world. The teaching profession is not isolated from humanity anytime or anywhere. Whatever affects people influences teachers and their profession.

These are exciting times in which to prepare for teaching. Nothing today is static. The changes that are occurring, at home and abroad, affect the lives of all. For those who teach, they pose new problems, add new responsibilities, and present new opportunities to influence the destiny of mankind. Learning to teach will be more exciting and rewarding if the teacher sees his efforts in relation to the total changing scene. Sensitivity to the meaning of events—wherever they may happen—and to the effect these events may have on the future generation being instructed in elementary and secondary schools will give the teacher added direction and incentive.

Examples of some of the important changes taking place that bear upon education and teachers generally include:

1. The population of the United States and the world is increasing at an accelerated rate as compared with the past.

2. Increasing population in combination with increasing emphasis on the importance of education has resulted in greatly expanded school enrollment.

3. The accelerating movement of people to urban communities

is bringing about continuing changes in these areas with serious attendant problems for urban schools and for school personnel. Meeting the needs of the underprivileged and those in need of remedial work are examples of such problems.

4. There has been a tremendous increase in the fund of knowledge in this century as compared with previous periods of time.

5. Notable technological advances have taken place and are continuing to occur.

6. The Federal Government has shown an increased sensitivity to the welfare of the individual. Its support of education has increased substantially in recent years.

7. New educational theory and technological advances have made possible educational procedures, instructional materials, and other resources that are revolutionary in potential.

Keeping attuned to forces such as these is the professional obligation of every teacher, regardless of his field of specialization. Learning how to hold the multiple signs of change in perspective is an assignment that properly should be undertaken during the program of clinical preparation.

SUMMARY

Student teaching is the most common means of providing clinical experience; however, the use of the internship is increasing. Benefits from the clinical experience include opportunities to develop teaching skills, understand children and youth, learn about schools, and determine whether or not one is suited for a teaching career.

Careful preparation for clinical experiences will make them more meaningful and more rewarding. In making this preparation, one needs to assess his qualifications in general education, in his field of specialization, and in his personal orientation.

In making preparation for clinical experience, the student will need to free himself insofar as possible of other time-consuming responsibilities. Emotional maturity, good health, a wide range of interests, and knowledge of current affairs contribute to success in teaching. Careful self-examination should be made; it will aid in determining adequacy in the foregoing characteristics.

To be effective as a teacher one needs to be aware of and study changing economic, political, and sociological conditions as they affect him, his students, and his world.

USEFUL REFERENCES

Association for Student Teaching. *Teacher Education in the Public Schools*. Cedar Falls, Iowa: State College of Iowa, The Association for Student Teaching, 1961, Chapter IX, "The Internship."

Association for Supervision and Curriculum Development. *Intellectual Development: Another Look*. Washington, D.C.: The Association, 1964.

Conant, James Bryant. *The Education of American Teachers*. New York: McGraw-Hill Book Company, Inc., 1963, Chapter VI, "The Theory and Practice of Teaching."

Hunter, Elizabeth and Edmund Amidon. *Student Teaching Cases and Comments*. New York: Holt, Rinehart and Winston, 1964.

Nash, Curtis E., Roy C. Hanes, and Alice Currie Harding. "They Lead Two Lives in Central Michigan University's Five-Year Teacher Intern Program," *NEA Journal*, LIV (April 1965), 12–14.

Sarason, Seymour B., Kenneth S. Davidson, and Burton Blatt. *The Preparation of Teachers: An Unstudied Problem in Education*. New York: John Wiley and Sons, 1962.

Smith, Elmer R., ed. *Teacher Education: A Reappraisal*. New York: Harper & Row, 1962, Chapter V, "Practice in Teaching."

CHAPTER TWO
THE CLINICAL
SITUATION

The college or university student who has made the kind of preparation suggested in Chapter 1 should be eager to begin working in a school. He will realize that, although certain broad, general characteristics are common to all schools, each school and each community has unique qualities. The chances for success and enjoyment of learning to teach will be increased if the prospective teacher obtains and utilizes in advance as much information as possible about the situation in which he will be working.

GETTING ACQUAINTED WITH SCHOOL
AND COMMUNITY

There are various ways, direct and indirect, to learn about a community and its schools. Those which bring the prospective teacher into direct contact with the life and work of the community are likely to be most fruitful. Descriptive material about a local situation, however, can be very useful; the college teacher placement office can help to locate such information.

Visiting the School

Some teacher education institutions require, and all encourage, the student teacher or intern to visit the school in which he is to work. The length of the visiting period may vary from a single day to several weeks. It may take place during the Easter vacation period of the college, during the late spring, or at another time when the student has been excused from campus classes. If visiting is a scheduled part of the institution's plan for preparing teachers, college officials take responsibility for making the necessary arrangements. If the student is making his own arrangements, it is important that he contact the school principal and supervising teacher well in advance so that a suitable date may be selected and the necessary planning completed.

When the student arrives at the school, he should go first to the principal's office and introduce himself, a custom of simple courtesy as well as a correct professional procedure. The principal or someone from his office will introduce the student to the supervising teacher with whom he will work. The principal and supervising teacher will be helpful in introducing the visiting student to other school personnel and giving him information about the school. He will probably be introduced to the group or groups of pupils with whom he will be working and to various staff members. He should anticipate these possibilities and be prepared to respond in a friendly and informal manner.

Most of the time during the visit will be spent in observation. There will be much to see—more than one can remember. This is a good time to start keeping a notebook so that important information will not be forgotten. Following are some points to keep in mind that can make the visit most beneficial.

1. *Pupils.* Typical attitude toward school, general intelligence and achievement level, home and family background, typical or persistent problems.

2. *Curriculum.* Subjects, areas, or units being studied, including what has been presented to pupils and accomplished by them to date.

3. *Instructional materials, supplies, and equipment.* Reading and reference materials available in classroom and library, educational supplies, duplicating equipment and services, storage and work space.

4. *Teaching aids.* Audio-visual aids, educational television, programmed instruction, auto-instructional devices.

5. *Records and reports.* Pupil-personnel records—what they in-

clude, how they are used. Reports to parents—kind in use, frequency.

6. *School plant.* Age of building, suitability for an adequate school program.

7. *Information about the school.* Existence and availability of handbook or file containing information about such items as fire drills, safety regulations, student government, and school publications.

8. *Teacher-pupil relationships.* Ways teacher and pupils work together—individually, in groups, as an entire group. Teaching procedures used. Ways of dealing with unusual situations.

This first visit provides an excellent opportunity for asking questions and obtaining suggestions from the supervising teacher. This may be done in several short conferences during the day, during a conference at the end of the day, or both. Special attention should be given to ways to prepare for, and to get started in, the clinical assignment. The following items may be useful as guides for planning:

1. Kinds of advance planning that should be done
2. How to obtain and assemble instructional materials
3. Possible methods of observation and participation at the beginning of the clinical assignment
4. Nature and frequency of conferences with the supervising teacher
5. Suggestions for developing good relationships with teachers and other school personnel
6. Professional activities in which there will be an opportunity to participate, such as faculty meetings, meetings of teachers' organizations, parent conferences, and Parent-Teacher Association meetings.

After each day of visiting, it will be helpful to crystallize one's thinking about the day's events and to relate them to the forthcoming clinical assignment. At the end of the period of visiting, if it lasts for more than a day, planning should be started for the clinical assignment. During the time before the assignment begins the student would be wise to collect material, to seek help from college professors, and to begin a program of reading related to the content to be taught. Attention should be given to characteristics of pupils and community as well as to methods of instruction appropriate to the age level and subject field.

Collecting Pertinent Information About the Community

Success in teaching depends, first of all, upon the ability to harmonize with the community. A recent study of problems of teaching in urban schools [1] documented the fact that only the teacher who can identify with the community served by a school and who can be accepted by parents and pupils as "belonging" has a chance to be effective.

Communities, like people, develop clusters of characteristics that give uniqueness to each. When such factors and their interrelationships are analyzed it is possible to know what a community is like, how its dominant groups may be expected to respond to various conditions. Communities are like the people who compose them in another way—they are always changing. Furthermore, the rate of change varies for different communities. Two school districts, side by side, may be very different in community composition and outlook and their rates of change may represent complete extremes.

The real personality of a community may lie beneath its exterior. Students preparing for clinical experience sometimes discover that as they come to know the community it differs markedly from their first impressions of it. Sensitive teachers who have taught in a community for years can recount the many changes that have taken place in community attitudes and responses. "This place is not the same anymore," is an expression every college student hears when he returns to his home community. How true that is likely to be!

[1] Raymond L. Jerrems, Ph.D. Dissertation, University of Chicago, 1965. Also see article by Ruth Dunbar, "Proposed Changes in Slum Schools," *Chicago Sun Times*, August 1, 1965.

The challenge to the teacher in understanding a town, city, or school district is to know which signs to look for and how to interpret them. Some of the pertinent guidelines for community study will be the broad general trends that affect all communities by differing degrees. The rapid trend toward urbanization is a good example. This general pattern of change has affected and will continue to affect every community and the life of every teacher. Most prospective teachers who graduate now and in the future will work in urban schools. According to a recent text on problems of urban education: "Already over two-thirds of all elementary and secondary school teachers work in metropolitan areas with total populations exceeding 100,000." [2]

The significance of the movement toward urban centers that has taken place during the past decade has been summarized as follows:

Seven of ten Americans live in cities, and one of five lives in the metropolitan areas of New York, Chicago, Philadelphia, Los Angeles, or Detroit. Not only do the problems of urban society touch most Americans daily but they have a great deal to do with the nation's future, both internally and as a world power. How to live with urbanization and how to marshal our human and material resources to improve it are urgent and difficult problems. [3]

Numerous characteristics need to be considered in studying a community. Space does not permit a discussion of all of these, nor can a prospective teacher be expected to approach the study of a community with the intensity or in the detail that a sociologist might employ. However, information on the following points will help the teacher relate to the community in a manner which can contribute to his success.

Economic patterns.   Is the industry primarily heavy industry, such as steel and large machinery, or does it engage in production of smaller items? Is the community dependent for the employ-

[2] B. J. Chandler, Lindley J. Stiles, and John I. Kitsuse, *Education in Urban Society* (New York: Dodd, Mead & Company, 1962), p. 195.
[3] National Education Association, Project on the Instructional Program of the Public Schools. *Education in a Changing Society* (Washington, D.C.: The Association, 1963), p. 76.

ment of labor primarily on one industry or is industry diversified?

Are most of the business establishments large or are they mostly small enterprises?

What is the pattern of vocations—primarily factory workers, management personnel, small business personnel, professional?

What are the income levels: range, unemployment, number on relief?

What about the strength, record of improvement of working conditions, strike experiences of labor organizations?

Ethnic groups. Does one nationality or race predominate in the community? Is there a single minority group or are there several?

What is the position of ethnic groups with regard to assimilation, integration, involvement in community life? What is the extent of barriers between national or racial groups? of progress toward elimination of barriers? Does the community practice de facto segregation?

Cultural and religious resources. What are the community's cultural and civic opportunities—community theatre, musical events, lecture clubs, art galleries, libraries, museums?

With regard to churches, what are the denominations, kinds of programs, opportunities afforded youth and adults?

What educational institutions—public and nonpublic schools, colleges, adult education programs—are in the community?

Physical resources—geographical conditions. What are the community's natural resources—mineral deposits, water supply, parks and other scenic areas? What are its geographical conditions—topography, rainfall, climate?

Political inclinations. What is the dominant political party? What are the trends in balance of power, strengths of extremist groups, influence of politics on progress?

Recreational facilities. What recreational facilities—parks, playgrounds, sponsored activities for children and youth, swimming pools, golf, bowling, motion pictures—are available in the community?

Other community resources. What are the community's public information resources, transportation facilities, health facilities, shopping facilities?

Attitudes toward schools and teachers. What is the predominant attitude toward schools? How about the community's interest in schools, financial support, the prevalence of private or parochial schools?

What are the attitudes toward teachers? Do teachers have opportunities to participate in community activities? Are they highly regarded by members of the community? What are the demands on teachers' out-of-school time?

The sort of information outlined above can be used as a basis for planning a program of study for pupils and taking steps to improve one's skill in teaching. For example, the child from an upper-middle-class home in which the pupil has access to a wide variety of stimulating reading materials is likely to profit from a different type of motivation in the classroom than the child of an unemployed parent in whose home there is literally nothing to read. Similarly, helping the child of a recent Puerto Rican immigrant to develop a wholesome concept of good citizenship may require an approach quite different from that used with the child in whose home continental American traditions and the responsibilities of citizenship are emphasized.

Identifying School and Community Leaders

Many of the conditions that prevail in a community are the result of the leadership the community has had. History, current conditions, and possible future developments can be understood better if one can identify school and community leaders. An example will illustrate this point. Throughout the period of unrest in many cities over the question of school integration, one city with a large Negro population experienced little or no disturbance. A study of the situation revealed that over a period of years, under the wise leadership of a strong and able superintendent of schools and prior to the United States Supreme Court ruling, integration had been taking place gradually. The vision, understanding, and courage of this capable leader had, with the help of competent school personnel, laymen, and the board of education, made it possible for the school and community to take constructive action.

The supervising teacher can often identify leaders within the community. Leaders in government, business, labor, and professional, cultural, and social fields are the "opinion makers" in most communities. Leaders in educational institutions other than public elementary and secondary schools should also be identified.

Information about community leaders may be obtained from college professors and from student teachers and interns who have already worked in the community. The news media will provide information about local events; some students subscribe to the community's newspaper in order to learn more about it and its leaders. Handbooks, printed community surveys, government reports, and material in school and community libraries are other sources of information about community leadership.

Living in the Community

Various factors influence the kinds of experiences the student will have in the community. He may be a temporary resident while working at his clinical assignment, he may be in his home community, or he may be a commuter. He may be working in the school full time or only a part of each day. The length of his assignment may be a few weeks, a semester, or a year.

The student should consider the benefits that come from living in the community where he is serving as a student teacher or intern. Some individuals resist an assignment if it is not in their home community or in the community where the college or university is located. This is a short-sighted attitude. When he moves into a new situation the young teacher becomes a more resourceful person than when he remains in one in which acquaintances and relationships are already established.

The individual who lives in the community in which he teaches is potentially a better classroom teacher than is the commuter. He is likely to become better acquainted with his pupils, and time which otherwise would be used in commuting can be devoted to professional work. He is more likely to make frequent contacts with parents and other citizens of the community, and he can become informed about community problems, issues, and daily community happenings in a way that would otherwise not be possible. For these reasons his classroom instruction can become more closely related to the experiences of pupils and more meaningful to them than would be possible if he lived outside the community.

Finding places to live may present a problem for temporary residents in a community. Help can be obtained from community sources, such as the housing bureau, the chamber of commerce, and local realtors. Increasingly, school systems are providing assistance. Frequently, members of the faculty make available rooms in their homes. The opportunity to live with a teacher or a parent should not be discounted, for much can be learned under such conditions from one's landlord. An important point about finding living accommodations is avoid the "do-it-yourself" urge. Time can be wasted and frustrations encountered by trying to be one's own rental agent.

Participating in Community Activities

Sometimes, the expectations of school personnel plus the desire of the prospective teacher for involvement in community activities may result in his overemphasizing community work to the neglect of important classroom duties. On the other hand, some individuals may find that their classroom responsibilities plus their lack of interest in the community inhibit or make impossible their participation in community activities. Balance is important; while learning, the prospective teacher will do well to follow a middle course.

Answers to two questions will aid in determining the optimum amount of community involvement. First, how much participation in and which kinds of community activities will help to advance the learning of your pupils? Second, which pattern of community participation will contribute most to your present and future effectiveness as a teacher and community leader? These questions should be discussed with the college supervisor prior to clinical practice in the school.

Many decisions about participation in community life will grow out of developments that occur from week to week. The following areas will give the student teacher or intern information about events and activities in the community while he is on the job.

1. *News media.* Reading the local daily newspapers and listening to the radio newscasts are indispensable habits. They provide information on what is happening and tell who is providing the leadership for each event.

2. *School-related community activities.* The school is the center for a wide variety of community activities, ranging from athletic events to musical concerts. Since the student learning to teach will find it impossible to attend all of the many worthwhile activities, choices must be made. A good rule to follow is to make sample selections from different categories of activities: (a) those that foster interactions with parents; (b) those that permit observations and associations with students in informal intellectual endeavors, such as a science club, an art appreciation group, or a discussion club; (c) events that bring associations with community leaders; (d) activities that involve the rank and file of community citizens; and (e) activities that are recreational in character.

Parent-Teacher Association meetings should be given a high priority under the first category of activities. This organization, national in scope, has long had strong influence on improvement of education. Being a partnership (as its name implies) between parents and teachers, its potentialities are unlimited. Learn this body's objectives, its organization, the work it does. Discover the ways in which it attempts to support the program of the school, and ways in which it may help the school to help the home and community.

Accepting active responsibility in community activities will be more beneficial than just observing them. If the supervising teacher is already involved in an activity, offer to help. Otherwise, offer to assist other teachers or parents who carry responsibilities. A good rule is to learn by first working behind the scenes. Let the local people play the starring roles.

3. *Organizations for children and youth.* Every community has a number of organizations established to promote the welfare of youth. Most such groups emphasize their own educational programs. Examples are such groups as Boy Scouts, Girl Scouts, 4H Clubs, Future Farmers, Y-Teens, boy's clubs, and girl's clubs. Observing the functioning of organizations of this type and participating in their work whenever feasible will give one added insight into the nature of the community.

In addition to organized groups there are unstructured and informal groups in most communities that exert influence on young people. This is especially true in the large urban community. The neighborhood gang, the group meeting at the pizza house, at the recreation center, or at an informal party can do much to mold the thinking and to establish values in the minds of children and youth.

4. *General and community organizations.* Service clubs (Kiwanis, Exchange, Rotary), farm organizations such as the Grange and Farm Bureau, labor organizations, and professional organizations are barometers of community life. Attendance at meetings of these organizations is by membership or invitation only. If an invitation to attend a meeting of one or more of these organizations comes, accept it if possible. The experience will add to your knowledge of community life.

5. *Religious organizations.* In most communities teachers are not under pressure, as they often were in the past, to maintain membership in a religious organization, to attend religious services, or to teach in religious education programs. However, religion is a vital force in most communities. Furthermore, religious organizations frequently conduct influential educational programs. As a professional person vitally interested in the education of youth and in school-community cooperation, the teacher

candidate should develop an understanding of the influence of religious organizations on the attitudes and beliefs of pupils. The question of attending religious services is, of course, a personal matter for each teacher.

6. *Other opportunities for community participation.* Many communities have Y.M.C.A. and Y.W.C.A. organizations. They offer programs and accommodations which often appeal to young teachers and they welcome membership from such persons. Membership presents opportunities to meet other citizens of the community in an informal situation which can contribute to mutual understanding.

The prospective teacher will undoubtedly be impressed with the number of drives for funds that are made by various organizations and agencies in the school and community. The degree of success of financial drives by the United Fund, Red Cross, and similar agencies will help one learn of projects the community considers important and the extent of community cooperation.

There was a time in the past when it was made clear to school personnel that they were expected to make purchases within the community. Although this is no longer true in most communities, the student learning to teach will find that visiting local stores and business establishments can help him to learn about the community. He can make assessments of standards of living in a community by the kinds of merchandise for sale. He can make tentative judgments, also, about the progressiveness and prosperity of the area by the way shops, stores, buildings, and streets are maintained and modernized.

Benefits of Community Participation

Members of all professions, by virtue of their education and the influence they exert on community life, are expected to participate in community affairs. Teachers, however, have a very special obligation in this area.

What personal and professional benefits can the prospective teacher expect from participation in community activities during his clinical assignment? If wise decisions are made with respect to the selection of activities and the apportionment of time to them, the following gains are possible.

1. *Leadership ability.* Participation can help the prospective teacher to develop leadership ability. For example, serving as a Scout, Y.M.C.A., or Y.W.C.A. leader can help one to learn to direct a group in informal, non-classroom situations.

2. *Community improvement.* Working with a group of laymen in the organization of, say, a "blood bank" or in encouraging the enforcement of school safety regulations can contribute to better living in the community.

3. *Improved public relations.* When a teacher participates in a community choral group or other local enterprise, he establishes a two-way relationship with the community. This communication may contribute to community support of a high-quality educational program in the school.

4. *Example for youth.* Young people are often influenced by the activities in which adults engage. They are frequently influenced by a respected teacher. The teacher's participation in community projects can encourage pupils to become participants too.

5. *Help to individuals.* In a number of instances, notably in congested areas of cities, capable but disadvantaged children and youth have acquired new purpose and sense of direction because a prospective or experienced teacher worked with them in some out-of-school activity. These contacts can occur in a community house, recreation center, or other youth groups.

UNDERSTANDING ROLES AND RELATIONSHIPS

Few professions require such continuous close contact with individuals and groups of people as does teaching. The medical doctor, the lawyer, the pharmacist, the nurse—all work with people, but mostly with one person at a time. The engineer works with mathematics and materials more than with human beings, unless he has administrative responsibility. The minister's work is similar to that of the teacher with respect to relationships with people, but his appearances before large groups are limited to a few times a week, and his individual contacts rarely approximate in number those of teachers.

The student entering into a clinical assignment confronts, in addition to the expected associations with pupils, parents, colleagues, and community representatives, certain special relationships that are integral to such a learning situation. Success in learning to teach will be advanced if the student develops a sound understanding of the roles and relationships that are possible and desirable and, in some instances, expected.

Coordinator of Clinical Experiences

The person in charge of administering an institution's over-all program of clinical experiences is the coordinator of clinical experiences (also called director of student teaching or coordinator of directed teaching). Whatever the title, the responsibilities of the position include negotiating with schools for clinical practice stations, providing general coordination for the program, and giving leadership to improve the program.

The student enrolled for clinical practice will likely have little relationship with the coordinator in large institutions. He should be aware, however, that such a position exists and he should understand the services it provides. In smaller institutions the person holding this position often functions in a dual capacity, serving as college supervisor for a particular subject field or the elementary area.

An important responsibility of the coordinator is to maintain good working relationships between the preparing institution and the cooperating schools. Each student has an obligation to help by following carefully the protocol that has been established.

College Supervisor (Clinical Professor)

Programs of clinical practice are offered as college courses, for credit, sometimes with marks or "grades" being assigned to indicate student achievement. The person in charge of the course is the college supervisor. Persons holding such positions are fre-

quently faculty members who teach methods courses, and, in
smaller institutions, other courses in either subject or pedagogical
fields. In his recommendations for improving teacher education,
Conant advocates employing for such assignments outstanding
teachers in elementary and secondary schools in liaison appoint-
ments between the college and the school system. His view is:
"The professor from the college or university who is to supervise
and assess the practice teaching should have much practical experience. His status should be analogous to that of a clinical professor in certain medical schools." [4] Dr. Conant recommends that
such a person be given the title "clinical professor." Northwestern
University, the University of Wisconsin, and others have moved
to establish positions of this type.

The college supervisor, whether or not he is actively engaged in
teaching as Dr. Conant recommends, of necessity must have a
background of experience in teaching at the level and in the subject fields for which supervision is provided. The college supervisor's assignment usually involves assisting supervising teachers
as well as helping students in preparation for teaching. He observes the student learning to teach and conducts follow-up
conferences with the prospective teacher and the supervising
teacher. He also may be available to advise the school principal.
In certain programs, including those of the Master of Arts in
Teaching type, the college supervisor may conduct seminars for
prospective teachers.

Often, an important responsibility of the college supervisor is
assisting in the assignment of students to clinical stations. The decisions made are based upon the student's record and his expressed preferences along with knowledge available about the
school and specific supervising teachers. Another duty often
assigned the college faculty member in this position is evaluation
of the prospective teacher's success and the assignment of marks
when they are used. In this function, the collaboration of the
school supervising teacher is essential, since he will have observed

the student teacher or intern on a day-by-day basis. However, the college supervisor will have the advantage of an overview of the student's work in the methods courses or clinically-related seminars and, also, will be able to compare the progress of one student with others.

The relationship between the college supervisor and the student enrolled in clinical practice is tutorial in nature. Much of the instruction takes place in individual conferences. Group presentations in methods of teaching are provided, of course, but the careful guidance required to help the student refine teaching skills is of necessity highly personal and usually is given privately. Because of this relationship, and because of the vital importance of clinical experience to the development of skill in teaching, the ties between the student and the college supervisor typically become strong and lasting. The recommendation given by the college supervisor is often the key factor in initial placement in a teaching position. The college supervisor's continued interest and encouragement motivates professional improvement and advancement well into the student's career as a teacher.

Supervising Teacher

The supervising teacher is the person who teaches pupils and also supervises the student teacher or intern. In some places he is called "cooperating teacher" and in others the formerly common term "critic teacher" is still in use. The prospective teacher works more closely with the supervising teacher than with any other person.

Because the role of the supervising teacher is so crucial in the development of the prospective teacher, his contributions deserve special consideration and will be discussed along with those of other members of the teaching team in Chapter 3.

Other School Personnel

Although the prospective teacher will have his closest contacts with his supervising teacher, he will no doubt become increasingly aware of the size, complexity, and interrelatedness of the school organization of which he is a part. He will soon discover that there are many individuals connected with the school who are interested in his success. This is true of school personnel for at least two reasons: first, school people are generally friendly and helpful individuals and, second, they are well aware of the need for a continuous supply of capable, well-prepared teachers and they are usually willing to assist in meeting this need.

One needs to be sensitive to the role of each of the many individuals who make up a school organization. They include the school principal, the superintendent, and classroom teachers other than the supervising teacher. Nonteaching staff members include supervisors or consultants, counselors, and the school nurse. There are also other specialized school personnel, such as food-service staff members and custodians. All play important parts in the education of youth.

Pupils of Grade or Class Group

The student learning to teach probably will have given more thought to his relationships with pupils than to other persons involved in his forthcoming clinical experience. This is understandable because, though relationships with staff members in the school are important, success in instructing pupils in the classroom is the primary objective.

The manner in which the teacher candidate is received by pupils in the class will depend on a number of factors. One is the kind of student teaching and the amount of instruction by prospective teachers to which pupils have been accustomed. If previous experiences with prospective teachers have been pleasant and profitable, pupils are likely to welcome another student teacher or intern. The supervising teacher can provide information about the orientation and past experience of the class.

In the last analysis, the kind of reception and the continued relationships that one will be able to establish with pupils will depend largely on the kind of person one is. Some individuals can achieve pleasant and satisfying experiences in almost any situation; others, in similar situations, may have serious difficulties.

The person who is intelligent, well grounded in his field of specialization and carefully prepared for his responsibilities, who understands and enjoys children and youth, who respects the roles and relationships of colleagues on the school staff, and who does not shrink from hard work should anticipate satisfying experiences during the clinical period. He should not be so eager to obtain the good will of pupils that he becomes "chummy" with them and solicitous of their good opinions. Some young teachers have tried this only to learn that such behavior resulted in loss of respect. Once lost, respect is difficult to regain. A better approach is to begin with a friendly, firm, sincere, and businesslike attitude. A casual but honest posture of self-confidence is important. One needs to remember that young people, most generally, are fair. They want a capable, pleasant, resourceful teacher who is in control of himself and who can help them develop self-control. They like to have a young and energetic teacher working with them, and they expect to receive helpful instruction from him.

Parents

The wholesome development of children and youth is most likely to be accomplished when there is a partnership between parents and teachers and when pertinent information about the pupil is shared. The teacher can work more effectively with each individual pupil in school if he understands how the young person uses his time and reacts to other family members at home. The parent can reinforce the work of the teacher to the advantage of the pupil if he knows how his child reacts in group situations and how he is progressing in school. The nature and frequency of opportunities to work with parents depend on the school viewpoint and parent attitudes. It is important to follow school policy in working with parents. The prospective teacher should welcome the opportunity to gain experience in this important aspect of teaching.

The attitudes of parents toward the developing teacher will depend largely on the amount and kind of experience they have had with them. If prospective teachers are new to the school, parents may have reservations about their value to the school. If parents have become accustomed to them, they are likely to be highly regarded. In either case, one will need to think of work with parents as a challenge to build good parent-teacher relationships and to provide the best possible instruction for pupils. In many communities parents consider the student teacher or intern as an additional staff member who is helping their children receive better instruction than would be possible without him.

RESPONSIBILITY FOR GOOD RELATIONSHIPS

The prospective teacher needs to assume his share of the responsibility for getting along well with others. The statements which follow crystallize what has been implied in previous sections and include additional suggestions for working in harmony with colleagues.

1. As early as possible be able to identify each position; obtain an overview of the entire school organization.

2. Be sure to understand the unique arrangements between the teacher education institution and the school system. Identify each position that functions in this cooperative arrangement.

3. Be sure to understand clearly what the teacher education institution expects in terms of course requirements, seminars, or other campus responsibilities, if any.

4. Clarify relationships with the college supervisor or other college representative. He will try to help, but he cannot always identify individual needs. Be forthright with him. Assist him by working harmoniously with the supervising teacher.

5. Do everything possible to profit from the help of the supervising teacher. The student teacher or intern should provide the supervising teacher with pertinent information about himself and should communicate with him about strengths and problems.

6. Assume that school personnel will want to be helpful. This will usually be true, but even if it is not, retaliation and ill will are unlikely to improve the situation. A friendly attitude and com-

petency as a teacher may change the views of others on the staff and result in the graceful acceptance of young teachers in the future. Avoid unfavorable remarks about school personnel.

7. Be careful to maintain self-respect and professional integrity. The thoughtful student of teaching will not compromise *with himself* on matters of principle. It may, however, be desirable, at times when good relationships are at stake, to be flexible in the interest of harmony with the individual to whom one is professionally responsible. These two positions are not incompatible. If one takes the long view of the development of his philosophy of learning and teaching, he will welcome opportunities to state and test his views.

8. Learn the names of pupils as soon as possible. Pupils, teachers, parents, and others in school and community will recognize and appreciate this interest. Be friendly and helpful to pupils, but maintain dignity and poise in working with them. Take a genuine interest in school and community activities and try to become an interesting person.

9. Become informed about school policies that are related to your work. When in doubt about how a policy should be interpreted, obtain help from the supervising teacher or principal.

THE NEW ROLE AS A PROFESSIONAL PERSON

When one begins the work of a teacher, he assumes a new role —the role of a professional person. He has been moving toward this role during the entire period of preparation for teaching, however long this period may have been (perhaps for some it began in the elementary school years). Nevertheless, when the prospective teacher enters the classroom he is accorded both privileges and responsibilities that were not his before. He must earn the right to retain these privileges, and he must be willing to assume the responsibilities that accompany membership in a profession.

The prospective teacher is privileged to instruct and provide leadership for youth and to be stimulated by, associate with, and receive the esteem of, creative and lively young minds. In most instances he is highly regarded by citizens in the community and his co-workers are usually pleasant and congenial. When he manages his time well his schedule allows for family life, study, and travel. He is privileged to receive benefits from a respected profession and to contribute to its strength.

The young person who is in the process of completing his college or university education needs to recognize that the mode of living on a campus is quite different from life in a school–community setting. By comparison he has been living in an artificial world which does not provide the best preparation for his future role. On campus he has had little or no contact with pupils, parents, a complex school organization, or a typical community. Campus customs relating to dress, conduct, and living in general make possible a kind of personal and academic freedom seldom found elsewhere in American life. As a student teacher or intern he will suddenly discover that pupils are all around him; he needs to fit into a complex school system staffed by more mature persons whose duties he may not quite understand; parents will seek information from him about their children. He may discover that people in the community have opinions about how and where he should find recreation, how he should dress, what community obligations he should assume.

The continuing trend toward urbanization has brought large numbers of pupils together in city schools. This situation has resulted in difficult problems for schools and teachers. In numerous congested slum areas classroom groups are often too large for effective instruction, buildings are crowded and inadequate, good instructional materials and equipment are lacking, and in too many instances pupils are undisciplined and have little respect for their teachers. Frequently these children have been denied the food, clothing, and housing that make decent living possible. Pupils and their parents may have little interest in schools and frequently are uncooperative or antagonistic toward teachers. Conditions such as these offer a challenge which requires unusual ability, courage, and resourcefulness. They also provide a setting in which teachers with these qualities can aid in brightening the future of many pupils whose chances for success in school and life might otherwise remain negligible.

The capable and alert young teacher who is sensitive to existing conditions will be prepared for hard work. He will understand that, unlike the craftsman who punches the time clock each day, does his job, and forgets his work until the next day, the member of a profession must plan, execute his plan, evaluate, and create. The professional teacher accepts *both* the privileges and the responsibilities of his profession. He is willing to contribute to community leadership. He exemplifies good, wholesome living—the kind of living that intelligent parents would like for their children.

In his new role the young teacher needs to recognize that the intellectual development of pupils is the primary goal of the school. He will set this goal for himself and will not be diverted from its attainment by those who might suggest unsound viewpoints, methods, and procedures.

Perhaps most important of all, the professional teacher, more than other citizens, will understand that the right kind of education for all people everywhere is the real hope for our people and others. He will accept the challenge before him, knowing that he has a crucial role to play in providing the kind of education that is needed.

SUMMARY

The prospective teacher is likely to find his work as a student teacher or intern more satisfying and successful if he becomes well informed about the school and community in which he is to work. Time spent in the school, prior to beginning the assignment, will provide information about pupils and colleagues that will serve as a basis for preliminary plans.

Each community is different, has its peculiar characteristics, and is constantly changing. One of the more significant changes in recent years is the trend toward urbanization. This change affects the life of every pupil and teacher. The teacher needs to understand the implications of urbanization for himself and as one who must help pupils prepare to meet changing conditions.

In making a study of the community, the prospective teacher needs to consider such factors as economic patterns, ethnic groups, cultural resources, physical resources, political institutions, recreational facilities, and community leaders. It is highly desirable that the student teacher or intern live in the community where he is teaching. This will help him provide instruction more closely related to the experiences of his pupils. The amount of his participation in community activities will depend upon how much is needed for effectiveness in teaching. The student teacher or intern may participate directly or indirectly through school-related community activities, organizations for children and youth, and general community organizations.

It is essential that the prospective teacher know the duties and responsibilities of those with whom he works in the school. He needs to discover as soon as possible his relationship to the following: coordinator of clinical experiences, college supervisor, other college representatives, supervising teacher, school supervisors, school principal, pupils, and parents.

The student learning to teach needs to assume responsibility for developing good relationships. Others will, no doubt, be cooperative and helpful, but skill in getting along with colleagues can contribute much to success in teaching.

As the student teacher or intern begins his work as a teacher he assumes a new role—that of a professional person. He must earn the right to privileges that are his in this capacity. This also involves assuming responsibilities required of a member of a profession.

USEFUL REFERENCES

Andrews, L. O. *Student Teaching*. New York: The Center for Applied Research in Education, Inc., 1964.

Blair, Lois C., and Paul Erickson. *The Student Teacher's Experiences in the Community.* Cedar Falls, Iowa: The Association for Student Teaching, 1964.

Chandler, B. J., Lindley J. Stiles, and John I. Kitsuse. *Education in Urban Society.* New York: Dodd, Mead and Co., 1961.

Conant, James Bryant. *Shaping Educational Policy.* New York: McGraw-Hill Book Co., Inc., 1965.

Fusco, Gene C. *School-Home Partnership in Depressed Urban Neighborhoods.* Washington, D. C.: U. S. Government Printing Office, 1964.

Greene, Gwynn A. *Problem Situations in Student Teaching.* New York: Bureau of Publications, Teachers College, Columbia University, 1959.

Kerber, August F., and Barbara Bommarito. *The Schools and the Urban Crisis.* New York: Holt, Rinehart and Winston, Inc., 1965.

McGeoch, Dorothy. *Learning to Teach in Urban Schools.* New York: Bureau of Publications, Teachers College, Columbia University, 1965.

National Education Association, Project on the Instructional Program of the Public Schools. *Education in a Changing Society.* Washington, D. C.: The Association, 1963. Chapter VII, "Urbanization."

National Society for the Study of Education. *Social Forces Influencing Education.* Chicago, Illinois: The Society, 1961. Chapter X, "Understanding Stability and Change in American Education."

Passow, Harry A. *Education in Depressed Areas.* New York: Bureau of Publications, Teachers College, Columbia University, 1964.

Scales, Eldridge. *Student Teaching in Higher Institutions of New York State.* Albany, New York: State Department of Education, 1964.

Woodruff, Ashael D. *Student Teaching Today.* Washington, D. C.: The American Association of Colleges for Teacher Education, 1960.

CHAPTER THREE
THE TEACHER DEVELOPMENT TEAM

Developing competent teachers requires team effort. The state department of public instruction gives support and leadership. It should encourage schools to help in clinical programs for student teachers and interns. In a few states financial reimbursements are made to schools for staff time devoted to clinical programs. The state department's responsibility includes, also, the encouragement of innovations and, in many ways, provision for high standards of excellence in teaching. School systems in local communities need to make available their resources, including faculty members and groups of pupils, to clinical stations. Increasingly, responsibility for supervision of prospective teachers, including evaluation of their progress, is being assumed by teachers, supervisors, and administrators in such schools. The academic and professional contributions of teacher education institutions are vital to provide a scholarly orientation, detailed planning and coordination, and integration with the total program of teacher education.

As was shown in Chapter 2, the student engaged in clinical preparation comes into contact with numerous types of people. In a broad sense, all of them make up a team for teacher development. The nucleus, however, consists of the college supervisor, the supervising teacher, and the student teacher or intern.

The relationship between tutor and student has always been a very special one. During apprenticeship in professional education the ties between the master practitioner and the apprentice are those of parent and child—in the finest sense. As preparation in the professions moved into institutions of higher learning, however, the responsibility for preparing new members of the profession became dispersed among many professors. The general trend of relationships between teacher and learner in all professions is clearly visible in teacher education. Much of the formal preparation for teaching, in the liberal arts as well as in the foundation courses in the professional sequence, is carried out in large classes that tend to nullify close ties between teacher and student. However, in the program of clinical practice and the related methods courses, the close ties between tutor and taught are still very much a reality. As programs of clinical practice have been moved out of campus laboratory schools into community school classrooms, the team has been expanded to include the supervising teacher in addition to the college supervisor and the student teacher or intern.

THE TEACHER DEVELOPMENT TEAM—STUDENT TEACHING

The Role of the Supervising Teacher

Much of the responsibility for the professional development of the student teacher rests with the supervising teacher. It should be helpful to identify ways to make this close association yield maximum results.

The competent classroom teacher instructs pupils; he is a curriculum builder, a guidance counselor, a consultant to parents, and a librarian who collects, catalogs, and files instructional materials. He is, also, a classroom manager, sponsor of co-curricular activities, usually serves on one or more committees, and participates in community activities. If the teacher works in a campus school he may also teach demonstration lessons and supervise the work of participating students during the pre-student teaching phases of clinical experiences.

When a classroom teacher accepts a student teacher, he assumes additional responsibilities. Unfortunately, it is incorrect to assume that the work load of the classroom teacher is reduced by the assistance provided by the student. In most cases, quite the opposite is true. The responsibility for guiding a young, inexperienced teacher is viewed by the capable and conscientious individual as a crucial and exacting assignment. And, as is true of any undertaking, it is more difficult to teach another to perform a task than it is to do it oneself.

The supervising teacher serves a dual function: he teaches children or youth and also supervises the work of a student teacher. In reality, his role is even more than dual: the capable supervising teacher is also a student; he must endeavor to increase his knowledge and skill, not only to teach pupils effectively but also to provide good instruction for the prospective teacher.

Why, in view of the additional work and responsibilities involved, does a classroom teacher agree to work with a student teacher? There is no single answer. Some feel a responsibility to pupils and the teaching profession for helping to provide a continuous supply of capable teachers. Thus, they make a professional commitment to help future teachers. Others are aware that guiding a young teacher compels them to keep alert to new and improved methods of teaching. Many simply like to work with young, ambitious, and energetic individuals who show promise of success; they enjoy the satisfaction that results when their protégés succeed. Certain teachers recognize that it is good for their pupils to have contact with college students who are learning to teach. Still others attest that they benefit personally from the help they receive from college supervisors to improve their own classroom teaching. It is probably true, also, that some teachers consent to work with a student teacher because of pressure from the school administration. Perhaps a few do so because of the small monetary payments made by the preparing institutions.

Whatever the reason an individual teacher has for accepting a student teacher, pupils benefit from being in classes in which students are learning to teach. They receive more help. The program provided is richer and more varied. Standards of achievement are uniformly higher.

The Role of the Student

The usual sequence in student teaching begins with planned observation (with some participation), followed by a variety of types of participation in classroom activities. The culminating phase is one in which teaching becomes a major responsibility. This progression is illustrated in Figure 1. Each prospective

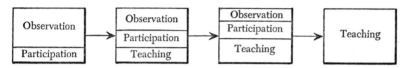

FIGURE 1.
Pattern of Induction into Teaching

teacher moves through this progression at his own rate, assuming responsibility for more involvement with pupils and greater independence in teaching as his readiness to do so is demonstrated. It should be noted, further, that in each stage of clinical work emphasis shifts, but the student teacher is involved in a number of activities at each stage. Thus, a student teacher may be engaged in participation as an assistant teacher to some extent while devoting major attention to observation. Similarly, as full teaching responsibility is being assumed the student may observe and give assistance to the supervising teacher.

Observing in the classroom. Observation is a special skill; it involves more than just watching what is going on. Alertness, sensitivity, and ability to identify and to assess crucial behavior and relationships are required. A key to useful observation in the classroom is knowing what should be seen. The supervising teacher or the college supervisor usually will provide guides to observers. An example of this type of guide follows. In using such a guide, each individual will have to decide how detailed a written record he can and should make. Some observers make the mistake of concentrating on taking too detailed notes. A wiser procedure is to record only significant information about important processes and procedures. If he concentrates on what is important at the time, the observer will subsequently be able to recall many unrecorded details.

OBSERVATION GUIDE

I. *Purposes of unit, lesson, or activity.* Why is this lesson taught?
   A. How do these purposes synchronize with goals for the semester or year?
   B. Is the purpose to develop skills, pass along information, or help the pupil develop attitudes, ideals, or appreciations?
II. *Content or subject matter.* What is being taught?
   A. What fields of knowledge are utilized in attempting to achieve the purposes listed in item I?
   B. How does this content synchronize with that of the semester, current year, preceding years, and with projections for future years?
   C. What is the source of subject matter—textbooks, other books, films, television, other?
III. *Teaching procedures.* What does the teacher do?
   A. What teaching techniques are used? Does the teacher lecture, lead in class discussion, ask questions, use audio-visual aids, give a test, use other techniques? Is one technique used exclusively, or is there a combination of techniques?
   B. How are pupils motivated?
   C. How does the teacher contribute to a stimulating intellectual climate in the classroom?
   D. What steps are taken by the teacher to foster a wholesome emotional climate?
IV. *Pupil activities.* What do pupils do?
   A. Are pupils interested, involved, active?
   B. Do pupils listen, discuss, give reports, write? In what other activities do pupils engage?
   C. What kinds of behavior are displayed by pupils?
V. *Physical factors.* How do physical factors contribute to learning?
   A. What provision is made for proper lighting, temperature, ventilation?
   B. How does the seating arrangement of pupils contribute to a good classroom situation?
   C. What use is made of chalkboards, bulletin boards, displays, instructional equipment?

VI. *Evaluation of teaching-learning situation.* Evaluation by teacher and/or pupils.
   A. Evaluation by teacher and pupils
      1. Was this the kind of situation in which teacher-pupil evaluation was feasible?
      2. If there was teacher-pupil evaluation, what was its nature?
         a. Was evaluation in terms of skills, knowledge, or attitudes developed?
         b. Was there evaluation of ways of working?
   B. Evaluation by the teacher in conference with the student teacher who was observing
      1. What aspects of the teaching-learning situation are considered good in terms of:
         a. Skills, knowledge, attitudes developed?
         b. Ways of working?
      2. What aspects of the teaching-learning situation might be changed or improved if it were possible to repeat it?
         a. Skills, knowledge, attitudes developed?
         b. Ways of working?

Observation requires critical analysis. The prospective teacher should remember, however, that his objective is to learn from observing rather than to assume the role of a critic. No two teachers will follow identical procedures. It follows, then, that there will be times when the procedures observed will contrast, or perhaps even conflict, with those favored in methods courses. In such situations, the ethical response is to assess the techniques employed within the context of their use and user, to observe their strengths and limitations, and to examine adaptations that might make them more effective.

The student teacher should feel free to discuss with both the supervising teacher and the college supervisor the possible use of techniques and procedures that neither the student teacher nor the supervising teacher employs. Approval should be obtained before they are put into practice as protection for the pupils being taught and for the student's relationships with those responsible for the program. It should be understood that the student teacher can pursue the course of action suggested here without compromising his views on sound principles of learning and teaching. He can, in fact, take advantage of his critical analysis of the teaching of others by using it to test his own theories and to crystallize his personal philosophy of education.

Participating in the classroom. The student teacher should become involved in teaching from the very first day he is with a group of pupils. He should be alert to take advantage of opportunities to participate in the work of the classroom—to assist the supervising teacher in teaching activities. This, of course, assumes that there has been adequate planning between the student and the supervising teacher and that there is a definite understanding about the role each will play. Neither pupils nor the supervising teacher will react favorably to a student who sits hour after hour without taking part in classroom activities. On the other hand, negative reactions are likely when the student is overly aggressive or dominating. He should be alert to opportunities to assist the supervising teacher in his work with the total group, to help individual pupils, or to work with a small group. Genuine interest and willingness to help will give the student teacher the feeling of belonging to, and being at ease with, the group. This interest, willingness to help, and initiative will lead naturally into more work with pupils and will contribute to the gradual professional growth of the student.

Participation may take various forms. Following is a list of some specific activities in which student teachers have engaged before assuming responsibility for the total classroom for an extended period of time.

1. Checked pupils' papers with them and helped them understand correct responses.

2. Read a story to the class.

3. Accompanied pupils to the playground.

4. Aided individual pupils and small groups of pupils in a mathematics class in understanding difficult problems and concepts.

5. Assisted pupils in the science laboratory.

6. Helped a group of pupils prepare a demonstration to be presented to the total classroom group.

7. Helped the clarinet section of the orchestra with a new musical selection.

8. Assisted the supervising teacher in working with small groups of pupils in a social studies class.

9. Assumed responsibility for carrying on the activities of the total classroom group for short periods of time. This was done with the supervising teacher present and also when he was called from the room for brief periods.

The amount of participation there should be at the beginning of the clinical period and the rate at which additional responsibilities should be assumed must be determined in each individual situation. The variables will include age, previous experience, and personality of the student teacher; the preference of the supervising teacher and the amount and kind of experience he has had with student teachers; and the age, ability, and degree of self-discipline of pupils.

Teaching. Most student teachers anticipate the time when they are permitted to "fly solo"—to take full responsibility for teaching the class. In most instances they achieve this objective so easily that they are hardly aware when it first happens. If communication between the supervising teacher and the student teacher is good, and if they work together harmoniously, the transition from observer to participant to teacher will be natural and pleasant. Difficulties that occur will be resolved in sequence, or adaptations can be made to minimize their impact. When it is agreed that the student teacher is ready to teach, the next decision will concern what is to be taught and whether the lesson will be presented to a part of the group or to the total class. These and other decisions about the first teaching should be made cooperatively. The student teacher's preference will be respected, but the supervising teacher must assume responsibility for the final decision. The student teacher should be prepared to express a frank and honest opinion, for only if he does so can the supervising teacher provide the maximum amount of assistance.

Students typically begin their first teaching of a group or class with a content unit in their area of greatest strength. The choice might be science or social studies for the teacher candidate in the elementary school, drama or the novel in a high school English class. Often student teachers develop poise by choosing first an instructional assignment that does not require difficult demonstration or leadership of the class by the teacher. Dictating a list of spelling words or supervising oral reading might be the selections of prospective elementary teachers. Vocabulary drill would be, perhaps, an example of a relatively easy assignment for a foreign language teacher. A student teacher in instrumental music might first choose to instruct the playing of sections of instruments before attempting to direct the entire band.

The length of time for the student teacher's first lesson will depend on the self-confidence of the student teacher and on general circumstances. He might teach for an entire class period, or he and his supervising teacher may agree to share the time.

Obtaining help through conferences.   If the student has had the opportunity to visit the school and classroom and to observe the supervising teacher before beginning the clinical assignment, he will very likely have his first conference at that time. (See Chapter 2 for a list of items for consideration during the preliminary visit.) If the student had no contact with the supervising teacher before beginning his clinical assignment, his program must be planned immediately in a series of conferences. A good practice is to set aside one or two hours each week for planned conferences. Also, unscheduled and informal conferences held during the lunch period, between classes, before or after school can be helpful. They are likely to occur naturally and to be problem oriented.

What do student teachers and supervising teachers discuss during conferences? Apparently, just about everything related to the school and its program for pupil learning. Subjects discussed during such conferences reported by both student teachers and supervising teachers include the following:

The philosophy of the school
Building regulations
Daily schedule and allotment of time
Classroom organization
Established classroom procedures and routine responsibilities of student teacher
Seating arrangements
Individual pupils—characteristics, abilities, problems
Involvement of student teacher—observation, participation, teaching
Relating previous preparation to classroom teaching
Specific teaching procedures to be used with each group of pupils
Planning for teaching—daily and long range
Use of textbook, selection and use of instructional materials and equipment
Evaluation of growth and development of pupils
Evaluation of growth and development of student teacher

The Role of the College Supervisor

The official leader of the three-member teacher development team is the college professor who serves as college supervisor. It is his design that determines the characteristics of the program of clinical practice. Responsibility for the success of the program and the quality of teachers produced rests heavily on his shoulders.

Planning and counseling. Long before the student has enrolled for student teaching, the college supervisor will have initiated plans with the supervising teacher. In some instances these two members of the team will have worked together over a period of years. It is not unusual for the supervising teacher to have taken his own student teaching under the guidance of the college supervisor. Whether or not they have worked together previously, the college supervisor will have planned the supervising teacher's relationships to the program. The importance of his leadership has been described as follows:

The college supervisor assumes a leadership role on the team which is concerned with the growth of the student teacher. He is the person who knows most about the roles and expectations of the others, of the objectives for student teachers, and about the student teacher himself. He is the key figure in establishing and maintaining a tension-free atmosphere for the student teacher in his new experience.[1]

The first contact between the college supervisor and the student will likely occur at the time of registration for student teaching. In some institutions the college supervisor becomes the faculty adviser for prospective teachers when they first enroll in the institution's teacher education program or when they decide upon their field of specialization. When the student teaching assignment is made, the college supervisor assumes responsibility for developing a functioning team—one in which each member understands his role and his relationships with the other two.

Developing a working team is frequently more difficult than might be assumed, particularly when the student teacher does not appreciate the necessity of division of responsibilities between the college supervisor and the supervising teacher. Insecure student teachers are sometimes guilty of attempting to play the supervising teacher against the college supervisor and to exclude the latter from team plans. The student teacher may find the supervising teacher a less rigorous taskmaster than the college supervisor—a natural tendency in view of the day-by-day personal relationships that develop and the limited contact the classroom teacher may have had with a variety of student teachers. When this happens, differences in appraisals of the student teacher's progress may interfere with healthy team relationships.

The student teacher bears a special responsibility for helping the team to function properly. He must not permit differences in

[1] Helen E. Edwards, *Building Good Relationships: A Major Role of the College Supervisor* (Cedar Falls, Iowa: Association for Student Teaching, 1961), p. 2.

philosophy and techniques of the college supervisor and supervising teacher or contrasting judgments of his work to weaken the team's strength. If this happens, the student teacher will be the major loser.

It is important that the student teacher realize that the college supervisor's job is to plan the program and to counsel both the student teacher and the supervising teacher. He needs also to appreciate the fact that the college supervisor bears professional responsibility to make constructive criticisms and to insist upon high standards of performance.

Supervisory assistance. The college supervisor maintains contact with and provides help to the student teacher through (1) periodic visits to the clinical station, during which teaching is observed; (2) individual conferences following visits and at other times; (3) group discussions with student teachers, usually regularly scheduled; and (4) in many instances, methods courses and seminars related to clinical practice. It is through such relationships with the student teacher that the college supervisor is kept aware of the program's problems and the student's progress and has opportunities to provide instruction and guidance.

The number of visits the college supervisor makes to observe a student teacher will depend upon various factors. One will be the division of supervisory responsibilities between the college supervisor and the supervising teacher. In some programs of clinical practice, the supervising teacher assumes most of these responsibilities; in others, the college supervisor does. The number of student teachers assigned to a college supervisor, the distance of their clinical stations from the college campus, other duties of the college supervisor such as teaching and research assignments—all bear upon the amount of help a college supervisor can give to each student teacher. Typically, however, the college supervisor will visit the student teacher near the beginning of the clinical assignment to help with his orientation. Other observations will be made at various stages of the student's teaching responsibilities. If emergencies develop, extra visits will be scheduled. A final visit for evaluation usually occurs near the end of the assignment.

It is natural for a student teacher to feel uncertain and perhaps ill at ease during the early visits and conferences with the college supervisor. Such feelings are due in part to the fact that teaching is a highly personal and, to some extent, artistic venture. The novice teacher will be apprehensive and keenly aware of his lack of experience. He should realize, however, that the college supervisor wishes to be helpful and is likely to be aware of the student's apprehensions. Visits usually will be scheduled so that the student teacher will know when to expect them; some, however, will be unscheduled. If he is not teaching when the college supervisor visits, the student teacher will want to greet the visitor quietly and to make him feel welcome. As quickly as possible the college supervisor should be informed about the schedule for the period. He can then decide how best to use the time that he has budgeted for the visit.

If the student teacher is not teaching, it may be an appropriate time for a conference between the visitor and the student teacher, or the college supervisor may prefer to become better acquainted with the classroom situation, to view available materials and equipment, or to confer with the principal. It is entirely proper for the student teacher to ask the college supervisor about his plans for the visit so that he too may plan for what is to occur. Usually the college supervisor will not request that plans be changed so that he may observe the student teacher as he teaches, though this request may be made, and the student teacher should anticipate it and be prepared to act accordingly.

There will usually be some kind of communication between the college supervisor and the other two members of the team on each visit to the school. On some occasions, if the visit is short and both team members in the local school are busy with teaching responsibilities and a conference has not been scheduled, the communication may be simply a brief informal conversation.

The student is sometimes disappointed if the college supervisor does not observe his teaching each time he comes. He should realize that the college supervisor can aid the student teacher's growth in other ways, such as conferring about problems and successes, providing help in relating theory to practice, and through three-way conferences between team members.

Conferences with the college supervisor, as with the supervising teacher, will be helpful to the extent they are approached in a spirit of cooperation and mutual respect. The student teacher needs to be prepared for each conference, regardless of whether it is prescheduled or unexpected, at the clinical station or on campus, with him alone or with his supervising teacher included. If the student teacher has been asked to keep a log or diary of his activities, frequent reference to them will call to mind topics for consideration. Points that the supervising teacher suggests for discussion with the college supervisor should also be noted as they occur and used to prepare for a conference.

It is common practice for the college supervisor to hold group meetings or seminars for the student teachers with whom he works. He and the student teachers may join with other prospective teachers and college supervisors in a large group, or the college supervisor may meet with five or ten individuals who are working in the same school or locality. Sometimes these meetings are held on campus, sometimes in the local school. In some group meetings of this kind the student teacher has an opportunity to meet with college staff members, supervising teachers other than his own, and administrative and supervisory personnel in schools other than the one in which he works.

Another Student Teacher on the Team

Though he was not listed as a member of the teacher development team, another student teacher in the classroom may be of great help. In a situation where more than one prospective teacher is assigned to a supervising teacher during the same assignment period, student teachers can plan, teach, and evaluate teaching together. When a student teacher watches a classmate instruct a group of pupils or direct individual learning, the observer can make helpful suggestions to the person who is teaching and, at the same time, learn more about teaching. The person who is being observed can benefit from the constructive criticisms of one of his peers. The student teacher–supervising teacher conference in which two student teachers working with the same supervising teacher participate can also be productive. An additional person is available to present constructive suggestions, raise questions, identify issues, and aid in evaluation.

THE TEACHER DEVELOPMENT TEAM—INTERNSHIP

The trend toward the internship, as distinguished from student teaching (see Terminology), as the basic route to teacher preparation is currently being accelerated by two developments. First, the Master of Arts in Teaching and similar programs have become widespread as alternate patterns to the four-year plan of teacher education. Second, many institutions that prepare teachers are incorporating into their four-year programs the unique features of the five-year programs.

Structure of the Internship

Internship programs, like those for student teaching, show wide variations from institution to institution. In terms of structure, however, they may be loosely classified in four broad categories.

1. Internship arrangements integrated into four- or five-year programs of teacher education in which student teaching is a prerequisite to the more advanced internship experience.

2. Master of Arts in Teaching internship programs, of one or two years' duration, of which one year is devoted to full-time clinical practice.

3. Post-baccalaureate programs leading to certification and possibly the master's degree, of twelve to eighteen months' duration, of which one semester is devoted to full-time clinical practice.

4. School-sponsored internship programs, of one or two years' duration, designed to orient new teachers to a system.

Features of Internship

The strengths and contributions of the internship to programs of teacher education include: (1) the added emphasis the prospective teacher is permitted to place on the study of the subject or subjects to be taught; (2) the telescoping of the professional sequence in and around the clinical practice; (3) the provision of real responsibilities for teaching as clinical practice.

Internship programs, as the name implies, give first priority to clinical experience. Many concentrate as much as 70 to 80 per cent of the time and college credits allocated to the professional sequence on clinical experience and related professional seminars that treat methods and problems of teaching. The clinical station for the internship typically provides for the intern to carry part of a regular teaching load for which a salary is paid by the school system. Such an arrangement frequently reduces or eliminates the observation and participation stages common to clinical practice in student teaching programs. It places the intern in a situation of reality from the first day he begins the clinical assignment.

Advantages claimed for the clinical experience aspects of the internship include the following: [2]

1. Because the intern is usually more mature than the student teacher and possesses a stronger background of scholarship in the teaching field, he typically has greater readiness and self-confidence for learning to teach.

2. The intern lives and participates in the life of the community and he is a full-time member of the school faculty; thus, he can learn more and faster about what teaching is like.

3. As a certified, employed teacher, the intern has the opportunity to become identified with the teaching profession.

[2] For a helpful discussion of the current status of the internship see: Judson T. Shaplin and Arthur G. Powell, "A Comparison of Internship Programs," *The Teacher Education Journal* 15:2, June 1964, pp. 175–183.

For a brief description of specific internship programs and the use of innovations in the internship see *The New Teacher: A Report on Ford Foundation Assistance For New Patterns in the Education of Teachers.* New York: The Foundation, 1962.

4. The intern's relationships with pupils and colleagues are the same as those of other members of the faculty since he is not viewed by either as a "student" teacher.

5. The study of methods and problems of teaching is more realistic, since it is conducted in concurrent seminars with college supervisor and supervising teachers that offer opportunities for consideration of ways to improve teaching.

6. The intern's close association with experienced teachers of the faculty, including in some situations participation in team teaching and other innovations, can lead to maximum professional development.

7. The intern gains from working in a program of clinical practice to which both the preparing institution and the school system providing the clinical station have made a strong commitment; the support and resources of both agencies are readily available.

8. The intern is awarded college credits, applicable to a master's degree in most instances, while obtaining valuable teaching experience and earning a salary.

Such advantages as these are accompanied by challenging responsibilities. In a real sense, the intern has many of the responsibilities of an experienced teacher without the equivalent background of knowledge for meeting them. However, the intern has the good fortune to be in a situation where he is confronted with the realities of the teaching-learning situation, is highly motivated to do his best, and can work with team members who are committed to help him do the best job of which he is capable.

Members of the Internship Team

The nucleus of the clinical practice team is essentially the same for the internship as for student teaching programs. Relationships and responsibilities, however, may differ. Depending on the situation, the college supervisor may take more responsibility for the supervision of the intern's teaching, since a supervising teacher will not be responsible for the classes taught as in the student teaching situation. On the other hand, in the internship arrangement the clinical practice team may be augmented by other faculty members and it may include other interns. The supervising teacher may be a clinical professor employed by both the school system and the preparing institution. If so, he will assume much of the responsibility of the college supervisor.

Perhaps more than in student teaching programs, all members of the faculty, particularly those in the same subject field or grade level, feel responsibility to help the intern. However, the commitment will not compare in intensity to that of the supervising teacher. Because he is a certified teacher and an employed member of the faculty, the intern will have more direct relationships with the principal, the departmental chairman, and the supervisory staff than he would if he were a student teacher.

A weakness that has been attributed to some internship programs is the failure of the teacher development team to function. The emphasis on giving the intern full responsibility for teaching certain subjects or a specific elementary grade may tend to put him on his own too much. With no supervising teacher giving day-by-day assistance, the intern's major source of help may be the college supervisor during the weekly seminars and other intermittent visits made by this official to the intern.

Here again, individual differences determine interns' needs. Many adapt well to the independence provided; others prefer more help. The intern faces a special obligation to assess his own capacities and difficulties and to seek help from colleagues or the college supervisor. A sound approach is for each intern to anticipate that he will need considerable assistance from the college supervisor during the initial stages of his assignment. This is likely to be especially true if the intern has not had the opportunity previously to engage in a program of clinical experience, including observation and participation, if not student teaching. The intern should be frank and forthright in asking for help whenever he needs it, but he will need to avoid consuming an undue proportion of the time of the supervising teacher or becoming dependent upon him. The intern in working with his supervising teacher needs to make a special effort to benefit from observing classroom teaching, engaging in cooperative teaching, and obtaining help through conferences.

The Value of Professional Seminars

Interns have found the professional seminar, scheduled once or twice weekly during the semester or year of clinical experience, to be one of the most helpful features of their preparation for teaching. It provides a unique opportunity to share successes and to obtain help with problems which arise in teaching. It serves as a channel for the exchange of ideas among all those who share in fostering the professional growth of the inexperienced teacher. Individuals who make contributions to the seminar include the college representative who conducts it, the intern, the supervising teacher, other teachers from local schools, local school administrators or supervisors, college faculty members from academic or professional fields, and specialists of many kinds from the local school or the college. Emphasizing the potentialities of the seminar, a committee from a highly regarded state council on teacher education made the following recommendations:

The seminar study that accompanies the intern teaching year ought to be seen as fundamental to the preparation of teachers. This continuing seminar should give attention to problems directly growing out of the teaching experience of the intern. Moreover, the seminar staff ought to introduce such professional content as is pertinent to the development of teaching competence. It is felt that out of such a seminar approach the staff should have opportunities to relate immediate problems to broad areas of professional learning, and that the intern ought to be helped to make generalizations about fundamentals of education from this classroom experience and this related instruction.[3]

The intern will receive maximum benefit from the seminar only when he assumes responsibility for making it a helpful learning experience. Some of the things he can do are listed here.

1. Understand the nature of the seminar. It is intended to serve as a forum where views are exchanged and solutions to problems

[3] California Council on Teacher Education, *The Place of Internship Programs in Teacher Education*. Sacramento, California: California State Department of Education, 1960, p. 25.

are sought. It is not a formal classroom situation where the instructor lectures and students listen.

2. Record in advance items to be considered in the seminar.

3. Attempt each day to relate what has been learned previously about learning and teaching to what is happening in day-to-day work in the school. Discussion in the seminar of instances where theory and practice do or do not synchronize can increase understanding and crystallize viewpoints.

4. Make careful preparation for each seminar meeting by

a. Keeping a notebook or log from which a brief résumé of what has happened each week can be prepared

b. Obtaining from the supervising teacher suggestions or questions which he believes need consideration in the seminar

c. Noting problems for which a solution is needed

d. Listing significant successes which when shared with others might be helpful to them

e. Giving thought to ways in which help may be obtained from the college supervisor, fellow interns, or others at each meeting of the seminar

5. Discuss with the supervising teacher what takes place at each seminar meeting. This will serve as an aid in obtaining benefits from the most recent meeting and in making preparation for the next one.

CLINICAL EXPERIENCE IN AN INSTRUCTIONAL TEAM

The foregoing discussion of the teacher development team has been concerned with the more standard arrangements for clinical experiences, either in the program of student teaching or in the internship, in which the prospective teacher is assigned to one supervising teacher and to one class group.

A recent innovation is the provision of clinical practice as an integral part of an instructional team engaged in team teaching. To perceive how this type of clinical practice is organized, it is first necessary to understand what is meant by both key terms: "instructional team" and "team teaching."

Instructional Team

An instructional team is a group of professional and para-professional workers whose members jointly and cooperatively develop and implement a system of instruction for groups of learners. The size and composition of the team will vary with the number of pupils served. Professional members in a large team might include one or more superior teachers; the part-time assistance of supervisory, learning, library, counseling, subject matter, sociological, and communications specialists; and student teachers or interns. Para-professional members may be instructional secretaries, technical assistants, teacher aides, or other types of workers whose services may be required. The smallest instructional team might be composed of a superior teacher, one intern as professional personnel, and an instructional secretary for para-professional support.

Team Teaching

The instructional team functions and organizes learning experiences for pupils through a process that has come to be called "team teaching." It has been defined as follows:

Team teaching is a type of instructional organization, involving teaching personnel and the students assigned to them, in which two or more teachers are given responsibility, working together, for all or a significant part of the instruction of the same group of students.[4]

A more detailed description of sample compositions of teams and the manner in which they conduct team teaching has been provided by Anderson:

At the elementary level, the team may include pupils of the same age or grade level or of adjoining age or grade levels. In general, each teacher in an elementary team teaches all subjects taught in her grade and works at one time or another with every child in the group. Each

[4] Judson T. Shaplin and Henry F. Olds, Jr., *Team Teaching* (New York: Harper & Row, 1964), p. 15.

teacher might, however, have special competency and interest in a curriculum area, so that the total team would include a number of specialists (e.g., one in science-mathematics, one in language arts, one in social studies, one in the creative arts), each capable of taking leadership for the planning and perhaps for a major share of the teaching in his area. However, because all teachers are involved in the total program, there would not be departmentalization in the usual sense.

The same principle applies at the secondary level, where teams may be organized in a number of different ways. Usually, teams are concerned with one subject field or a familiar combination of fields (e.g., English-social studies or science-mathematics), but sometimes they are multidisciplinary. There is also variation in the age-grade levels with which teams work: some teams deal only with pupils in a single grade (e.g., tenth-grade science or eighth-grade all subjects), while others work with pupils in several levels. For example, a team of three language-arts specialists might, in a small junior high school, handle all English instruction for the pupils in seventh, eighth, and ninth grades.[5]

Under the instructional team arrangement one or more prospective teachers, one or more supervising teachers, and other personnel function as team members. They work in close cooperation toward the goal of helping developing teachers to become competent classroom teachers and, also, experienced members of instructional teams. The University of Wisconsin has pioneered in the use of the instructional team to provide clinical experience for interns. Its intern-in-team plan involves the cooperation of schools throughout the state; a number of other colleges, public and nonpublic; and the state department of public instruction.[6]

Only in the past few years, however, and only in a few schools has the prospective teacher had the opportunity to serve as a member of a *teaching team* in the sense that the term is defined by Shaplin and Olds. The number of school systems engaging in team teaching has been increasing, however, and colleges and

[5] Robert H. Anderson in *Individualizing Instruction*. Yearbook, National Society for the Study of Education, Part I. (Chicago: The Society, 1962), p. 257.
[6] *Administrative Handbook on the Teacher Internship Program in Cooperation With Other Colleges and Wisconsin School Systems* (Madison, Wisconsin: University of Wisconsin, 1963), pp. 23–26.

universities are alert to this newer, effective way of preparing teachers for the kinds of situations in which they may later work.

PERCEPTION AND ASSIMILATION OF RESOURCES FOR CLINICAL TEAMWORK

The prospective teacher entering into a program of clinical practice, whether in a program of student teaching or of internship, should not lose sight of the reason for working with pupils in a classroom and with other members of the clinical practice team. Everything focuses on the development of a competent teacher. To make the most of the team resources the student teacher or intern needs to assess the elements in the total situation, to perceive what is happening, and to comprehend the impact all has on pupil progress as well as on the professional development of the prospective teacher.

A diagramatic outline of teamwork during clinical practice is presented in Figure 2. By visualizing the resources and relationships available, the potentialities of the teacher development team may be better realized.

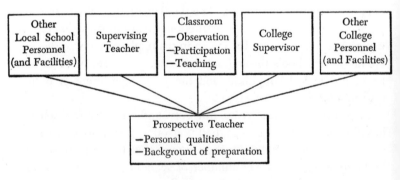

FIGURE 2.

Resources and Teamwork for Clinical Experience

Clearly, the resources for teacher development are almost unlimited. The astute and thoughtful student will search for and seek to utilize the potentialities that exist. Otherwise, the time and energies of the various members of the clinical team will be dissipated. More critically, for the individual student teacher or intern as well as for the profession of teaching and the society it serves, teaching talent—one of the world's most precious commodities—will go undeveloped.

SUMMARY

The student teaching team is composed of the student teacher, the supervising teacher, and the college supervisor. The internship team is composed of the intern, the supervising teacher, and the college supervisor.

The student teacher needs to understand the complex role of the supervising teacher. It is a dual role in that the supervising teacher is a teacher of children and a guide for the prospective teacher. Working with a student teacher is an added responsibility for which the classroom teacher's load usually is not reduced, nor is adequate financial compensation made.

The student teacher has unusual opportunities for learning by observing, participating, and teaching. He needs to become actively identified with pupils from the beginning of the clinical assignment. He should assume additional responsibilities as rapidly as he and his supervising teacher believe he is ready. As he approaches the end of the assignment period he engages in teaching much of the time.

The student teacher should expect to receive help from his supervising teacher through scheduled and informal conferences. It is his responsibility to prepare for them and to make them of maximum value.

The college supervisor is the leader of the three-member student teaching team and holds a strategic position in the education of teachers. If the student teacher understands the role of the college supervisor and works in close cooperation with him, he can benefit from the help available through visits, conferences, and the seminar which the college supervisor usually directs.

The internship team is composed of the intern, the supervising teacher, and the college supervisor. Internships have been classified into four broad categories. Regardless of the structure of the internship or the manner in which the internship team is constituted, three conditions usually exist. The intern receives a salary, receives supervision and assistance from both local school and college personnel, and enrolls in a seminar.

In elementary schools it is common practice for the supervising teacher to devote full time to supervision of interns. He teaches a group of children at times while the intern observes, but he does not hold a regular classroom teaching position. At the secondary level he customarily works with the intern and also teaches.

The college supervisor has major responsibility for the internship program at a particular grade level or in a subject field. He is the connecting link between the local school and the teacher education institution. He works with the other two members of the teaching team to coordinate the efforts of all. The professional seminar is a formal means of dealing with teaching problems as they arise.

The intern-in-team pattern of clinical practice provides for the prospective teacher to become a member of an instructional team and to participate in its program of team teaching. Such a plan has certain advantages not found in most programs of student teaching or the internship.

USEFUL REFERENCES

Association for Student Teaching. *Concern for the Individual in Student Teaching.* Cedar Falls, Iowa: The Association, 1963.
———. *The Supervising Teacher.* Cedar Falls, Iowa: The Association, 1959.
Boyan, Norman J. "The Intern Team as a Vehicle for Teacher Education," *The Journal of Teacher Education* 16:1 (March 1965) 17–24.
California Council on Teacher Education. *The Place of Internship Programs in Teacher Education.* Sacramento, California: California State Department of Education, 1960.

Corman, Bernard R., and Ann G. Olmsted. *The Internship in the Preparation of Elementary School Teachers.* East Lansing, Michigan: College of Education, Michigan State University, 1964.

Edwards, Helen E. *Building Good Relationships: A Major Role of the College Supervisor.* Cedar Falls, Iowa: The Association for Student Teaching, 1961.

Hunter, Elizabeth. *The Cooperating Teacher at Work.* New York: Bureau of Publications, Teachers College, Columbia University, 1962.

Shaplin, Judson T., and Henry F. Olds, Jr. *Team Teaching.* New York: Harper & Row, 1964.

Wisconsin Improvement Program, *Making Teaching and Learning Better.* Madison, Wisconsin: Wisconsin Improvement Program, 1962.

PART TWO
LEARNING
TO TEACH
THROUGH CLINICAL
EXPERIENCE

CHAPTER FOUR

PLANNING
FOR LEARNING

Every good school has an over-all plan for the organization of the curriculum. Decisions will usually have been made about what content should be included in the instructional program and at what age or grade level certain portions of this content will be presented to pupils. This information is usually available in a curriculum guide or course of study for the school system.

Wise educational planning is based on sound methods of teaching, with consideration of relevant factors in the local school. In this chapter we will examine the kinds of planning that will lead to successful instruction; in Chapters 5 and 6, the methods for carrying out the plan and for evaluating its success will be discussed.

FOUNDATIONS OF PLANNING

The Local School System and Planning

What are existing curriculum requirements for pupils from kindergarten through grade twelve? What have been the curricular experiences of pupils one will instruct and what is prescribed for them in the future? What existing school policies influence the school curriculum? These are questions which relate to a teacher's planning and for which he should seek answers.

Learning about the curriculum of the total school. As background for intensive planning the prospective teacher will need to become informed about the content prescribed in the curriculum guide for the grade level or subject area in which he will be working. For example, the sixth-grade teacher needs to know more than that he will be teaching social studies. He needs to know more specifically whether he will be teaching about the Old World, the Americas, the Far East, or his individual state. The ninth-grade science teacher needs to know specifically what areas or sections of the subject his pupils will study. Both also need to know, in broad outline at least, what is prescribed in each grade from kindergarten through grade twelve. This is essential so that the teacher can help the pupil to achieve unification and integration of what is learned. This cannot be accomplished if each teacher is concerned only with content for his own group of pupils and teaches what he chooses without regard for the total instructional program.

Synchronizing present instruction with previous and future instruction. The individual who is working in a school for the first time needs to relate his planning to the instruction the group has received in the recent past and to that which the group is likely to receive in the foreseeable future. Some teachers who have failed to make such relationships have made extensive preparation for the instruction of pupils only to hear them say, "We have had that before." Others have received the disapproval of staff members who have taught the same group of pupils at a later time and found that their prescribed content has already been presented. The curriculum guide or course of study indicates what is to be presented to the group each year. Use of this information will prevent serious overlapping and enable the teacher to utilize every opportunity to relate what is taught during the current year to previous and subsequent instruction.

Discovering school policies on instruction. Each school system and individual school has goals or policies directly or indirectly related to instruction and instructional planning. They may be stated in the school handbook or curriculum guide, or they may not be stated in writing. In some schools it may be an unwritten policy for each staff member to determine what is to be taught. The student teacher or intern has the responsibility as a professional person to discover and adhere to such school policies.

The following questions indicate some of the areas in which policies are frequently formulated.

1. Is reading taught in the kindergarten to those who are ready for it, or is it delayed for all children until later?

2. Is phonics emphasized in the teaching of reading, is it used as it seems to be needed, or is it seldom used?

3. When do pupils change from manuscript to cursive writing? Is the change to be made at a fixed point in the child's progress, such as grade three, or is it to be determined on an individual basis?

4. Is spelling instruction based on a prescribed list of words given at predetermined intervals, or is it based on the needs of each individual child?

5. Is mathematics instruction based upon traditional mathematics or is emphasis placed upon "modern mathematics"?

6. Is emphasis placed on the use of new methods, devices, and techniques such as educational television, programmed instruction, and auto-instructional devices?

7. Is homework emphasized or discouraged?

8. Is organization of instruction around units encouraged? Are resource units developed cooperatively?

9. What is the place of the textbook in the instructional program? Is it adhered to rigidly in all areas or is there considerable flexibility in its use?

10. Is there an abundance of supplementary instructional material, or are there limited instructional resources? Is there a school library? How is it utilized?

11. Are excursions and field trips to be used, or are they discouraged?

12. What is the policy about the use of specialists and assistants other than teachers in the instruction of pupils?

13. Are teachers encouraged to experiment and search for ways of improving the instruction of pupils or are they expected to adhere to more conservative practices?

The individual who expends the time and effort necessary to discover in advance of detailed planning the existing policies and practices which are related to instruction will very likely save time, avoid embarrassment, and work in harmony with both faculty members and pupils.

Discovering and Using What Is Known About Pupils

The effective teacher discovers as much as possible about the group of pupils with which he is working and makes use of this information in planning for their instruction. He knows that his purposes in making plans will be affected by individual needs of group members and by the environments in which they live.

In preparation for teaching a fourth-grade group a young intern discovered that children in her group were living in a low-income area where there was considerable unemployment. It was apparent that some children in her group were not receiving an adequate diet and some frequently came to school without breakfast or returned for the afternoon session without lunch. After conferring with her supervising teacher and principal, she planned instruction in health and science classes to help pupils meet some of the problems confronting them. Children learned of the foods which meet nutritional needs and of their relative costs. They prepared simple, nutritional, low-cost menus and took them home. They worked with the school nurse, home economics teacher, and cafeteria personnel in planning adequate and low-cost school lunches. With the intern's help they obtained films and filmstrips for their own use and arranged to have them shown at Parent-Teacher Association meetings.

A student teacher working with a group of tenth-grade pupils in a world history class had a different and less satisfying experience. In a methods course taken prior to student teaching, he prepared a very complete unit on the countries of Western Europe to be used during his student teaching or later in his first year of teaching. His assignment was in a school located in a prosperous suburban residential community where many of the residents were business and professional people employed in a neighboring city. His pupils were privileged individuals from homes which provided many educational advantages for their children. In preparing his unit he had made provision for motivation on the assumption that he would be teaching a group which knew very little about the countries to be studied. He was surprised and disappointed to discover that pupils did not respond enthusiastically to the motivation techniques he had planned. He soon learned that the lack of interest and enthusiasm resulted from the fact that a number of the group had traveled in Europe. Some had visited Europe several times and several had been there during the previous vacation period. He was quick to change his plans. He took advantage of the experiences of class members who had been to Europe as a means of motivating study of the unit and making it real and meaningful to all members of the group. The necessity for changing plans caused him some embarrassment and considerable added time and work which might otherwise have been used more profitably. The shift necessitated a change in his tentative timetable for completing the unit, wasted some of the pupils' time, and caused a temporary loss of his status with pupils. This was a costly learning experience for him. These unproductive results could have been avoided if he had spent time and effort to learn about the experiences of his pupils before he introduced the unit.

The Time Element in Planning

It is important to establish a classroom setting in which teacher and pupils recognize that there is relationship and sequence between the various topics, problems, or units that comprise the instructional program. This necessitates both long-range and short-term planning.

Superior teachers take the long view of instruction. They think of their goal as helping the individual pupil become an integrated personality as he progresses through the elementary and secondary schools. This is in sharp contrast with the attitude of the teacher who merely "keeps school" and views each school day as a separate period of instruction in which he dispenses the subject matter that is most conveniently available without considering the needs of pupils. Long-range planning is essential for good instruction. This may require making plans for a month, a semester, a year, or even several years. For the student teacher or intern long-range planning is likely to encompass a semester or year at the most, and, often, a shorter interval.

When long-range plans have been formulated, the teacher is ready to make short-term plans. They may be for a week, one or more days, or for part of a day. In some schools the course of study will indicate that a specified amount of time is to be allotted for a topic, unit, or area of instruction. In other schools the teacher is encouraged to make his own time schedule and to use the time available in a manner which is likely to be most productive. The preparation of a daily plan from a long-range plan is illustrated later in this chapter.

The Preparation of Plans

An analysis of well-constructed plans will reveal certain basic components which are common to most of them. Each component is essential in long-range, daily, short-term, or unit planning. They are: objectives, content, instructional materials, pupil activities, and teaching procedures—including motivation, and the assignment when it is needed.

The work of the prospective teacher will be influenced by the extent to which he will be expected to follow a predetermined curriculum. He should remember that the situation in which he will work at some later time as a fully certificated teacher may be quite different from that in which he is involved during his clinical assignment. Thus, it is important to know more about planning than may be needed in the present situation. This help is provided in the following sections.

Objectives. Sometimes a beginner becomes so eager to start teaching that he fails to give careful thought to what he hopes to accomplish by his instruction. He may see little need for a statement of objectives and may not even realize that he is working toward an objective.

A beginning student teacher in charge of a sixth-grade group during a language arts period was asked by the college supervisor what she hoped to accomplish during the half hour she was teaching. She replied that she was asked by her supervising teacher to pronounce a list of spelling words. She had failed to comprehend the fact that the list she was using had been prepared cooperatively by pupils and teacher and consisted of words the group had misspelled in their written work during the previous week. She had failed to pinpoint the objective of her teaching—to help pupils master words they did not spell correctly and which they needed to spell in order to communicate properly.

It is possible with thought and practice to become so skillful in selecting and stating attainable objectives that the student learning to teach, his supervising teacher, or any knowledgeable teacher will know what outcomes are intended. A study of the work of a group of researchers should assist the student in achievement of this degree of clarity. They have classified and defined educational objectives in the following manner.

1. *Cognitive:* Objectives which emphasize remembering or reproducing something which has presumably been learned, as well as objectives which involve the solving of some intellective task for which the individual has to determine the essential problem and then reorder given material or combine it with ideas, methods, or procedures previously learned. 2. *Affective:* Objectives which emphasize a feeling tone, an emotion, or a degree of acceptance or rejection. 3. *Psychomotor:* Objectives which emphasize some muscular or motor skill, some manipulation of material and objects, or some act which requires a neuromuscular co-ordination.[1]

Content. Content is the vehicle by which objectives are reached. It becomes the basis for determining the instructional materials to be used, the activities in which pupils will engage, and the procedures the teacher will employ. Good content is essential to good planning and good teaching. Just as high-quality

[1] David R. Krathwohl, ed., *Taxonomy of Educational Objectives: The Classification of Educational Goals.* Handbook II: *Affective Domain* (New York: David McKay Company, Inc., 1964), pp. 6–7.
See also Handbook I: *Cognitive Domain,* edited by Benjamin S. Bloom, and published in 1956 by Longmans, Green and Co.

ingredients are essential in the preparation of a superior meal or the production of a precision instrument, the most appropriate, accurate, and challenging content is essential to good planning, teaching, and resultant learning. Just as the skill of a good cook or craftsman is not fully utilized when inferior raw materials are used, so even the superior teacher cannot achieve the results of which he is capable unless the best content available is selected.

The person who wishes to become a competent teacher will not be satisfied to include in his plans only content that is prescribed in the course of study or that which happens to be easily available. He will be alert to up-date what is found in textbooks; he will read widely and thus discover and use new pertinent information, and he will search continuously for subject matter that is pertinent for his pupils. He will keep in mind that the subject matter selected must be in terms of the objectives he has selected for his plan.

Instructional materials.   Good planning includes provision for specifically identified and listed instructional materials. Materials will include those which will be assigned to pupils as well as those to which they can refer as they do individual work and research. Provision needs to be made for all available instructional materials that can be used effectively. There is such a wealth of good material available today that the teacher has little excuse for using materials that are of slight value. The busy teacher may be tempted to use mediocre instructional materials because of the large quantity always available. Chapter 7 is devoted to the selection and use of instructional materials.

Pupil activities.   A plan should provide for the involvement of pupils and should indicate ways to do this. If the teacher waits until actual instruction begins to decide what activities pupils are to engage in, their involvement is likely to be haphazard, resulting in poor instruction and little learning.

Provision needs to be made for a variety of activities. At times —for example, when high school pupils in a laboratory are working on an individual experiment and interest is high—it will be profitable for pupils to continue with the same activity for an extended period of time. However, as the thoughtful prospective teacher learned from professional courses and contacts with pupils, it is normal for them to tire when they engage in any activity for a long time without a change of pace.

Teaching procedures. The good teacher knows that before starting to teach he must determine which of the many procedures he might employ will be most likely to help him reach his objective for each phase of instruction included in his plan. This does not mean, however, that his plan will be so rigid that procedures cannot be changed to adapt to changing circumstances.

A teacher needs to be aware of the numerous techniques, devices, and procedures available today. He should avoid the error of using the same few procedures over and over, day after day, until pupils (and often the teacher himself) become bored from lack of variety. He should not limit procedures to the commonly followed routine of the lecture, assigned reading from a textbook, and questioning. He needs to use procedures which at any given time are most likely to result in appropriate learning. If he decides that a lecture will stimulate thought about a topic, he should expect an attentive response from his pupils. If it becomes evident that pupils are uninterested or inattentive, the procedure should be changed to one that is likely to obtain better results.

Motivation and planning. Careful planning should include provision for motivation. The teacher needs to achieve two objectives in the area of pupil motivation. One is long-range and continuous. With this goal in mind he attempts to help the pupil understand that he has a continuing opportunity to improve himself through school attendance and that he must assume some responsibility for his own education. A second objective is to stimulate pupils' interest each time a lesson, topic, or unit is introduced.

The kind of motivation to be included in planning will be determined by such factors as age, ability, home background, and breadth of experience of pupils. It is important to start a lesson, project, or unit with an item of interest to the group and to build upon that interest. The near at hand can be used to interest pupils in the far away; the tangible or concrete can be utilized to motivate pupils to understand and learn about the intangible and the abstract. The following examples illustrate procedures that have been used to motivate pupils in various situations.

A beginning French class in junior high school viewed a film portraying a day in the life of a French villager.

In a social studies class in lower elementary grades a mail carrier talked to a group which was beginning a study of community helpers.

In a mathematics class in senior high school the manager of a computer center spoke to the class about the changing mathematics and its implications for future living.

The teacher of a literature class in upper elementary grades read sections from *Huckleberry Finn* to illustrate the fact that there are many interesting good books in the school library which may be chosen for recreational reading.

A science class in junior high school was taken on a field trip to the municipal water treatment plant to increase pupils' interest in a study of ways science benefits mankind.

A short walking excursion in the vicinity of the school building was taken by a language arts class in lower elementary grades to encourage each child to select a topic about which he would write briefly.

The teacher of a social problems class in senior high school asked each pupil to make a list of conditions in the community which needed improvement. This was to motivate a study of how community improvements are brought about.

The person who wishes to become a superior teacher will continually explore possible ways of motivating pupils. He will keep in mind that pupils learn the things that interest them. He will put forth every reasonable effort to make his classroom one to which pupils like to come because they are challenged to learn. The teacher needs to distinguish between the kind of satisfaction the pupil experiences when he masters a difficult concept or skill and that which results from merely enjoying pleasant associations. Some beginning teachers have been guilty of viewing their major goal as making their classroom a place where pupils "enjoy" themselves. This is a superficial view of the teacher's role. The truly great teachers are those who succeed in motivating each pupil to learn to the limit of his ability. This kind of motivation takes the learner beyond the "enjoyment" stage to the stage where the real reward results from having undertaken and mastered tasks that are both important and difficult for him.

Assignment and planning. In planning for effective teaching consideration must be given to making assignments. The assignment should have the following characteristics.

1. It should be appropriate to the objectives the teacher has in mind or that teacher and pupils have agreed upon. It is important to distinguish between assignments that are mere busywork and those that are related to a specific purpose. For example, the skillful teacher who is attempting to help a group of elementary school children master a specific skill in arithmetic will attempt to assign each individual enough meaningful practice to help him acquire that skill. He will not ask all pupils to "work the problems on the next three pages" regardless of individual needs.

2. It should be challenging and geared to the abilities of individuals in the group. The teacher should not insult the intelligence of his pupils by assigning tasks that are much too easy for them to accomplish without effort. On the other hand, he should avoid assignments that are too difficult or impossible for them to complete satisfactorily.

3. Each assignment should be made with the purpose of contributing to the total development of the pupil. Demands are made upon the pupil by other school personnel, and many pupils have responsibilities at home and elsewhere during out-of-school hours. The teacher should learn to know his pupils and school policies relating to homework so that he can avoid overloading as well as lack of challenge.

4. Assignments must be clear and definite. Pupils should be

taught to pay attention to the assignment as it is being made. They have a right to expect their teacher to tell them exactly what is expected, to give illustrations when necessary, and to answer pertinent questions which are needed for clarification.

5. The assignment should provide for motivation. It should help the pupil see the need for the work assigned. He should be led to see the relationship between what has been completed and what lies ahead.

6. Prospective and beginning teachers are concerned frequently about when the assignment should be made. It should be made whenever it will be most likely to facilitate learning. This time will vary, depending upon a number of factors. If a teacher is following a textbook rather closely, he may need to made an assignment every time the class meets—perhaps near the end of the class period. If he is teaching a group in a science laboratory, the assignment may need to be made whenever a project or an experiment is finished. In some subjects such as art, home economics, or social studies where pupils may be working on individual or small-group projects, assignments may need to be made infrequently or on an individual basis. The teacher should be alert to determine when interest is high among his pupils and when there is a need to move forward.

7. Assignments should be made in the light of availability and accessibility of learning resources needed to complete the assignment. The student teacher or intern needs to be informed about instructional materials and learning resources available in the school and should help his pupils make good use of them. He should be sure that all reference and supplementary material to which they are referred is readily available to them. He should work in close cooperation with the school librarian and others who make resource materials available so that unreasonable demands are not made upon them and so that they will know in advance of requests that will be made by pupils.

Evaluation. Teaching plans should include provision for evaluation. Procedures, instruments, or techniques should be selected in terms of how well they are likely to determine the extent to which objectives have been achieved. If, for example, the plan is for a single lesson in a mathematics class and the main objective is mastery of certain specific skills, provision for evaluation might include only a brief written test to determine if skills have been acquired. On the other hand, if the plan is for a unit in a content subject such as science or social studies which is to cover an extended period of time, provision for evaluation will need to include a list of various evaluative procedures for determining how well the several objectives listed in the plan have been met. For example, assume that a high school teacher of American History has made plans for a unit in which the content deals with a period of time following World War II. He might use the evaluative techniques indicated below to determine how well the hypothetical objectives mentioned have been reached.

OBJECTIVE	MEANS OF EVALUATION
To develop attitudes of world-mindedness.	List of questions sampling beliefs held by pupils to be asked before the unit is taught and again *when it is completed.* Changes to be noted.
To develop mastery of historical facts and an understanding of their implications.	Written test to determine if facts were learned and if an understanding of their implications was acquired.
To help pupils grow in ability to work cooperatively.	Oral and written statements by pupils about their own effectiveness or lack of it. Teacher states his own evaluation and discusses it with pupils.

The Unit and Planning

Teachers have discovered advantages in using a unit as they plan for instruction. The unit makes possible systematic organization of subject matter to be taught and facilitates careful long-range planning.

In the *Dictionary of Education* a unit is defined as "an organization of learning activities, experiences, and types of learning, around a central theme, problem or purpose, developed cooperatively by a group of pupils under teacher leadership." [2] This has come to be known as a *teaching unit* or *learning unit* as contrasted with a *resource unit*. The teacher will observe that the unit as defined here provides the framework into which the components of a plan, as discussed in previous sections, can be placed. The teaching unit makes it possible to plan for unity of instruction to a greater extent than is possible when unrelated lessons are prepared day after day. It makes possible a systematic means of listing objectives, content, instructional materials, pupil activities, teaching procedures, and evaluation, regardless of whether the central theme is to extend over a considerable period of time or only last for a short period. The unit also makes possible and facilitates teacher-pupil planning without consuming an unwarranted amount of time for teacher and pupils.

The following definition of a *resource unit* will help the prospective teacher to gain understanding of its possibilities in the preparation and use of the teaching or learning unit.

The resource unit is a comprehensive study usually developed by a group of teachers or college students on some topic which is taught at a given grade level. The topic may be as broad as "South America" or as limited as "Wireless Communication." Following the same arrangement or organizational areas identified in a teaching unit, a group of teachers usually makes an exhaustive study of the selected topic. Thus, the resource unit becomes a source of ideas and materials readily available for use at the time needed by the teacher in developing some phase of learning related to the topic. Expediency becomes paramount when the teacher is involved in actual classroom teaching. Therefore, the resource unit which is usually developed during workshops or extended work days beyond the teaching year provides the teacher with an invaluable time-saving resource.[3]

The prospective teacher may or may not work in a school where resource units are available for his use. In most schools he is likely to find that the teaching or learning unit is being used by

[2] Carter V. Good, *Dictionary of Education* (New York: McGraw-Hill, 1954), p. 436.
[3] Albert H. Shuster and Milton E. Ploghoft, *The Emerging Elementary Curriculum* (Columbus, Ohio: Charles E. Merrill Books, Inc., 1963), pp. 111–112.

some of the teachers. At any rate, he will be better prepared for teaching in any situation if he makes sure that he has had experience in the preparation of units.

Aids to Planning

The student teacher or intern must be alert to assistance in planning that he may obtain from sources other than the supervising teacher.

Illustrations of plans. The illustrations which follow have been used in the classroom by prospective teachers. They illustrate the components of a plan but without the usual detail, which is omitted because of space limitations. Because a good *resource* unit must of necessity be detailed and voluminous, no illustration of that type is included. Illustrations of resource units will be found in references included at the end of this chapter.

TEACHING UNIT [4]

Subject: English
Topic: Paragraph building
Grade: Nine

Introduction

This unit was designed to fit the needs of students of high ability who are preparing for college. A fundamental aspect of this preparation is practice in writing. The development and mastery of a good paragraph is the first step in becoming a good writer. Since this is a ninth-grade class, we will deal only with paragraphs. It is important that pupils obtain a background in the different types of paragraphs and their use. This is the primary purpose of this unit.

I. Objectives
  A. General
    1. To set up a standard for written work
    2. To make good writing a habit
    3. To show importance of writing as a means of communication
    4. To stimulate logical thinking which may be transferred into written English
    5. To foster self-evaluation

[4] Adapted from a unit prepared by Delores Fagg, a student at Indiana State University while she was engaged in student teaching at Bosse High School, Evansville, Indiana.

B. Specific
   1. To develop recognition and use of various types of paragraphs
   2. To correct grammatical errors and poor writing habits
   3. To develop accuracy and good organization in paragraphs
   4. To develop a proficiency in spelling and enlarge the vocabulary of the student

II. Materials
   A. Text: John, Mellie and others. *Building Better English,* Grade 9. Evanston, Illinois: Row, Peterson, and Company, 1957.
   B. Student supplement: Paragraphs from magazines, newspapers, and other books
   C. Teacher supplement: Cross, E. A. and Elizabeth Carney. *Teaching English in High School.* New York: Macmillan, 1950. Flesch, Rudolf and A. H. Lass. *The Way to Write.* New York: McGraw-Hill, 1955. Schutt, Warren E. *Effective Written English.* Princeton, N. J.: D. Van Nostrand, 1949. Smith, Reed. *Learning to Write in College.* Boston: Little, Brown and Company, 1940.
   D. Audio-visual materials: Bulletin board displays and poster on how to construct good paragraphs.
   Examples of well-written paragraphs.
   Chart: Check Your Spelling of These Words (words that have been misspelled by the group). Examples of correct form to be used in written work.

III. Procedure
   A. Diagnosis
   This unit is for the ninth grade. The students are on the college preparatory curriculum. They have not had much experience in writing except for some work on book reports. I hope this unit will enable them to recognize and use various types of paragraphs.
   B. Presentation and motivation
   1. Writing is fun!
   2. There are many different ways in which one may write.
   3. One who writes well is one who gets more pleasure from the works of other people.
   C. Long-range planning
   This unit was designed to cover these areas:
   1. Purposes for writing
      a. To inform
      b. To persuade

      c. To define
      d. To compare and/or contrast
      e. To entertain
    2. Sources for writing
      a. Imagination
      b. One's experience
      c. Factual data
    3. Types of paragraphs
      a. Descriptive
      b. Narrative
      c. Expository
      d. Argumentative
    4. Organization of paragraph
      a. Topic sentence
      b. Relevant material
      c. Sequence of ideas
      d. Unity
      e. Clincher sentence
    5. Grammatical construction of paragraphs
      a. Sentence structure
      b. Verb forms
      c. Punctuation
    6. Vocabulary and spelling used in paragraphs
      a. Level of vocabulary
      b. Specific and vivid words
      c. Troublesome spelling words
D. Summary
By adopting this means of developing paragraphs, one will find that he is bringing about better communication with his reader. This, in turn, brings pleasure to the reader and to you, the writer.
E. Activities
    1. Selection of different types of paragraphs from magazines, newspapers, and other books
    2. Oral exercise in recognizing each type of paragraph
    3. Practice in writing different types of paragraphs
    4. Review of rules on grammar and sentence construction
    5. Oral exercise in selecting vocabulary to use in writing paragraphs
    6. Brief written drill on spelling of troublesome words
    7. Selection of specific words for general terms and more vivid forms of words
    8. Selection of meaningful, life-related topics for paragraphs

IV. Evaluation
   A. Pupil-based upon:
      1. Improvement as writing progresses
      2. Handing in assignments on time
      3. Accuracy and neatness of work
      4. Class participation
   B. Teacher-based upon:
      1. Maintaining objectives
      2. Recognizing weaknesses and strong points of unit
      3. Understanding students' individual needs in order to correlate the unit with these needs

DAILY PLAN [5]

Subject: English
Topic: Paragraph building (from preceding unit on paragraph building)
Grade: Nine
   I. Objectives
      A. To determine the students' writing abilities
      B. To discuss the purposes, sources, and types of writing in paragraphs
  II. Procedure
      A. Pupils will write a paragraph in class on following topics:
         1. "My Ideal ————"
         2. "How I Would Like to Spend My Vacation"
         3. "Why I Should Study"
         4. "My Viewpoint on Going to College"
         5. "What Is Truth?"
         6. "My Best Friend"
         7. "Why I Like or Dislike ————"
      B. Discussion of their purpose for writing.
         Explanation of five purposes for writing:
         1. To inform
         2. To persuade
         3. To define
         4. To compare and/or contrast
         5. To entertain
      C. Discussion of sources from which they gain information for writing:
         1. Imagination

   [5] Adapted from a plan prepared and used by Delores Fagg, a student at Indiana State University while engaged in student teaching at Bosse High School, Evansville, Indiana.

2. One's experience
3. Factual data
D. Explanation of different types of paragraphs:
   1. Descriptive
   2. Narrative
   3. Expository
   4. Argumentative
E. Exercise in trying to identify the type of parapraph from the selections the teacher reads in class

III. Assignment
   A. Bring to class examples from magazines or newspapers of the different types of paragraphs
   B. Write a descriptive paragraph

IV. Class Activity
   A. Writing paragraph in class
   B. Discussion of various aspects of paragraph writing considered
   C. Exercise in identifying different types of paragraphs

V. Evaluation
The students accepted the introduction of this unit very enthusiastically. It was challenging to them to identify the different types of paragraphs. I had told them that they would write a paragraph in class so they were prepared. I found the class to be very responsive.

OUTLINE FOR A DAILY LESSON PLAN [6]

I. Objectives
   A. Concepts—what pupils are expected to learn
   B. Symbols—what new words, dates, or titles are important

II. Materials and resources
Arrange for all material to be used in teaching the lesson, such as maps, audio-visual material, books, or resource persons

III. Time estimate
Estimate time to be used in teaching the lesson

IV. Method
Teaching procedures and pupil activities to be employed
   A. Introduce lesson (motivation)
   B. Pertinent questions
   C. Provide for pupil activities such as
      1. Discussion

[6] Adapted from an outline prepared by Mary Frances Gooldy for use in working with a student teacher. Mrs. Gooldy is a fifth-grade teacher in the Nicholson School, Crawfordsville, Indiana.

    2. Practice to acquire skills

    3. Reading and study

V. Evaluation

    A. Testing

    B. Checking understanding of symbols

    C. Discussion of what has been learned

VI. Assignment

    A. Designation and clarification of responsibilities

    B. Textbook assignment, resource book assignments, and other assignments

    C. Provision for individual differences

Guide for planning. The teacher will find a guide or check-list useful as an aid in making plans. A number of prospective teachers have found useful the following list of questions which incorporate the essential components of planning.

I. What am I going to teach?

II. Why am I going to teach this unit or lesson?

III. How am I going to teach this unit or lesson?

    A. How shall I make motivation effective?

    B. What pivotal questions shall be used?

    C. How shall I discover what the pupil already knows about this subject?

    D. What past experience shall I draw upon to introduce new concepts?

    E. What materials, references, and resources shall I use for enrichment?

    F. What individual assignments or follow-up activities shall I use to follow this unit or lesson?

    G. What suggestions shall I give to stimulate further research by pupils?

IV. How shall I check the results of my teaching?

    A. Did I accomplish my purpose?

    B. What objectives did I accomplish?

    C. What will I need to reteach?

    D. Which pupils need individual instruction as revealed through evaluation?

    (Part IV is used, after the unit or lesson is taught, in making plans for instruction to follow.) [7]

[7] From a guide sheet originally prepared by Janice Hankins, a student teacher at Indiana State University while she was engaged in student teaching at Deming School, Terre Haute, Indiana. She was assisted by her super-

PLANNING WITH THE SUPERVISING TEACHER

The supervising teacher more than any other person is likely to influence the thinking of the student teacher or intern in the area of planning. The prospective teacher should take full advantage of every possible opportunity to utilize this assistance.

Obtaining Help in Planning

To fully utilize the help of the supervising teacher the prospective teacher should do the following things, among others:

1. Discover and understand clearly the instructional plans that already exist for the group with which one is to work.

2. Take the initiative in seeking help from the supervising teacher.

3. Discover expectations of the supervising teacher. This requires free and frank communication. Such questions as these need to be answered: When do I start to plan? Do I plan alone or with the supervising teacher? How rapidly will I progress toward full responsibility for teaching and, consequently, for extended planning? How frequently will I be called upon to take charge of a part or all of the classroom group without advance notice?

4. Become knowledgeable about individuals in the group. Who is the brilliant one, who the dull one, the lazy one, the shy one, the extrovert, the bookworm?

5. Learn about the kinds and qualities of instructional materials and aids available. Where are they located? What policies and regulations are to be followed in using them?

Written Versus Unwritten Plans

The type of plan and amount of written detail will vary, depending upon the classes to be taught, the ability and judgment of the young teacher, and the judgment of the supervising

---

vising teacher Gertrude Dinkel, members of the Deming School faculty, and Dr. Otto J. Shipla, College Supervisor at Indiana State University. Adapted by Edgar M. Tanruther.

teacher. Beginners are sometimes displeased when they are asked to prepare written plans. They should be made aware that many of the best, most experienced teachers write down what they plan to do when instructing a group. This compels the teacher to be definite and specific rather than indefinite and vague as he might be when he relies on his memory to guide him.

Good planning is essentially making sure one knows what one is doing when instructing pupils. Both supervising teacher and prospective teacher need to understand clearly what is to be taught while the student is in charge of the group. The written plan provides the best means for this understanding. The supervising teacher can make helpful suggestions and the student can obtain help on questions which may be in his mind. The student learning to teach should welcome the opportunity to prepare written plans as one of the best ways to crystallize his own thinking about good teaching and to obtain assistance from a capable and experienced teacher.

It is common practice for the amount of writing to decrease as ability to plan and teach increases. What one should do as an experienced teacher will be determined by his own ability and the situation in which he works.

Thoroughness in Planning

Some beginners, perhaps because they have attempted to carry an overload of other activities or are only interested in "getting by" during their clinical assignment, have not made the careful plans that are essential to good teaching. This is a dangerous practice. If one continues to meet pupils in class and "gets by" even though he has feelings of inadequacy, there is danger that this will become an established pattern of procedure. The result may be that succeeding groups of pupils receive inferior instruction. In making plans the prospective teacher should take care to make adequate provision for content, instructional materials, and pupil activities during the period covered by the plan. Failure to do this may result in a situation in which pupils are left "with nothing to do" and both pupils and teacher lack a sense of direction. The individual who discovers that he has planned more thoroughly than actual teaching requires will find he has a reserve of information and enthusiasm which will help him succeed the next time he meets the group.

Providing for Flexibility

A good plan will include provision for adaptation to changes that may need to be made. The competent teacher plans for what he expects will happen as he teaches, but is prepared to meet the unexpected and to take advantage of learning opportunities that may arise. The following incidents illustrate this point.

An elementary student teacher had made careful plans for teaching spelling to his group for a period of one week. He used the list of words and procedures prescribed by the local curriculum guide, but discovered that his pupils were having difficulty with many of the words encountered in the science unit being studied. With the approval of his supervising teacher he changed his plans so that the spelling assignment also included science words misspelled by the group and, for each individual, a list of words troublesome for him.

An intern responsible for a history class in high school had made extended and detailed plans for his group. His plans did not include the use of a resource person. However, when he discovered that the father of one of the members of the group previously had worked as an engineer in Venezuela as an employee of an oil company, he changed his plans. With the approval of the supervising teacher, his revised plan included an invitation to the father and a planning conference with him. This change in plans resulted in valuable learning experiences for pupils, which both teachers agreed would not have been possible if the original plan had been followed rigidly.

Planning for Extending the Range of Responsibility

The prospective teacher should experience continuous growth in ability to plan as he assumes more responsibility for instruction. Regardless of whether his initial planning is for teaching a single lesson for a short class period or the preparation of a unit designed to continue over an extended period of time, he should make certain that by the time his clinical assignment has ended he is capable of planning for instruction as a responsible teacher. The supervising teacher will usually take the initiative in encouraging the novice to obtain experience in planning for instruction in a wide variety of situations. However, the developing teacher has a responsibility for obtaining it. This need is illustrated by the experience of a first-year elementary teacher. She found that one of the most difficult problems she faced in her teaching was planning so that each individual in several small groups could be kept profitably busy without continuous assistance from her. This, she discovered, was a problem for her because as a student teacher she had resisted the repeated efforts of her supervising teacher to encourage her to make adequate plans for instruction when pupils were divided into small groups.

Evaluating Effectiveness in Planning

Evaluating what one has done is a good learning experience. This is true of learning to plan for instruction. Self-evaluation should follow each instance in which one has been responsible for directing the learning of pupils. This can be a simple exercise in reflection on what was good and what was not good, or it can take the form of a more detailed and careful analysis. The student teacher or intern should find it helpful to ask himself such questions as the following which are stated in terms of the components of a plan mentioned earlier in this chapter.

1. *Objectives.* Did I choose the right objectives for the topic or problem selected? How well were the objectives attained?

2. *Content.* Was the content assigned appropriate for achieving the stated objectives? Was it sufficiently wide in scope to challenge pupils of all levels of ability? Was it up to date?

3. *Instructional materials.* Was the textbook used effectively? Were sufficient supplementary materials available to make it pos-

sible for pupils to accomplish what teacher and pupils sought to accomplish?

4. *Pupil activities.* Were pupils actively and purposefully involved in worthwhile activities? Was there provision for a variety of worthwhile and useful learning activities, or was there a boring sameness to what pupils did?

5. *Teaching procedure, including motivation and needed assignments.* Were teaching procedures appropriate to accomplishment of the stated objectives? Was thinking stimulated by procedures used? Did procedures encourage thoughtful involvement of pupils or were they passive listeners?

PLANNING WITH PUPILS

The alert and resourceful teacher will discover ways of approaching topics or problems for study by talking *with* pupils as well as *to* them. He will not underestimate the importance of planning with pupils. By obtaining experience with each type of planning he can achieve a satisfactory blend of planning both for and with pupils.

Understanding Roles

When a teacher undertakes to involve pupils in making plans for learning he needs to understand clearly, and to help them to understand, the proper role of each. The teacher is charged with the responsibility of leadership. This means that he, not the pupils, determines what is to be taught. This determination of content is made in terms of school policy as reflected in the course of study. It is within this framework that the teacher involves pupils in instructional planning. Some who have not understood this distinction between the roles of teacher and pupils have been embarrassed as a result of their experience with teacher-pupil planning.

While engaging in teacher-pupil planning, the student teacher or intern needs to keep in mind his own role in relation to his supervising teacher. He will support, not disrupt, any plans for the instruction of pupils which the supervising teacher may have projected and will involve pupils in planning within that framework.

Working Together in Planning

When pupils assume some of the responsibility for planning they can discover more clearly what they need to learn and why they need to learn it. They can be encouraged to discover problems and to think carefully and logically as they help to solve those problems. Pupils' involvement in planning can also help the teacher gain insight into the kind of thinking being done by each individual pupil. This knowledge can help the teacher to individualize instruction.

The prospective teacher should have no illusions about the ease with which teacher-pupil planning can be employed. Good teaching is more difficult than poor teaching, and involving pupils in planning is more difficult than planning by the teacher alone. This is especially true if pupils have not had such an experience previously. How does one introduce teacher-pupil planning? The approach will vary, depending on the specific learning situation. The following example will illustrate one approach.

A student teacher in an elementary school, responsible for teaching a unit on weather, conferred at length with her supervising teacher about how pupils might be involved in planning for a study of the unit. She introduced the unit by telling pupils that the course of study provided an opportunity to learn about how living in their community was influenced by weather. She suggested that they think about the topic, talk about it at home, and come to science class the following day prepared to help make plans for learning as much as possible during the time tentatively allotted for study of the unit. During the science period the next day they proceeded as follows:

1. The teacher listed on the chalkboard the questions to which answers were needed in a thorough study of the topic. In doing

this the teacher helped formulate the questions as they were raised by pupils and teacher so that they would be clearly stated and pertinent to the topic.

2. Pupils and teacher made a list of sources of information, including the textbook, supplementary material in their own room, materials available in the library, and possible sources in their own homes and elsewhere in the community. (Individuals were to be contacted as resource persons.)

3. They made a list of ways they would work together. They decided which items listed on the chalkboard all members of the group would study and which would be investigated and reported by individuals or small working committees.

4. They talked briefly about how they would check to discover whether they had found correct answers to questions listed on the chalkboard. They agreed that the teacher should give them a written test and that there should be oral questions. They also decided that the teacher and pupils would need to discuss occasionally how well they were working together and that the teacher would confer with individual pupils as needed.

In carrying the unit to completion, the group met each day during the regular science period. Although the student teacher and her supervising teacher were careful to use no more total time than had been allotted for science instruction, it was necessary to have a flexible science period. On some days more than the allotted time was needed to complete effectively what had been started; on other days less than the regular period was used. Some changes from plans outlined in the original planning session became necessary, but in each instance the teacher and pupils working together decided what the changes should be and how they were to be executed.

Evaluating Teacher-Pupil Planning

The individual who engages in teacher-pupil planning must recognize that he, with the assistance and cooperation of his supervising teacher, must assume responsibility for the effectiveness of planning. As indicated in the illustration, however, pupils must have the opportunity and the responsibility for evaluating their own planning. The prospective teacher must assume a dual role. He will help pupils evaluate their own effectiveness in planning, and he will need to evaluate the over-all results to determine whether or not children have really learned what should have been learned in terms of his stated objectives for the topic, problem, or unit under consideration.

SUMMARY

The kind of planning done by a teacher affects, directly or indirectly, everything that occurs in his classroom. Wise planning contributes to good instruction. Factors to consider in planning include synchronization of classroom work with the curriculum of the school, synchronization with previous instruction and planned future instruction for the group, discovering of school policies on instruction, and utilization of what is known about learners and the learning process.

The teacher needs to become skillful in making long-range plans. He should become proficient in planning and using both teaching and resource units and in making and using good daily plans.

In making long-range plans, in building a good unit, or in making daily plans that achieve good results, the developing teacher must make provision for the essential components of a plan: objectives, content, instructional materials, pupil activities, teaching procedures (including motivation and assignments), and evaluation.

Illustrations were given of a long-range plan, a unit, and a daily plan.

The student teacher or intern will profit by working closely and cooperatively with his supervising teacher in planning for instruction. He can discover what his supervising teacher expects from him in the area of planning. He can obtain information about instructional plans that have already been determined for the group. He can learn much about individual pupils that has implications for instructional planning. He can ascertain the availability of instructional materials.

The supervising teacher recognizes his responsibility for assistance in learning to plan wisely. However, this help cannot become effective unless it is welcomed—even solicited. When the young teacher does welcome assistance he can develop competency in the use of written and unwritten plans and can acquire an optimum amount of flexibility in his instruction. He can learn to plan for extending teaching responsibilities, until he is finally making plans for full-time instruction of his group of pupils. He will also learn to evaluate the effectiveness of his planning.

In learning to plan with pupils as well as for them, one needs to understand the role of teacher and pupil and to develop skill in working with pupils while helping them to share responsibility for making plans.

USEFUL REFERENCES

Alberty, Harold B., and Elsie J. Alberty. *Reorganizing the High School Curriculum*, 3d ed. New York: Macmillan Co., 1962.

Association For Supervision and Curriculum Development, *Individualizing Instruction*. Yearbook. Washington, D. C.: The Association, 1964.

Leese, Joseph, Kenneth Frasure, and Mauritz Johnson, Jr. *The Teacher in Curriculum Making*. New York: Harper & Row, 1961.

National Education Association, Project on the Instructional Program of the Public Schools. *Planning and Organizing for Teaching*. Washington, D. C.: The Association, 1963.

Petersen, Dorothy G. *The Elementary School Teacher*. New York: Appleton-Century-Crofts, 1964.

Shuster, Arthur H., and Milton E. Ploghoft. *The Emerging Elementary Curriculum*. Columbus, Ohio: Charles E. Merrill, 1963.

Thornton, James W., Jr., and John R. Wright, eds. *Secondary School Curriculum*. Columbus, Ohio: Charles E. Merrill, 1963.

White, R. W. "Motivation Reconsidered: The Concept of Competence." *Psychological Review*, 66 (1959), 297–333.

CHAPTER FIVE
DIRECTING
LEARNING

One frequently hears pupils, teachers, principals, or parents speak of some member of a school faculty as a good teacher. In each of these instances there is usually the implication that a good teacher is one who helps pupils learn what they need to know. The good teacher is a director of learning; he helps to determine what should be learned and he is skillful in teaching it.

The prospective teacher has had an opportunity to consider the theoretical aspects of teaching, and he has had numerous opportunities to observe the teaching of others. He has probably taken advantage of opportunities to participate in classroom activities prior to his assignment as a student teacher or intern. As he becomes more deeply involved in the activities of the classroom and assumes more responsibility for what occurs there, his opportunities for becoming a competent teacher also increase.

CHALLENGING THE LEARNER

The capable teacher not only obtains and holds the attention of the learner, but also helps him use his time and energy wisely.

Helping Pupils Discover Needs and Opportunities

Learning is facilitated when pupils are aware of their needs and opportunities, and it is the responsibility of the teacher to help pupils recognize them. The following needs of pupils are illustrative of those to which teachers should be sensitive.

1. *The need to communicate effectively with others.* Individuals at all levels, kindergarten through high school and in adult life, need to communicate with others if they are to be successful. This is true for the laborer, the craftsman, the businessman, the professional person, and the homemaker. Pupils need to be led to understand that they can meet this need to communicate by learning to speak, write, and spell properly.

2. *The need to become well informed in many fields.* To become a useful, well-adjusted, and reasonably happy pupil or adult one needs knowledge in the broad fields of learning such as science, social science, and literature.

Many pupils who drop out of school might not have done so if they had understood more clearly what is needed to achieve success and if they had been encouraged to take advantage of their opportunities.

3. *The need to locate pertinent and useful information.* The teacher can help pupils develop an awareness of their need to locate accurate and appropriate information. He can help them appreciate and take advantage of the services of librarians and other staff members who can assist them. He can aid pupils to realize that opportunities to acquire knowledge are presented through textbooks, supplementary books, materials in the library, and other instructional aids. The pupil's attention should be called to the extensive sources of information available through associations with knowledgeable people. Youth of all ages can be led to understand that education is important for them and that it is their individual responsibility as well as that of their teachers to see that they make progress in the various areas in which they are receiving instruction.

Working Toward Effective Motivation

It is often difficult to discover techniques that will be effective in interesting a specific group of pupils. Real success in teaching, however, is achieved only by those who reach this goal. The effort needed to recapture the interest of a group after interest has been lost is much greater than would have been necessary if the group had been motivated properly in the beginning. How does a teacher obtain the attention of a group of pupils and keep them interested? One way to obtain help in answering this question is to consider procedures used by prospective teachers which resulted in difficulties for them and to suggest how those procedures might have been improved.

1. A poorly made and explained assignment—"tomorrow we will take the next ten pages" or "for the next lesson you will complete the problems on page 90"—provides poor motivation for learning.

The teacher might explain how content to be studied is related to that just completed and how it relates to the unit or larger area of content being studied. There should be opportunities for questions to determine if the assignment is clear to pupils. There could be alternative assignments to meet varied abilities and interests.

2. If there is no opportunity for pupil involvement, if the teacher is concerned about how *he* can get through the class period and is not much concerned about what happens to pupils, many of them will feel unchallenged.

Provision for teacher-pupil planning can be an instrument of motivation. Pupils can help to determine what needs to be learned and can suggest procedures to be used in learning it. They can participate in determining how well learning has progressed.

3. Pupils may lose interest rapidly if the teacher asks too many factual questions that can be answered with very little thinking ("In what year did the Civil War end?").

The teacher needs to formulate the kinds of questions which will require thought and which will imply a need for further interesting information. He should encourage pupils to ask questions to which they need answers.

4. Only half the learning team is in use if the teacher is active, working hard to do a good job, while pupils are inactive and passive.

Pupils need to be made to feel responsible for their own learning and for contributing to the proper functioning of the group. Each pupil, or a small group of pupils, can be made responsible for answering specific questions the group has raised. Individual or small-group reports can be prepared on either a voluntary or an assigned basis. Useful written work can be assigned all pupils.

5. Exclusive use of the textbook does not provide maximum opportunities for challenging pupils. Pupils can be motivated more effectively by the use of a wide range of instructional materials and devices such as supplementary and reference books, appropriate audio-visual aids of all kinds, and perhaps programmed material.

6. Interests of pupils are affected by a variety of factors, and the teacher may not be relating instruction to those interests. The environment is one factor which may be used for illustrative purposes. Whether the group lives in an urban area where there are many disadvantaged pupils, in a farming area, or in a privileged suburban area, the teacher should relate content to their own living.

7. Exclusive use or overuse of the lecture, questioning, or any other procedure becomes boring and monotonous to pupils. A variety of appropriate teaching procedures and pupil activities can bring the opposite results.

8. If content is either too difficult or too easy, if it is not geared to the ability of the group, pupils will not be motivated to learn.

The teacher must quickly discover the ability of individual pupils and of the group as compared with other groups and make adjustments accordingly.

PROVIDING A WHOLESOME LEARNING ENVIRONMENT

Most pupils spend more time in the classroom than in any other place except their homes. This fact provides teachers with an opportunity to make a continuous and positive impact on the life of each member of the classroom group. The classroom should have a homelike yet businesslike atmosphere. It should be an attractive, pleasant, and comfortable place in which to work.

Establishing a Good Emotional Climate

Classroom living should contribute to the emotional stability and emotional maturity of each person in the group, including the teacher. The atmosphere should be friendly and relaxed, yet orderly, rather than hostile, tension filled, and confused. Consideration should be given to factors which affect the emotional climate, such as competition, uniform assignments, emphasis on marks, and interpersonal relationships.

One factor which should not be overlooked is the attitude of the teacher toward the nonconforming, rebellious, belligerent, uncooperative, or generally difficult member of the group. The wise teacher by actions and words will make it known to the pupil that he is accepted and will help obtain group acceptance of him. At the same time, he will make it clear to the pupil and to the group that *undesirable behavior* is *not* accepted. This may require extreme effort, but if the teacher can achieve it it will contribute greatly to good feeling in the classroom.

The shy, retiring, unresponsive pupil also needs the attention and assistance of the teacher. He frequently needs recognition and encouragement. Attention by the teacher to the withdrawn pupil can result in his involvement in the work of the class in a manner which will benefit him and other members of the group.

In short, every pupil is entitled to attention and consideration.

Providing Desirable Physical Conditions

Lighting, temperature, and ventilation affect comfort and thus, indirectly, the attitudes and behavior of the pupils. Although it is true that in some buildings the teacher has limited control over physical factors, he does have at least some control in most. He can, for example, do what some teachers fail to do, namely, turn on the lights when pupils' eyes might be strained by insufficient natural light. He can, in many buildings, adjust the thermostat or otherwise regulate temperature and ventilation to obtain optimum working conditions for pupils. The intern who made the following statement had discovered the importance of maintaining good working conditions for pupils.

It is a necessity for the teacher to regulate the physical aspects of the room for the benefit of all. Such things as good lighting, elimination of glare on the chalkboards, and proper temperature contribute to the total achievement of the class.

Building a Stimulating Intellectual Climate

Perhaps the greatest contribution a teacher can make to the maintenance of a wholesome learning environment for pupils is to encourage a stimulating intellectual atmosphere in the classroom. Each individual in the group should be motivated to work to the limit of his ability without being frustrated with an overload. In order to accomplish this goal the teacher must learn to distinguish between "busywork" and keeping pupils busy with worthwhile and rigorous tasks. He must learn how to motivate pupils to attack difficult tasks because their intellectual curiosity has been aroused, rather than being satisfied if they meet easy minimum assignments. Superior teachers at all grade levels have been meeting this challenge successfully for a long time, and the neophyte need not feel that the goal is impossible or unrealistic for him, either. One student teacher had discovered a measure of this feeling of accomplishment when she said, "Pupils strive to meet our expectations." Another prospective teacher attained some realization of the potentialities of pupils when he stated, "I was really amazed at the amount of work the pupils turned out."

Using Time Wisely

With the tremendous increase in discovery of knowledge in recent years, it has become more important than ever that careful thought be given to the selection of content to be included in the school curriculum. However, even the most carefully planned curriculum loses its effectiveness if the time of pupils is wasted in the classroom by unthinking teachers. In actuality, the curriculum for any individual pupil is what takes place in his classroom day after day. For that reason, the teacher has unlimited opportunities to help pupils use time wisely and acquire useful rather than useless skills, knowledge, and attitudes. He can, for example, encourage individual study and research in skill subjects, rather than using games for motivation. He can encourage pupils to record and master their own misspelled words, rather than rigidly concentrating on general lists that include words they already know.

The time available for teaching and learning should be devoted to content and procedures which will neither insult the pupil's intelligence nor waste his time.

Organizing Classroom Routines

Routine activities in the classroom should be managed so that the time and energy of pupils and teacher may be used in the most profitable manner. The following are some of the tasks that may be reduced to routine:

Housekeeping responsibilities

Collecting money in connection with such activities as school banking, school lunch, or miscellaneous fund-raising drives

Checking attendance

Distributing and collecting materials, papers, and assigned material

Issuing supplies and/or equipment

Serving as room or class librarian

Serving as messenger to other rooms or to the school office

Providing a standardized form or heading to be used in written work

Children and youth who are underprivileged because of home or community environment may profit to a greater extent than more fortunate individuals by participating in some of the above activities. It is important that routines be organized and administered so that individual pupils will not be exploited and that the group will benefit. This suggests a rotation of responsibilities among members of the group. It is not good procedure to permit the performance of routine activities to consume so much of any pupil's time that his opportunities for learning are reduced.

Procedures for carrying out routines must be understood by all members of the group. One needs to be consistent in administering them. The feeling of security that results from knowing what to expect in matters of classroom organization contributes to a good learning environment; the reverse is true when pupils are uncertain about what is to occur.

FACILITATING INDIVIDUAL GROWTH

Individual learning can be facilitated when the teacher discovers as much as possible about each pupil in the group, when he is skillful in working with groups of pupils in his class, and when pupils are motivated to work independently.

Obtaining Information About Each Pupil

The teacher can easily acquire inaccurate impressions about pupils in a group when he starts to work with them. They may be categorized as "dull," "bright," "well-disciplined," or "ill-mannered." However, in order to know an individual well and to help him, the teacher needs many more kinds of information than the initial impression provides.

Ability and school achievement. In every group, even when homogeneous grouping is employed, there are wide differences in ability and school achievement. From the first days in the classroom even the novice teacher will observe that some pupils learn quickly, others slowly. This general and superficial observation should be followed by study of each pupil.

Teachers sometimes fail to utilize individual cumulative records and spend considerable time working with pupils before they discover some of the things that might have been learned from the records before instruction was begun. Scores on individual or group intelligence tests, if considered as clues rather than as absolute facts, are helpful. Marks received in the various subject areas are of value when used with similar reservations. Progress through the school—whether a pupil has been accelerated or retained—can also be noted. Anecdotal information relating to ability and achievement should be studied.

Test results which may not be recorded on the individual's cumulative record can provide useful data. Noting an individual's rank in relation to the median on general and special subject tests will reveal strengths and weaknesses in achievement and, perhaps, a pattern of consistent or inconsistent performance.

The prospective teacher can learn a great deal about the ability and achievement of each pupil by developing ingenious ways of working with individuals in day-to-day classroom contacts. Some teachers keep a file or folder for each pupil. This file might contain such information as tests results, results of oral questioning, participation in class discussions, and samples of the pupil's work. Other teachers ask each pupil to keep samples of his own work; these are used at various times by teacher and/or pupil to note how well the pupil is progressing.

Out-of-school experiences.   The things that happen to pupils during the time school is not in session have direct bearing on their learning, behavior, and growth in school. The teacher needs as much information as can be obtained about the out-of-school segment of the pupil's life. His family structure, home surroundings, neighborhood, financial status, employment, and use of leisure time are all pertinent. Some of this information can be obtained from the cumulative records. Some can result from close observation of each individual. Teachers who have worked with the group previously will know much about individual pupils and will be willing to share their knowledge. This sort of information should, of course, be treated as a confidential matter.

Relationships with others.   The success or failure of an individual often hinges upon his ability to get along well with others.

The individual who is not accepted by the group needs help in discovering why this is true and how he can alter that situation. The individual who is overly aggressive needs help in improving his ways of working with others. The capable but shy and retiring pupil may need assistance in building self-confidence and in becoming actively identified with his group.

Careful observation of pupils in classroom and informal situations will help the prospective teacher to learn much about each individual. Anecdotal information in the cumulative record may reveal much about a pupil's relationships with others. Some teachers through casual conversation with a pupil have become skillful in learning why he has desirable or undesirable relationships with his peers. Before or after school, in the corridor, at recess, or on the playground the teacher can take advantage of opportunities to *listen* to what pupils say about themselves and others.

The sociogram has been used to obtain information about relationships between pupils. The teacher may be puzzled about why a specific pupil is either ignored or is a favorite when pupils work in groups, on a committee, or on a panel. In an attempt to find an answer, the teacher might tell pupils it would help in establishing committees for the study of a forthcoming topic if each pupil would indicate a first, second, and third choice of persons with whom he would like to work. Building a sociogram by tabulating the responses can provide information which will help a teacher to understand each individual. The results obtained from a sociogram should be considered clues rather than absolute facts. The relationships between individuals in a group are always changing; therefore, the tabulations on a sociogram can be considered valid only at the time responses are made.[1]

Physical status. The student teacher or intern should assume responsibility for learning about the health needs of his pupils and should do what he can to meet them. Optimum use of cumu-

---

[1] For suggestions in the use of sociograms see Georgia Sachs Adams, *Measurement and Evaluation in Education, Psychology, and Guidance* (New York: Holt, Rinehart and Winston, 1964), pp. 281–292.

lative records, careful observation, conferences with the school nurse, and communication with parents are means for obtaining information about the physical status of pupils. The youth with boundless energy, the child with poor vision, the youngster with a hearing loss, the anemic child, the adolescent with a heart condition, the pupil with insufficient sleep at home, and the undernourished pupil all need to be identified, understood, and helped.

Individual objectives.   Knowledge of the goals the pupil has set for himself can be helpful to the teacher. This information is often difficult to obtain. The pupil is frequently unaware of the reasons for his behavior and this behavior often puzzles teachers. It is the job of the teacher to try to understand what motivates each pupil to act as he does, to encourage him in attaining desirable goals, and to aid him in changing his objectives when they do not appear to be leading toward desirable ends. The pupil who has decided that he wants very much to engage in one of the professions and knows that high school and college education are essential in reaching his goal may take full advantage of the learning opportunities available to him. A pupil who comes from a home where circumstances provide little stimulation or little hope for the future may take quite a different view toward learning. This is a problem of real concern for teachers in many crowded urban communities.

One pupil may overestimate his own ability, whereas another may be much more capable than he thinks himself. Both may need help from the teacher in making the most of their abilities.

The prospective teacher needs to study the ways pupils are motivated by their peers and by adults both in school and out of school. The brilliant high school girl who is not working to capacity because she seeks the approval of a less capable boy friend may need guidance in taking the long view of the future. The equally brilliant elementary child who has no friends because he is impatient and sarcastic with his less capable peers can profit by appropriate counsel from his teachers. The lazy pupil who mistakes the tactful prodding of his teacher for extreme dislike of him may need help in learning to think more objectively.

Working with Groups

The learning and growth of the individual can be facilitated, at times, when the total classroom group is divided into smaller groups. In the past division into small groups has been more common in elementary than in secondary schools, though there, too, it has been a useful practice. The greatest opportunity for the pupil to receive help from the teacher would exist if each group consisted of one pupil. In this hypothetical and impractical situation the full attention of the teacher could be focused on the individual. A workable and useful compromise between this situation and the other extreme of little or no individual instruction is the use of groups. First consideration is given here to situations common to elementary and secondary schools in which a classroom group may be divided into subgroups each consisting of approximately five pupils. This is followed by a brief discussion of the common practice in the elementary school of dividing the classroom group into two, three, or four subgroups.

The prospective teacher is not likely to succeed in working with groups, and thus in meeting individual needs, unless he has a real purpose for formulating groups and until he has given thought to how groups can be guided to work effectively. Groups can be formed for such purposes as making plans for the study of a topic, problem, or unit; gathering information; organizing information; study of a problem; developing a skill; making a report; or completing some special task. The following points should be kept in mind.

1. Teacher and pupils should understand clearly why the group has been organized.

2. There are advantages in changing the personnel of groups on different occasions and for differing purposes.

3. The role of individual pupils and the role of the teacher usually change as the membership of groups is changed.

4. The membership of each group may be determined by the teacher, by the pupils, or cooperatively by teacher and pupils. It

should always be done under the supervision of the teacher and without needless waste of time.

5. Pupils can profit from an opportunity to work with individuals who differ in ability, sex, age, attitudes, and interests.

6. When a group is to remain intact for more than one or two class periods it is important for group members to formulate a simple set of ground rules to guide each individual in his behavior as a member of the group.

In guiding the work of individuals in groups the teacher should:

1. Encourage, but not demand, the involvement of each individual in the work of the group.

2. Help pupils learn to plan effectively and to carry plans through to the stated goal.

3. Discourage any individual from dominating the group and take tactful and appropriate action when it becomes necessary to prevent such a situation.

4. Take the necessary steps to see that materials and resources needed for carrying out the purposes of the group are available.

5. Help each pupil learn effective ways of working with others as a result of group membership. This should include learning to serve as a leader as well as a constructive group member when not a leader.

6. Help pupils learn to profit by mistakes when the purposes they have established are not met.

7. Help pupils learn to evaluate the results of group work in an objective manner.

Although some secondary teachers follow the practice of dividing the classroom group into subgroups which continue over an extended period of time, this procedure is used more frequently in the elementary school. The discussion which follows relates primarily to the elementary school. Younger children especially can profit from the guidance and closer supervision provided when two, three, or four groups are functioning within the classroom. The number of subgroups will vary depending upon the size of the classroom group, the ability and maturity of pupils, and the subject matter being taught. There will, of course, be times when all pupils will function as a total group.

The sequence one intern followed during a typical day in working with an intermediate grade class as a whole and divided into small groups is listed below. There were thirty pupils in the group. The day may be considered typical in the sense that it illustrates work with the total group and subgroups. It should not be inferred that subgroups are to be used only in the subject areas indicated.

Before formal opening—pupils worked at their seats, worked on special projects, visited, or engaged in outdoor play.

Opening exercises and planning for the day—total group.

Social studies—five groups. Each group was given a specific assignment requiring individual reading needed in preparing a group report.

Science—three groups. Two small groups were to be responsible for preparing and giving a demonstration relating to the topic being studied. The third and largest group was to work at obtaining information from the textbook and supplementary books so that its members might contribute to a discussion of the topic under consideration.

Noon intermission.

Mathematics—total group. The period was devoted to a discussion of a concept introduced by the teacher the previous day, followed by individual application of the concept. The teacher assisted individuals and answered questions.

Language arts, spelling—total group. Pupils studied words from a list of their own misspelled words of the previous week. Teacher worked with individuals.

Language arts, reading (and health)—three groups. Because the school was committed to teaching reading in the intermediate grades through the content subjects rather than as a separate subject, special emphasis was placed on reading skills in the health class. The three groups were formed primarily on the basis of reading ability. A textbook was used along with supplementary materials of various kinds. The teacher worked with one group in the front of the room while pupils in the other groups worked at their seats.

Art, music, physical education—total group. These were scheduled on a regular basis throughout the week and were taught by special teachers. The room teacher worked closely with the special teacher in attempting to meet individual needs.

In working with groups the elementary teacher will need to keep in mind both what is good for the individual and what is good for the total group. The overly aggressive or ill-tempered child, for his own good and the welfare of others, should not be kept in the same group for an extended period of time. The timid child, and perhaps his peers, will benefit if he is shifted occasionally from one group to another. It is good practice to form different groups for each subject rather than placing children in the same group for all subjects.

The prospective teacher is reminded that one of the chief objectives in small-group work is that the needs of each individual be met. The teacher's goal should be to encourage each pupil to work up to the limits of his capabilities. Most teachers would agree that it is easier to make a single assignment than to prepare an assignment that will challenge each group and, hopefully, each individual. Perhaps this is why some teachers who work with several groups search for activities which will "keep pupils busy" and "out of mischief." The emphasis, however, must be placed upon stimulating pupils to attack and complete worthwhile tasks rather than to dawdle with busywork.

Helping Pupils Work Independently

One important aspect of growth is the ability to think and act as a rational and logical individual. Frank Lloyd Wright, when asked what factors contributed to his accomplishments as a creative designer of unique buildings, replied that as a boy he was compelled by circumstances to spend considerable time alone in a rural setting with no children and few adults with whom to associate. There were few distractions, and he was forced to take advantage of opportunities to explore his surroundings and think for himself. Today the typical pupil is in a situation greatly different from that in which Mr. Wright found himself. Certainly this is true of the disadvantaged child living in crowded quarters in a low-income section of a large city. To an increasing degree the teacher needs to encourage each pupil to work independently.

The ability to make decisions is perhaps of minor importance for one living under a dictatorship, but for citizens who live under a democratic form of government it becomes of prime importance if that form of government is to function effectively. They need to decide how they will earn and spend their money, where they will live, and for whom they will vote in selecting public officials. Learning to think and act so that one can make wise decisions does not occur in a vacuum or under the guidance of an inadequate or dictatorial teacher. Children in elementary and secondary schools need to be given opportunities for independent thought and action and they need to learn to make decisions.

A student teacher or intern can learn and practice much that will help pupils learn to work independently. The suggestions which follow should aid in accomplishing this purpose.

1. The attitude of the teacher sets the tone for the group. The teacher who insists on perfection in every detail is likely to discourage individual initiative. The teacher who gives pupils the impression that he assumes they will perform well on their own encourages independent action.

2. A pattern for the organization of class routines which involves pupils aids them in learning to work independently. Checking attendance, checking their own papers at times, preparing a book report file, arranging a bulletin board, serving as classroom host or hostess—all illustrate this point.

3. A well-organized plan for the use of groups for instructional

purposes provides many opportunities for independent thought and action on the part of pupils. Serving as a leader, a responsible group member, an evaluator, or making a report for a small group—all provide opportunities for initiative and self-expression.

4. The use of a variety of teaching procedures and many instructional materials can provide opportunities for independent work. Serving on a panel, introducing a resource person, writing a report for the school paper, presenting an oral report, being challenged by several instructors on an instructional team, being stimulated by educational television or programmed instruction can encourage individual initiative.

5. Mastery of study skills can give the pupil a feeling of self-confidence which will encourage him to act on his own. The ability to skim what he reads, to get the central idea from a paragraph, to summarize, and to read with speed and comprehension contribute to this end.

6. The attainment of skill in the location of information encourages wide and careful reading and can lead the pupil to think independently. Learning to use the card catalogue and reference materials in the library and tables of contents and indexes in books will help in development of individual initiative.

DETERMINING METHODS OF TEACHING

How does the prospective teacher decide which methods to use in his teaching? What are the methods available for use?

Identifying Sources of Information About Method

Some experienced teachers when asked how they arrived at a decision about teaching methods have found the question difficult to answer. They may indicate that they did the things that "seemed to be natural" or "seemed to work" for them. A few find it possible to explain why they use the methods they employ. The following are sources of help in determining method: (1) procedures used by a former teacher, (2) professional courses taken in college, (3) the supervising teacher, (4) teachers in one's school other than the supervising teacher, (5) a study of the reports of research in the area of teaching.[2]

It is sometimes argued that the prospective teacher is so involved in the mastery of subject-matter content and in getting acquainted with the personnel and surroundings of his school that it is impossible for him to give thought to specific methods to be used. The discerning individual who is determined to succeed in teaching *should* engage in this kind of thinking lest his professional viewpoints become rigid and inflexible.

Analyzing the Components of Method

As the student teacher or intern attempts to think his way through all that has been spoken and written about method, he will find it helpful to make a distinction between the *organization of learning experiences* and *teaching procedures.*

Content must be organized in some manner for presentation to pupils. The nucleus for this *organization* may be a topic, unit, problem, or project. In presenting this content to pupils, *teaching procedures* must be used. Some of these teaching procedures are the lecture, class discussion, questioning, and the use of audio-visual aids. *Method* for the individual teacher consists of the way or ways he combines the nuclei for the organization of content (e.g., topic, unit, problem, or project) and teaching procedures (e.g., lecture, class discussion, or questioning).

Understanding Viewpoints of Other Teachers

One of the professional responsibilities of a classroom teacher is to work harmoniously, to the extent this is possible, with other members of the faculty. In some schools a great deal of emphasis is placed on the improvement of instruction and the in-service ed-

[2] The inexpensive bulletins "What Research Says to the Teacher," prepared jointly by the Department of Classroom Teachers and the American Educational Research Association, both departments of the National Education Association, are helpful for keeping informed about useful research. They may be obtained from the National Education Association, Washington, D.C.

ucation of teachers. In other schools these are not emphasized and self-improvement becomes a matter of individual initiative. In some schools emphasis is placed on developing a common viewpoint toward methods of instruction; in others, diversity is encouraged.

The prospective teacher may be puzzled by the fact that there are wide differences in methods used. One teacher may follow the unit plan of organization and use a wide variety of teaching procedures while another rigidly follows the textbook as a means of organizing content and relies almost exclusively on the lecture as a teaching procedure. Both may be considered good teachers by their colleagues and the principal. A third teacher, very unorthodox in using all the flexibility permitted by the school curriculum guide in organizing content and following no discernible pattern of teaching procedures, may be considered one of the school's best teachers. The prospective teacher should realize that in observing these variations he can learn how other individuals combine a plan for *content organization* and *teaching procedures* into effective methods of teaching. He should also observe that there is no one best method to be used by all teachers and under all conditions.

Resolving Conflicts Between Professional Preparation and Existing Conditions

The student teacher or intern will be less than realistic if he is not prepared to meet differing viewpoints in the realm of methodology. He may discover that some of the things he has learned in professional courses are in conflict with what is practiced in his school. One writer comments on this situation as follows: "The teachers defend what they do as practical, they talk shop and they would initiate the novices into this society and their culture. The college teachers talk theory, question practice, and would make novices into experimental teachers." [3]

It is unlikely that the student learning to teach will find himself

[3] E. Brooks Smith in *The College Supervisor, Conflict and Challenge,* Yearbook of the Association for Student Teaching (Cedar Falls, Iowa: The Association, 1964), pp. 168–169.

in a hostile or unfriendly situation. Personnel in teacher education institutions are careful to place the student teacher or intern in a situation where working relationships between school and college are reasonably harmonious. The college representative who works with the local school will usually have exchanged viewpoints with the supervising teacher and will work in close cooperation with him. Nevertheless situations sometimes arise in which differences about learning and teaching occur. The prospective teacher should seek help when he is concerned about conflicting viewpoints. He should discuss these differences with his supervising teacher and college supervisor in a forthright manner. The issues which follow are illustrative of differences in viewpoint which sometimes exist between what the prospective teacher has learned about teaching and practices in local schools.

The organization of content

The use of the results of research

The amount of pupil involvement in planning, administering, and evaluating instruction

The question of what is considered theoretical and what practical

The degree of acceptance of new knowledge as it relates to both content and methodology

The amount of "discipline" or "control" to be exercised in dealing with pupils

If the prospective teacher should find himself differing with his supervising teacher on these or other issues he should ask for a conference to discuss the conflict. This will provide an opportunity for becoming further informed about the position of the supervising teacher and the school. It frequently happens that when differences are identified and discussed they are of less magnitude than had been imagined. It is important that discussions be confined to issues and not be allowed to result in serious personal differences. If, after careful thought and adequate discussion, professional differences persist, the prospective teacher is ethically obligated to be guided by the position of his supervising teacher. Though he may find it impossible to accept the views of his supervising teacher, he should not permit this fact to interfere with the performance of his professional responsibilities.

A similar procedure should be followed when differences in viewpoint develop between the prospective teacher and other members of the school staff. One needs to avoid developing a militant attitude or leaving others with the impression that he is a fervent fighter for a "cause." It is much better for the prospective teacher's personal, emotional, and professional development to view differences as learning opportunities. By rethinking his views, by further study of issues, and by continuous search for excellence he can become a more capable teacher and can earn the personal and professional respect of his colleagues. He will also earn the right to present his views with some degree of authority and self-confidence.

Developing Professional Individuality

Good teachers are alike and yet they are different. They are alike in that they have acquired the competency that results from skillful use of method, from knowledge of pupils, and from being proficient and keeping up to date in their fields of knowledge. They are different because each possesses peculiar traits and characteristics which mark him as an individual. Just as good schools and good teachers help to make pupils different as each grows toward the limits of his capacity, so a good teacher tends to become different from all others as he extends his own capability. He becomes different not because he is striving to be different, but because his potentialities for growth are unique. He searches for ways to extend his potentialities and utilizes opportunities which make this possible.

The prospective teacher must understand and respect established procedures which have become matters of policy in his school. He should, however, be projecting himself into the future role he hopes to fill as a capable and experienced teacher. He should guard against the danger of becoming a carbon copy of his supervising teacher. If he does not take precautionary steps he may suffer a fate similar to that of many other carbon copies which so often are destined to reside permanently in the "dead file." His supervising teacher will help him adapt to his present situation and at the same time develop his potentialities for becoming a unique individual.

The developing teacher needs to observe how his supervising teacher organizes content, the procedures he uses, and the results which follow in terms of pupil behavior and development. As he works the student teacher or intern can learn how to combine a plan for the organization of subject matter with teaching procedures in a manner which will result in good instruction. While this is taking place he can profit not only by making the combination he employs function well, but also by reflecting about how other ways of combining the organization of content and teaching procedures might work. He can discover ways to improve his teaching as a student and to prepare himself for an interesting career as a teacher with professional individuality. Study of the following questions should aid him in this discovery and preparation.

How can the teacher help pupils acquire difficult concepts?

What teaching procedures should be used when one's goal is to help pupils acquire desirable attitudes, ideals, and appreciations?

How does one utilize out-of-classroom resources effectively to facilitate learning?

What does the teacher do to encourage pupils to think logically?

What are the various ways to organize content? In what situations is it preferable to organize learning experiences around problems? around projects? in the form of units?

How does one proceed to obtain an optimum amount of interaction in the classroom so that a maximum amount of real learning results?

How can a variety of useful instructional media be used to obtain best results in the classroom?

How can a classroom teacher and others work together effectively as members of an instructional team?

The teacher who is interested in continuing his search for improvement in his methods of teaching will find much has been written to help him in his study.[4]

The best teachers are creative teachers—creative in the sense that they find unique ways to employ methods to help pupils make the greatest progress possible during their years of school attendance. The great inventor Thomas A. Edison has been quoted to the effect that creativity is 1 per cent inspiration and 99 per cent perspiration. If this is true, it would appear that many teachers who are not considered creative by themselves or others might become so by expending a bit more effort in the search for creativity. The individual who wishes to develop creativity in teaching will find that the period spent as a student teacher or intern is an excellent time to prepare for reaching that objective. The development of creativity in teaching is discussed in Chapter 12.[5]

SUMMARY

The good teacher is a director of learning. This is the view of educators and laymen alike. Directing learning in the classroom requires skill in several areas of activity; these include challenging the learner, providing a wholesome learning environment, facilitating individual growth, working with groups, helping pupils work independently, and determining methods of teaching.

[4] N. L. Gage, ed., *Handbook of Research On Teaching* (Chicago: Rand McNally and Company, 1963). *The Journal of Teacher Education,* 14:2, September 1963.

[5] For helpful references on creativity in teaching see the following:

Mary Lee Marksberry, *Foundation of Creativity* (New York: Harper & Row, 1963).

National Education Association, *Step Beyond: Creativity* (Washington, D.C.: The Association, 1964).

In preparing for a good beginning as a director of learning, the prospective teacher needs to establish purposes for his teaching, understand the content that is to be taught, know the group with which he is working, and know how to apply effectively what has been learned about how to teach. If learners are to be challenged to work up to capacity, they must be led to discover their own needs and opportunities and to assume responsibility for their own learning. This makes it imperative that the student teacher or intern be effective in motivating pupils.

For a wholesome learning environment a good emotional, physical, and intellectual climate must pervade the classroom. The teacher must know how to provide these conditions. He must know how to use his time and that of his pupils wisely. This requires the establishment of efficient classroom routines.

Methods of teaching influence learning. In order to determine methods to be used and to employ them effectively the student teacher or intern must go to the available sources of information about methods. An understanding of the components of method is essential. The prospective teacher must understand the views of his colleagues about method and be able to resolve conflicts which may develop when his views do not harmonize with existing conditions. Perhaps most important of all, he needs to develop his own professional individuality as it relates to directing learning. To become an effective teacher one must develop skill in fostering individual pupil growth, in working with groups of pupils, and in helping pupils learn to work independently.

USEFUL REFERENCES

Association for Student Teaching. *The College Supervisor, Conflict and Change*. Yearbook. Cedar Falls, Iowa: The Association, 1964.
Association for Supervision and Curriculum Development. *Individualizing Instruction*. Yearbook. Washington, D. C.: The Association, 1964.
————. *Learning and Mental Health*. Yearbook. Washington, D. C.: The Association, 1966.

Broudy, Harry S. and John R. Palmer. *Exemplars of Teaching Method.* Chicago: Rand McNally and Company, 1965.

Gage, N. L., ed. *Handbook of Research on Teaching.* Chicago: Rand McNally and Company, 1963.

Macdonald, James B. and Robert R. Leeper, eds. *Theories of Instruction.* Washington, D. C.: Association for Supervision and Curriculum Development, 1965.

Marksberry, Mary Lee. *Foundation of Creativity.* New York: Harper & Row, 1963.

Meierhenry, W. C. "Implications of Learning Theory for Instructional Technology," *Phi Delta Kappan.* 46 (May 1965), 435–438.

National Elementary Principal. Entire issue is devoted to "Cooperative Teaching." 44 (January 1965), 3–102.

National Society for the Study of Education. *Theories of Learning and Instruction.* Yearbook, Part I. Chicago, Ill.: The Society, 1964.

Rippey, Robert M. "How Different Classroom Environments Affect Learning," *Phi Delta Kappan.* 46 (June 1965), 525–527.

Witty, Paul A. "Recent Publications Concerning the Gifted and the Creative Student," *Phi Delta Kappan* 46 (January 1965), 221–224.

CHAPTER SIX
EVALUATING
PUPIL PROGRESS

The ability to evaluate the progress of pupils is an essential component of good teaching. Skill in evaluating desirable learning is considered, by teachers and laymen alike, an important criterion in determining the success of a teacher. This chapter is devoted to a consideration of the nature, purposes, and procedures of evaluation.

MEANING OF EVALUATION

Many beginning and experienced teachers consider the evaluation of pupil progress their most difficult task. This important aspect of teaching can be made less difficult when one understands what is meant by "evaluation." The following definition is helpful: "Educational evaluation is a process in which a teacher commonly uses information derived from many sources in order to arrive at a value judgement." [1]

Measurement and Evaluation

In attempting to assess the progress of pupils the teacher soon discovers that some aspects of growth can be determined with a considerable degree of definiteness; this specific kind of appraisal is called *measurement*. Other aspects of growth can only be estimated; this more general appraisal is commonly called *evaluation*. "Evaluation" is a broad term which includes the more narrow term "measurement." By way of illustration a teacher might

[1] J. Stanley Ahmann and Marvin D. Glock, *Evaluating Pupil Growth* (Boston: Allyn and Bacon, Inc., 1963), p. 13.

find it relatively easy to determine how much progress a pupil has made in mastering certain mathematical skills by administering an objective test before and after teaching the skills. He has used measurement to obtain a reasonably accurate estimate of the amount of learning which has occurred. However in attempting to evaluate the total accomplishment of the pupil the teacher would probably wish to consider additional information such as ability to use the skills in appropriate situations, understanding of terminology, and meaningful application.

The teacher who is interested in fostering the balanced development of pupils finds that he must appraise the amount of growth which appears to have been made in areas where precise measurement is difficult or impossible, but where information he has obtained makes evaluation both possible and necessary in helping pupils make progress. This point can be illustrated by referring to a situation common in work with children in the kindergarten or first grade. The beginner who is an only child and the center of attention at home sometimes finds it difficult to work in cooperation with his peers at school. The skillful teacher will try to help the child correct this inability to get along well with other children. A teacher is not likely to find a test available which will measure accurately the amount of cooperation the child exhibited when first entering school and again after a period of time—perhaps a semester or a year. However, by collecting and using information obtained through observation, conferences with him, and meetings with his parents, the teacher can arrive at a judgment as to the amount of progress he has made in working harmoniously with his classmates. The teacher has *evaluated* the pupil's growth, or the lack of it, toward the goal of increased cooperation with his associates. In doing so he has found it possible to help the pupil, even though the amount of change cannot be *measured*.

Evaluation as Learning

Teachers sometimes overlook the fact that the pupil can and should be led to understand that evaluation of his performance in school by himself and/or his teachers is an important element in the learning process. The student teacher or intern who understands that good evaluation can facilitate desirable learning has acquired a valuable tool in directing growth. The pupil who views evaluation of his work as a means of increasing his own effectiveness is also increasing his intellectual and emotional maturity. The following examples illustrate the kinds of situations in which teacher and/or pupil evaluation can facilitate learning.

1. A child in the lower elementary grades realizes that his ability to read is increased because the teacher has checked carefully the amount and quality of his silent and oral reading and has suggested additional suitable books for him to read. He has discovered the increased progress and satisfaction which result from additional reading, as contrasted with the lack of growth and satisfaction that results when he completes only the minimum assignment in reading.

2. An upper elementary pupil discovers that the continuous checking by teacher and pupil of written and oral language used in all subjects has identified areas in spelling, handwriting, and composition that need improvement. The pupil builds on his own individual needs and improvement is the result.

3. A ninth-grade pupil learns that through the use of a programmed textbook, a teaching machine, and the guidance of his teacher he can discover his personal needs for improvement in mathematics. He utilizes the information obtained through this kind of evaluation with the result that both the rate of learning and the extent of his understanding are improved.

Objectives and Evaluation

The skillful teacher endeavors to obtain evidence of all significant changes in every aspect of pupil growth. He is hopeful that his pupils will master skills, obtain knowledge, and gain understanding; he knows that changes of this kind can be *measured*. He is hopeful, also, that pupils will acquire desirable attitudes, ideals, and appreciations; he recognizes that although growth in these areas may not be measured, it can be *evaluated*. Thus, the good teacher attempts to appraise both tangible and intangible changes in pupils.

Evaluation should be made in terms of the objectives the teacher has included in his long-range or daily plans. He should make certain that his instruction and subsequent evaluation are compatible with the objectives of the total situation in which he is working.

UTILIZING EVALUATION DEVICES AND PROCEDURES

Teachers need to know about the various devices and procedures which may be used in evaluation. The wide variety of instruments available will be classified in the following discussion as standardized tests, teacher-made tests, and informal devices. Consideration will also be given to the use of pupil self-evaluation.

Standardized Tests

The student teacher or intern is not likely to be involved in the planning that precedes the administration of a system-wide testing program, but he should take advantage of opportunities to assist and participate in administering, scoring, and interpreting results of standardized tests given to pupils with whom he works. Standardized tests may be subdivided into aptitude, achievement, and personality tests.

One of the most widely used, and perhaps the most frequently misused, aptitude test is the type used to determine scholastic aptitude and more commonly known as the intelligence test. When correctly administered and interpreted the scholastic aptitude test can be useful. This is especially true of the type designed to be given to the individual, for example, the well-known *New Revised Stanford-Binet Tests of Intelligence*. Caution is necessary in the use of the group pencil-and-paper test of mental ability. Some teachers have assumed wrongly that the results of a single testing of an individual with a group intelligence test provides an accurate measure of a pupil's mental ability. This is not true. There are so many variables involved in selecting, administering, scoring, and interpreting a test of this kind that the results as they relate to an individual should be considered clues rather than facts. In consideration of the status of a pupil the findings of a test of this kind should be considered as one bit of information along with many others such as scholastic accomplishment, home conditions, and general health. When used in this manner the scholastic aptitude or intelligence test can be a useful instrument of evaluation. The accuracy of results obtained as they relate to an individual are increased when tests are administered at intervals throughout the school life of the pupil. In some school systems this is done on a regularly scheduled basis, e.g., annually, biannually, or every third year.

A second type of standardized test, one with which the developing teacher is most likely to become involved, is the achievement test. Most schools administer achievement tests according to some pattern. The prospective teacher should discover the pattern used in his school and take advantage of opportunities to learn how tests are selected, administered, scored, and interpreted. He will profit by participating in the various stages of the testing program whenever feasible. Whenever possible he should make use of test results to facilitate learning.

Personality tests represent a third kind of standardized test now being used in schools. As with intelligence tests, the teacher will need to learn of the values and limitations of these tests. Some are designed to be administered and interpreted by specialists only, whereas others are prepared for the use of the classroom teacher. There appears to be a trend toward limited use of personality tests and test results by the typical classroom teacher, unless the counsel of a specialist in evaluation, such as the school psychologist or other individual charged with responsibility for coordinating the evaluation program is involved.

Teacher-Made Tests

Instruments for appraisal by the teacher allow him to construct devices which can be used at any time and which are appropriate to his objectives. They help the teacher discover individual pupil progress, they can provide clues to success in teaching, and they can be used to encourage pupil self-evaluation.

Written tests are used less extensively in primary than in upper grades. Their use increases with the maturity of pupils.

If tests are to be useful to the teacher and also helpful as self-evaluative devices for the pupil, they must be constructed with a great deal of care. Through experience in the construction and use of tests and test items, the conscientious teacher can discover those which meet the needs of pupils. He can retain for use with other groups those which prove to be most worthwhile. This practice, if followed over a period of years, can reduce the time needed for test construction, but it will require good judgment and self-discipline if the teacher is to avoid the use of inappropriate items merely because they are available. References listed at the end of this chapter contain useful information on the construction of tests.

The essay test.   Prior to the 1920s the essay test was used almost exclusively as a means of written evaluation. Although it has been replaced in many situations, it continues to be valuable when appropriately used. It is valuable in determining how well a pupil can organize his thinking and express ideas in written form. It is also useful in appraising his understanding of concepts and his ability to think creatively. Its limitations include lack of objectivity, limited sampling, the fact that it is time-consuming for pupils—especially young pupils—and that much time is required for scoring. With all these limitations, the essay test appears to have regained some of the popularity it lost during the period when objective teacher-made tests were introduced.

Objective tests.   During the 1920s, when emphasis on educational research greatly increased, the objective test idea was introduced. Objective teacher-made tests continue to be widely used, though their limitations are recognized by thoughtful teachers and other educators. There can be little doubt that some teachers who found themselves burdened with reading large numbers of essay examinations seized upon the quick-scoring objective test as a time saver, overlooking the fact that considerable time is required to construct the items that comprise a good test. The result has been the use of poorly constructed tests in many instances. The misuse of a good instrument should not, however, detract from the fact that the objective teacher-made test is an excellent means of evaluation when correctly used. These tests— sometimes known as short-answer tests—include (1) the simple-recall question, (2) the completion question, (3) the true-false question, (4) the multiple-choice question, and (5) matching items.

Some of the advantages of objective tests are that they make possible a wide sampling of subject matter to be tested, correct answers or their absence can be easily recognized, a comparatively short period of time is required for administering and scoring, and they do not penalize the pupil who knows the subject matter over which he is being tested but cannot organize or write well. Some of the limitations of teacher-made objective tests are that they do not require creative thinking, writing ability, or skill in organizing ideas. Some teachers believe that they encourage memorization rather than reflective thinking.

Informal Devices and Procedures

The teacher needs to consider possible ways of evaluating progress of pupils in all aspects of growth. He needs to appraise the development of attitudes and the degree to which pupils adjust to their environment. This should be done not only because sound attitudes and adjustment to one's surroundings represent desirable long-range goals, but also because both are important to pupils' success in day-to-day activity.

Prospective teachers, especially those who are most concerned about the successful academic acomplishment of pupils, sometimes shy away from attempts to appraise growth in areas other than those which are strictly academic in nature. This is often because they have not learned of ways to appraise the aspects of growth which cannot be evaluated with objective devices such as standardized tests or objective teacher-made tests. Prospective teachers in this category should find the following procedures and devices helpful.

Informal observation.   Informal observation has long been used by teachers interested in improving the attitudes and adjustment of pupils. The teacher should take advantage of as many opportunities as possible in classroom, laboratory, corridors, lunch room, on the playground, and in various co-curricular activities. One can learn about the behavior and attitudes of a pupil by observing him as he works with other pupils both in the classroom and in social situations.

As the teacher seeks to become an effective observer, he will find it helpful if he attempts to:

1. Give attention to *all* the pupils in the group he is instructing.

2. Become an unbiased observer who is not influenced by such factors as appearance, home background, or status of a pupil within his peer group.

3. Make brief notes about significant behavior of each individual. Some teachers use a notebook or card file for this purpose.

4. Observe for a purpose. The over-all objective will no doubt be to help the individual pupil become a well-adjusted person with wholesome attitudes, but there will be more specific reasons for observing some individuals at any given time.

5. Continue to improve skill as an observer. This can be accomplished in a number of ways, including reading how others have become successful observers and conferring with colleagues.

Anecdotal records.   Informal observation is greatly enhanced when the teacher records his observations. With other pertinent information they can become a valuable *anecdotal record*. This record might include statements or descriptions of significant incidents in the school life of a pupil which, if kept with reasonable care and regularity, can become a useful source of information.

The teacher who utilizes anecdotal records needs to learn to record objectively what he observes. It is desirable to emphasize exactly what occurred without interpretation. Analysis and interpretation can be made better after a series of incidents has been recorded. With such a series the teacher will be in a much better position to understand the pupil and take constructive action than if he acted on the basis of one incident or even several incidents not viewed as part of a pattern of behavior.

The suggestions which follow can help the teacher in writing anecdotal records.

1. Start by selecting one or two students for intensive study.

2. Each week describe as many significant incidents as possible.

3. Do not try to interpret every incident. Make a summary analysis at convenient periods and look for developmental trends in behavior.

4. Concentrate on describing those types of behavior which you believe to have a bearing on the student's difficulties.[2]

Teachers who have learned to use anecdotal records with a minimum of time and effort have found them helpful in several ways. They contribute to a better understanding of pupils, they aid in the appraisal of individual pupils, and they provide information which is useful for conferring with, and reporting to, parents.

Informal conferences and interviews. Specialists in evaluation make considerable use of projective techniques in the study of personality. In using these procedures and devices "the person is not asked questions about himself but is asked to respond to vari-

[2] Georgia Sachs Adams, *Measurement and Evaluation in Education, Psychology, and Guidance* (New York: Holt, Rinehart and Winston, 1964), p. 273. The suggestions appeared originally in Theodore L. Torgerson, *Studying Children* (New York: Holt, Rhinehart and Winston, Inc., 1947), pp. 88–89.

ous stimuli and his responses are interpreted as indicating significant personality trends." [3]

There are those who believe that projective techniques should not be employed by classroom teachers but should be reserved for use by specialists in these techniques. It is true, however, that capable teachers who understand pupils and know how to communicate effectively with them have used some of these techniques, including informal conferences and interviews, with excellent results. The classroom teacher who wishes to be successful in conducting a conference or interview should become informed about basic principles to be employed. Among the most important points to be kept in mind are the following:

1. Prepare for the conference or interview. Plan possible lead questions, study the pupil's record, and organize materials that may be needed.

2. Greet the pupil in a friendly manner and encourage him to feel at ease.

3. Encourage the pupil to talk in a free, relaxed, and informal manner.

4. Listen to what the pupil has to say. The real purpose of a conference or interview is to learn how the pupil thinks and feels.

5. Help the pupil understand that the teacher is really attempting to be helpful and that he can further his own growth by cooperation in this and future conferences.

The sociogram discussed in Chapter 5 is also a useful informal evaluative device.

Pupil Self-Evaluation

It has been mentioned that the pupil who views evaluation of his work, either by himself or by his teacher, as a means of in-

[3] J. Wayne Wrightstone and others, "Educational Measurements," *Review of Educational Research*, 26 (June 1956), p. 276.

creasing his own learning is also increasing his intellectual and emotional maturity. It is reasonable for the classroom teacher to expect pupils to develop increased skill in *self-evaluation* as they progress through the school. Pupils are not likely to develop this skill, however, without help and encouragement from the teacher. Pupils should be involved in evaluative experiences frequently. How and under what circumstances can this be accomplished?

1. Pupils should be encouraged to view evaluation as facilitating their own growth. They need help in understanding that growth is an individual matter and that discovering one's own strengths and weaknesses is a starting point for self-improvement.

2. The pupils must be made aware of the goals toward which they should be working. In some classroom situations pupils will need little help in keeping the objective(s) in mind. In others, appraisal may call for new plans which necessitate new goals which, in turn, may require that the cycle of appraisal, planning, and working toward new goals needs to be repeated.

3. The teacher should make clear that he and the pupils can work *together* in evaluating their performance. This may be done on a *person-to-person* basis between teacher and pupil. For example, the teacher of a fourth-grade pupil might administer a spelling test consisting of the pupil's own most commonly misspelled words. The pupil could check the results with the dictionary and have his paper checked by the teacher. This check could be followed by suggestions for improvement. Cooperative self-evaluation can also take place between the teacher and a *group* of pupils. To illustrate, a tenth-grade social studies group set the goal of learning as much as possible about an assigned topic through the preparation of individual reports on various aspects of the topic. Each individual was asked to make note of the knowledge gained and of the effectiveness of his own and others' reporting procedures. The teacher administered a test to determine to what degree the knowledge sought had been acquired. Together the teacher and the group discussed the strengths and

weaknesses of reporting procedures. Plans for the future were made on the basis of the combined evaluation.

4. Pupils should be helped to evaluate their own performance with a minimum of guidance by the teacher. Pupils at almost all levels in the elementary and secondary school can be encouraged to keep a cumulative folder containing samples of their work at various stages of their development throughout the year or semester. Each individual can compare his work with checklists prepared by the group or teacher, and the group can determine whether or not it is functioning in accordance with predetermined ground rules.

5. It is important that pupils understand that their over-all purpose in learning is to acquire knowledge and skills and to develop right attitudes, and that it is *not* the accumulation of grades.

6. Pupils should be assisted in learning to compete with their own record—to improve their own performance, rather than to overemphasize competition with others. The teacher can help pupils see the need for cooperation with other pupils.

7. Pupils should be encouraged to view self-evaluation as a continuous process and a part of almost everything they do in school, rather than as something to be accomplished in a separate or isolated period set aside infrequently for evaluation. Pupils need to view self-evaluation as closely related to self-direction.

REPORTING TO PARENTS—AN ASPECT OF EVALUATION

The chief purpose of evaluation is to facilitate the growth and development of the pupil. The developing teacher needs to become aware of the important role that parents can play in evaluation when they are well informed about their child's progress and when there is good communication between parent and teacher. He needs to develop skill in reporting to parents.

Teacher–Parent Cooperation

Reports of a pupil's progress represent a significant contact, often the most significant contact, between the school and the parent. In most schools reports to parents are made at stated intervals. Teachers, however, recognize that effective pupil evaluation is a continuous process and that if it is to be most effective, teacher and parent must work together in encouraging and appraising pupil progress. Free, frequent, and perhaps informal communication between the teacher and parent of a pupil makes possible an exchange of views relating to the experiences of each. The teacher sees the pupil in a group situation where he is associated with those of his own age group who have interests similar to his own. The parent, on the other hand, views the pupil as a member of the family and of other groups where he is associated with individuals and with groups of a more heterogeneous nature than his peer group in school. Each may observe interests or behavior of the pupil which might not come to the attention of the other without an exchange of views.

Methods of Reporting

There are three types of reports to parents: report cards, letters or narrative statements, and conferences. There has been a relatively recent change in some schools in reporting procedures, from the formal report card using letter ratings to the pupil–parent–teacher conference. The prospective teacher will be hopelessly confused if he is not aware of the wide variation in reporting procedures. The reporting practices used by a school system are a reflection of the philosophy of the school, and thus it is not surprising that there are countless variations of the three general types of reports mentioned above. In some instances there are variations within the same school system as individual schools experiment with different systems of reporting. There are also instances where variations exist within one school. The student teacher or intern will benefit by study of, and involvement in, reporting procedures in his school.

Report cards.   There has been a movement away from the use of numerical marks such as 95, 84, and 76. This is in recognition of the fact that honest evaluation cannot be made within a small range of percentage points, for example, the once common practice of using 100 for "superior" and below 75 for "failure." Similarly, in the use of report cards there has been a movement away from letter marks—commonly A,B,C,D, and F—toward the use of terms such as "superior," "above average," "average," "below average," "poor," and "failure." Others use such terms as "excellent," "good," and "satisfactory." There is a trend toward the use of descriptive words or phrases and/or a checklist providing information about qualities or traits exhibited in the school life of the pupil. These may be in addition to, or may replace, the mark or grade in academic subjects commonly used in the past. School marks have been eliminated more frequently in elementary schools than in secondary schools.

There are continuing efforts to improve report cards. There is also a tendency for school systems and individual teachers to supplement the report card with other means of reporting such as conferences or exchange of informal notes by teacher and parent.

Letters or narrative statements.   Some schools have found the informal letter valuable in reporting to parents. When properly written, it has the virtues of directness and informality not possible with the formal report card; and where a carbon copy is made, as should always be done, a record is readily available in the pupil's individual file. In this latter respect the informal letter is superior to the parent–teacher conference. An obvious advantage of the letter is that it is focused on the individual pupil. It can also emphasize specific strengths, needed improvements, and ways in which teacher and parent can cooperate in facilitating progress. It eliminates competitive school marks.

Letters have the disadvantage of requiring a great deal of the teacher's time. This can be burdensome for the elementary teacher who has a large number of pupils and impractical for the secondary school teacher who is responsible for several large classes. Though the parent may be asked to reply, he seldom does so by written communication. When letters are used in reporting to parents, it is important that teachers and school officials work together to provide guidelines for their preparation. Experience has shown that where this is done the quality of the reporting procedure is greatly increased.[4]

Conferences. During recent years the use of the parent–teacher conference has increased as a means of reporting pupil progress. This has come about through a growing recognition of the limitations of report cards and the dissatisfaction with letters expressed by some teachers who have found the writing of them burdensome. A more positive explanation is the fact that parents and teachers have in many instances come to realize that there can be no adequate substitute for two-way, face-to-face communication.

The conference provides an excellent means for focusing on the accomplishments and needs of a single pupil. The parent has the opportunity to present his views, obtain answers to his questions, and make what he considers constructive suggestions for furthering the desirable intellectual, physical, and social growth of his child. The teacher has similar opportunities and, perhaps most important, an opportunity to listen and learn about the pupil as viewed through the eyes of the parent. He also has an opportunity to help the parent obtain additional information about the principles of child and adolescent growth and development. When conferences are well planned and properly conducted, the groundwork can be laid for cooperative action in advancing pupil welfare.

In some schools the conference has been expanded to make it a parent–pupil–teacher conference. When proper attitudes on the part of all concerned have been developed, this three-way conference can be useful in facilitating pupil growth. It will usually be desirable to supplement the three-way conference with a conference in which the pupil is not present.

[4] For a list of helpful "Suggestions for Writing Letters to Parents" see J. Stanley Ahmann, and Marvin D. Glock, *Evaluating Pupil Growth* (Boston: Allyn and Bacon, Inc., 1963), pp. 571–572.

A decision to use conferences as a means of reporting to parents should be preceded by careful study of this method's values and limitations. School systems which adopt the conference as a means of reporting must also launch a program to help the teacher develop skill in preparing for, conducting, and evaluating the conference. The following list of suggestions has been used for this purpose.

1. Make careful preparation.
2. Insure privacy.
3. Have an informal setting.
4. Set a time limit.
5. Overlook parents' critical remarks.
6. Establish rapport.
7. Encourage the parent to talk.
8. Listen attentively.
9. Begin on a positive note.
10. Develop attitude of mutual cooperation.
11. Delay making definite suggestions.
12. Let suggestions come from parents.
13. Build on parent suggestions.
14. Summarize points covered.
15. Make plans together.
16. End on a note of continuing cooperation.
17. Make notes after parent leaves.[5]

The Prospective Teacher and Reporting to Parents

The student teacher or intern will be either directly or indirectly involved in reporting to parents. He should welcome opportunities to participate in the reporting process as it is carried on in his school. The following are practical suggestions for studying and using reports to parents.

1. It is important to operate within the established framework. The student teacher or intern does not change the form of reporting even though he may not be in complete agreement with the educational philosophy on which it is based.

[5] U.S. Office of Education, *Reporting Pupil Progress to Parents*. Education Briefs, No. 34 (Washington, D.C.: Department of Health, Education, and Welfare, Office of Education, December 1956), p. 18, mimeographed.

2. There are many variations in reporting procedure. A knowledge of the basic types and possible adaptations of them will aid the prospective teacher in using the procedures employed in his school.

3. The capable and well-informed teacher will not permit limitations of the reporting system to restrict his efforts to communicate effectively with parents. Working in a professional and ethical manner, he will supplement a restrictive or inadequate reporting instrument with procedures which will make reporting effective. Notes, letters, or conferences might be used to supplement the formal report card.

4. Good reporting provides for two-way communication between parent and teacher. In the past some teachers have viewed reporting as nothing more than a means of informing the parent about the school performance of his child. Effective reporting encourages the parent to provide useful information for the teacher.

5. The pupil whose work is being evaluated should be involved in the reporting process. This may be done in a number of ways, including, when feasible, a three-way conference of parent, pupil, and teacher.

6. Cooperative action among parent, pupil, and teacher for the purposes of facilitating the progress of the pupil should be encouraged. Reporting procedures should not only report the situation as it exists, but should also lay the groundwork for improvement.

7. There has been greater change in reporting procedures in elementary schools than in secondary schools, but desirable adaptations can be made—and, in fact, are being made—in some secondary schools. The adoption by secondary schools of such procedures as letters and conferences has been resisted in some instances by parents and pupils. There is also the factor of teacher load. Some secondary schools are supplementing the report card with other reporting procedures. This trend can be accelerated as parents who have been involved with flexible reporting procedures in elementary schools have children in secondary schools, as secondary school teachers recognize their value, and as secondary

school administrators and guidance staff members discover ways to aid teachers in finding time to carry out more flexible reporting procedures.

8. In the preparation of reports to parents it is desirable to be forthright, direct, honest, and tactful. Following are some suggestions:

   a. Strive to make each report individualized and personal.
   b. Take time to prepare a meaningful report. This will necessitate the use of information in the cumulative file, test results, and other evaluative instruments discussed in this chapter.
   c. Help the parent discover what he can do to aid in the progress of his child. Regardless of how difficult the problems which confront the child may be, steps can be taken to help him. The difficulties should be stated and positive steps for solving them should be mentioned. Suggestions from the parent should be solicited.
   d. Avoid the use of terms that will not be understood by the parent. Use simple, nontechnical language. The parent is likely to resent a superior or condescending attitude on the part of the teacher. Cooperation is enhanced when the parent recognizes that the teacher has a sincere interest in his child.

SUMMARY

The capable teacher is skillful in evaluating the progress of those he instructs. To do this he needs to understand the meaning of evaluation, to use the devices and procedures of evaluation with skill, and to know how to report to parents in a manner which will facilitate pupil progress.

The evaluation of pupil growth should be in terms of established objectives. Teacher and pupils should consider evaluation an important aspect of learning. Wise appraisal makes provision for the use of standardized tests, teacher-made tests, informal devices and procedures, and self-evaluation by pupils.

Reporting to parents is both an important and a difficult aspect of evaluation. It is most satisfactory when there is close parent–teacher cooperation—when parent and teacher work as partners in appraising pupil progress and in taking constructive action to encourage desirable growth. Report cards, letters, and conferences are the basic methods of reporting, though there are many variations and combinations in their use. The student learning to teach has many opportunities to participate in reporting pupil progress. Thoughtful study of, and participation in, the reporting process by the prospective teacher can contribute much to his present understanding and can result in improvement in the future.

USEFUL REFERENCES

Adams, Georgia Sachs. *Measurement and Evaluation in Education, Psychology, and Guidance.* New York: Holt, Rinehart and Winston, Inc., 1964.

Ahmann, Stanley, and Marvin D. Glock. *Evaluating Pupil Growth,* 2d ed. Boston: Allyn and Bacon, Inc., 1963.

Burns, Paul C., and Daniel H. Brown. *The Student Teacher Evaluates Pupil Progress.* Bulletin No. 19. Cedar Falls, Iowa: Association for Student Teaching, 1962.

Educational Leadership. Entire issue is devoted to "Testing and Evaluation," 20 (October 1962), 2–80.

Educational Testing Service. *Making the Classroom Test: A Guide for Teachers.* Princeton, N. J.: The Service, 1961.

Gage, N. L., ed. *Handbook of Research on Teaching.* Chicago: Rand McNally & Company, 1963.

Noll, Victor H. *Introduction to Educational Measurement,* 2d ed., Boston: Houghton Mifflin Company, 1965.

Rothney, John W. M. *Evaluating and Reporting Pupil Progress.* What Research Says to the Teacher No. 7. Washington, D. C.: National Education Association, 1955.

Thorndike, Robert L. *The Concepts of Over- and Under-Achievement.* New York: Bureau of Publications, Teachers College, Columbia University, 1963.

U. S. Office of Education. *Reporting Pupil Progress to Parents.* Education Briefs, No. 34. Washington, D. C.: Department of Health, Education, and Welfare, Office of Education, December 1956.

CHAPTER SEVEN

USING
INSTRUCTIONAL
MATERIALS AND
TEACHING AIDS

Teachers with extensive experience can recall the lack of adequate instructional materials when they started teaching. The beginning teacher finds himself in a much different situation today. He is fortunate to have available an array of instructional aids. Books are more authentic, attractive, and usable than ever before. Pictures, maps, globes, charts, films, recordings, filmstrips, flannel boards, programmed materials, television, auto-instructional devices, and many more instructional tools comprise an imposing list of teaching aids from which teachers today may select those most appropriate to their needs. The following definition of teaching materials is accepted for purposes of this discussion.

An Instructional Material may be defined as any medium of communication used by teacher and pupil to advance learning. Under this definition, all teaching tools are Instructional Materials. Library books, audio-visual aids, television and radio, glass slides, filmstrips, flat pictures and maps, real objects, and community resources are some of the classes of teaching tools of extreme importance to education.[1]

It is the purpose of this chapter to assist the prospective teacher in selecting and using these resources effectively.

[1] Lois Shores, *Instructional Materials* (New York: Ronald Press Company, 1960), p. 3.

LEVELS OF COMMUNICATION AND
INSTRUCTIONAL MATERIALS

Pupils learn best through actual, direct, and lifelike experiences. Actually seeing an elephant is more meaningful than viewing a film about elephants or reading about an elephant. Riding on a train conveys sights, sounds, and sensations one does not receive when reading even the best-written account of a train trip. One learns much more by visiting an oil field and viewing oil being pumped from the ground than when one hears another person describe such a visit. If time, transportation, communication facilities, funds, and personnel for adequate planning were not limiting factors, perhaps arrangements might be made for pupils to learn through *direct* experiences alone. Perhaps communication between teacher and pupil would then be more complete and verbalism greatly reduced. Because it is impossible for schools and teachers to rely solely on direct experiences, communication media and instructional resources of various kinds are needed. The following statement is useful for comprehension of the various types of existing resources:

> For our purposes of inspecting teaching materials it is convenient to consider experiences on three levels:
> The first, the basic, level involves *real-life* experiences.
> The second level includes experiences intended to *substitute for real life*, but here we refer to experiences that do not use words alone. Instead on the second level we are concerned with the use of such media as arranged lifelike projects, field trips, real-life materials for exhibit and demonstration, models and mock-ups, dramatics, puppetry, sociodrama, motion pictures, television, photographs, drawings, and filmstrips.
> Our top, or third level, involves experiences that are *exclusively verbal*—ones that we read or hear about.[2]

SELECTING INSTRUCTIONAL MATERIALS

When the textbook and the chalkboard constituted the major teaching aids, there was no problem in deciding which instruc-

[2] R. Murray Thomas and Sherwin G. Swartout, *Integrated Teaching Materials* (New York: David McKay Co. Inc., 1963), p. 10.

tional materials should be selected. As the job of the teacher has become more complex and as the number of materials, aids, and devices has increased, he is compelled to decide which media will be used to achieve the best results under any set of circumstances.

Selection in Terms of Goals

No single teaching material or instructional aid is best and to be advocated under all circumstances. The teacher should avoid forming the habit of overusing any kind of instructional material or teaching aid to the exclusion of others because he likes to use it and uses it effectively, or because it is more readily available than others. Frequently, for example, a teacher will rely almost completely on the textbook because he has become accustomed to using it, there is a book in the hands of every pupil, and less effort is required in preparing for its use than would be required if additional media such as supplementary books, reference books, or audio-visual aids were used. The teacher should not avoid using an appropriate instructional aid because he has not used it previously and feels insecure about attempting its use. The capable teacher will become proficient in discovering and using the instructional media most likely to achieve the goals he has set.

Two simple examples will illustrate how instructional aids may be selected in terms of goals. An elementary teacher who was introducing common fractions supplemented the explanatory material in the textbook, his own comments, and his sketches on the chalkboard with paper pie plates which were cut into fractional parts showing, among other things, that if half a pie plate is cut into four parts each part is one eighth of the whole. Similarly, an apple was cut into sections. A high school teacher of world history was attempting to help pupils understand how people in the Stone Age were able to provide themselves with food, clothing, and shelter under primitive conditions. In addition to the textbook and numerous supplementary and reference books, she was able to locate a filmstrip and synchronized recording which illustrated and described how ancient man lived and the tools and instruments he used in obtaining food and clothing. She also located a sound film which made similar contributions to the understanding of her pupils. In addition she borrowed objects, drawings, and pictures from the city museum. In each of these situations the teacher was attempting to help pupils form concepts; real materials, drawings, and pictures were used to reinforce the spoken word and printed page.

Sources of Instructional Materials Within the School System

The capable teacher needs to know where to turn for instructional materials which will be useful in teaching. He should consider ways to obtain them from sources both inside and outside the school in which he works.

Schools differ in the ways instructional materials are made available to teachers and pupils. The following are possible sources of instructional materials which may be found in the school.

Classroom. Some classrooms, especially self-contained classrooms in the elementary school, contain a wealth of instructional materials; others contain very few resources. This situation may be the result of school policy or it may reflect the attitude of the teacher. If one is fortunate enough to work where many resources are available, he should become informed as soon as possible about their location and ways of using them. If an inventory list is available, it will provide the information needed. If not, a list using broad general headings can be made in a short time.

School office. In some schools, especially those in which there is no teaching materials center or adequate library, the office contains files of various types of instructional materials and, in some instances, actual materials. Catalogs of school-supply firms from which needed materials may be ordered are frequently on file in the school office.

School library. Schools vary greatly in the amount and quality of service provided by the library. This variation ranges all the way from no library of any kind to one with extensive content and services. In some schools the library is a part of a teaching materials center or teaching aids laboratory.

Teaching materials center. In some school systems, especially larger ones, the teaching materials center or instructional materials center is operated independently of the library and is used primarily by the instructional staff rather than by pupils. Instructional materials and teaching aids of all kinds are made available to individual schools or individual teachers as needed. The following statement is helpful in understanding the teacher's relationship to the teaching materials center:

> The Materials Center can, therefore, be seen as a school-wide Instructional Materials program that parallels the organization of the school system itself. Necessary to its functioning are adequately prepared personnel at every level. A director or supervisor of Instructional Materials is needed at the system level for over-all planning. Librarians or building-level coordinators are required in each of the schools to work directly with teachers and pupils. But fundamental to a successful Instructional Materials program are the teachers at the classroom level who know Instructional Materials well enough to use them intelligently in their teaching. This knowledge includes a familiarity with the potentials and limitations of the various classes of materials and an understanding of methods of procurement, organization, and distribution. It consists further in some skill in the handling of the materials and of the equipment that accompanies some of them. In particular, this knowledge necessitates sufficient competence to enable the teacher to select and utilize Instructional Materials for a given subject area and age level.[3]

Sources of Instructional Materials from Outside the School System

Sources of instructional materials from outside the school system will vary a great deal. However, some exist with sufficient consistency to deserve consideration.

Teacher education institution. Some colleges and universities, through one or more agencies on the campus, make certain instructional materials and teaching aids available to prospective teachers. Some institutions' audio-visual centers lend a wide vari-

[3] Lois Shores, *op. cit.*, p. 13.

ety of films, filmstrips, slides, and recordings to student teachers and interns. In at least one institution they are listed in a catalog which is updated each year and which makes selection easy for the user. The same institution through its teaching materials center makes a large variety of instructional materials, such as books, pictures, units, clippings, and charts, readily available.

Public library. Some school systems have worked out cooperative arrangements with the local public library which facilitate the use of instructional materials by pupils and teachers. Even in situations where such formal arrangements have not been made, those in charge of public libraries encourage use of the library by all citizens of the community, including, of course, school pupils and teachers. It is sound practice for a teacher new to the community to become acquainted with library policies and personnel.

State traveling library. A number of states maintain a central library supported by state funds. This is frequently done to serve those areas of the state which do not have a local library or in which library facilities are inadequate to meet the needs of residents. In most instances the central library has a division of school libraries which makes loans to schools for an extended period.

Community. The community is a valuable source of instructional materials and one often overlooked by teachers. Frequently the school library, the instructional materials center, or the principal's office contains a file of community resources that may be used by teachers. In others, much of this information will be incorporated in a curriculum guide. In still others, little or nothing has been done to help the teacher become acquainted with the community and use it as a learning laboratory. Included in the possibilities that might be explored with a view to classroom use are natural resources; the industrial, recreational, and cultural activities of the community; and the many human resources that are found in every community.

Commercial organizations and agencies. Many corporations make it a practice to supply schools with information about their company or industry. Associations sponsored by industries such as the life insurance, railroad, or dairy industries provide schools with informative publications, displays, or exhibits. Chambers of commerce, travel bureaus, and many similar agencies represent another source. There are numerous lists and catalogs of free or inexpensive materials available to aid the resourceful teacher in obtaining useful instructional material.[4]

Professional organizations for teachers. Ordinarily, the prospective teacher has affiliated with one or more professional organizations for teachers and has discovered that they can be helpful in suggesting materials which are useful in teaching. The National Education Association, the largest organization of a general nature for teachers, through its magazine, the *NEA Journal*, and its many other publications, provides suggestions relating to instructional materials and teaching aids. Organizations of a more specialized nature, such as the Association for Childhood Education International, National Science Teachers Association, and National Council for the Social Studies, suggest materials of instruction useful in their respective fields.

Selection as a Cooperative Process

The student learning to teach has many opportunities to work with others and to obtain assistance from them in selecting instructional materials. He also has an opportunity to learn how pupils can be involved in this important learning task.

Selection with the supervising teacher. As a capable and experienced teacher, the supervising teacher has discovered ways of selecting instructional materials that have been effective in his teaching. He will usually be quite willing to share these ideas. The prospective teacher, on the other hand, as a result of his

---

[4] Illustrative sources are:

Educators Progress Service, Randolph, Wisconsin. *Educators Guide to Free Films* (Other titles also available).

George Peabody College For Teachers, Nashville, Tennessee. *Free and Inexpensive Learning Materials.*

Rubidoux Printing Company, Riverside, California. *Catalog of Free Teaching Materials.*

campus contacts with the teaching materials center and up-to-date sources of information relating to materials, can make helpful suggestions for increasing the resources available to pupils. As a result of this cooperation one sixth-grade student teacher left his student teaching assignment with considerable experience in the selection and use of instructional materials. Information obtained included the following:

A list of textbooks for each subject, including teacher's manuals for some of them.

A list of supplementary books used in each subject.

A list of books, rocks, insects, and other items collected by pupils for a science corner.

A list of books which children, teacher, student teacher, and parents had lent for the room library during the semester. A card for each book was made and filed by pupils.

A list of motion pictures, slides, and filmstrips viewed by pupils.

A list of records and tapes heard by the group.

A record of ways the tape recorder had been used for recording presentations of individual pupils and group discussions.

A list of flat pictures available in the file of the supervising teacher.

A list of units which the supervising teacher had used in the past and kept on file.

A list of books and magazines contributed by parents.

A list of the Midwest Airborne Television lessons viewed by the group.

A record of materials used in each science experiment and demonstration.

A record of materials included in each bulletin board display by supervising teacher, student teacher, and pupils.

A record of displays obtained from the teaching materials center at the college or prepared by pupils.

A record of models prepared by pupils in social studies and other classes.

A copy of the form used by pupils in keeping their own card files of books each had read. A list of all titles read by children in the group.

Selection with other school personnel. The effective teacher in an effective school does not work alone. He recognizes that "everybody knows more than anybody."

With the guidance of his supervising teacher, a social studies major working as a student teacher in a junior high school discovered that working in close cooperation with others could be helpful in obtaining suitable learning resources for the pupils he instructed. He received the following help.

The college supervisor obtained several resource units provided by the director of the curriculum laboratory at the university. These resource units helped the student teacher to prepare learning units for his pupils.

The coordinator of the instructional center for the school system helped select films, filmstrips, and slides to be used in his units.

The vice-principal, who was a member of one of the local service clubs in the city, made arrangements for him to contact a fellow club member, an industrialist, who served as a resource person in providing information his pupils were seeking.

The school librarian prepared a list of reference books and made them available to pupils for use in connection with the units studied.

Another member of the faculty who had examined social studies textbooks while serving as chairman of the textbook selection committee for the school system offered suggestions for supplementary books to be used with topics being considered.

Selection with pupils. The skillful teacher can help pupils to participate in the selection of instructional materials. Such involvement can become an excellent means of motivating learning and encouraging pupils to assume some responsibility for their own education. One group of authors suggests ways pupils can participate in the selection of materials.

1. Bringing from home concrete and printed materials that will help in the studies being pursued at school. Such instructional materials include articles for exhibits, science specimens, books, pamphlets, clippings, maps, charts, pictures.

2. Bringing to school materials that can be used in construction activities. These might include items such as wood, cardboard, tools, paper, paint, cloth.

3. Bringing to the group materials for aesthetic enjoyment. Story books, poems, prints, recordings, art objects, and the like are examples.

4. Choosing from the library printed materials that will help the group in their research.

5. Locating further sources of information for the group. This might include places to visit, persons to interview or to speak before the group, community projects to investigate.

6. Sharing with the group objects which the children themselves have created. This could include models, constructions such as bird houses, scientific experiments, miniature gardens, terrariums, paintings, creative writing.[5]

USING A VARIETY OF INSTRUCTIONAL MATERIALS

Basic Techniques

After a teacher has decided which instructional materials or devices are to be used, he needs to consider how they may be used to achieve best results. This will usually require preparation, presentation, summarization, clarification, reflection, and, finally, evaluation. It will be helpful here to examine these steps to the most effective use of instructional materials in some detail.

Preparation.   There are two important aspects of preparation for using a learning resource. One relates to the steps the teacher takes in preparing himself; the other, to ways he prepares the pupils he is instructing.

The detailed steps the teacher takes to prepare himself will vary with the medium to be used, but it is essential to become well informed about each instructional aid. If printed materials

[5] James B. Burr, Lowry Harding, and Leland B. Jacobs, *Student Teaching in the Elementary School* (New York: Appleton-Century-Crofts, Inc., 1958), p. 307.

such as textbooks, reference books, or supplementary books are to be used, each should be read or scanned before assignments are made to ensure the material is appropriate in terms of purpose, difficulty, and interest. When audio-visual materials are to be used they should be heard and/or viewed prior to use with pupils. If equipment is to be used, it should be obtained and checked for proper functioning in advance of use. If the teacher is to operate the equipment himself, he must be certain that he knows how to operate the specific make and model available for his use.

A teacher is sometimes unsuccessful in using instructional aids because he neglects to prepare his pupils for using them. Below are some of the things he can do that will contribute to the best preparation of pupils:

1. Help pupils relate what is to be studied, viewed, or heard to their previous learning.

2. Call attention to similarities or differences in the use of the instructional medium as compared to others previously used.

3. Help pupils obtain a general idea of what is to be seen, heard, read, or used.

4. Help pupils understand the purpose for which the resource is used, e.g., for enjoyment or to obtain information.

5. Ask individuals, small groups, or the total group to obtain answers to either general or specific questions as they view, listen, or read.

6. Ask individuals, small groups, or the total group to list issues or problems that are raised as the instructional resource is used.

7. Request that each pupil make an effort to discover points with which he agrees or disagrees, or to discover portions he either likes or dislikes.

8. Assign to individuals or the group the responsibility for determining how well the group meets previously determined standards for effective use of the medium.

Presentation. Information relating to the presentation of instructional materials is discussed later in the chapter as the various types of materials are considered. There are, however, certain important points that may be appropriately mentioned here.

1. *Timing.* The successful use of any instructional material often hinges upon whether or not it has been introduced at the most opportune time. Should a film on community helpers be shown before or after the postman speaks to a second-grade group? How much informative reading material should a ninth-grade science group be assigned before making an excursion to the city sewage disposal plant? The teacher needs to be sensitive to the abilities, interests, and needs of the group as guides in the matter of timing.

2. *Physical conditions.* Beginning teachers sometimes overlook the importance of maintaining optimum conditions of temperature, ventilation, and lighting. Pupils need to be seated so that each can see and hear. An overheated room, poor ventilation, improper lighting, and overcrowding should be avoided.

3. *Classroom management.* A pleasant and businesslike classroom atmosphere should be maintained. Interruptions and distractions should be held to a minimum, and pupils should be encouraged to learn to focus their attention on the medium being used.

Summarization, clarification, reflection. A third step in the use of an instructional resource such as a filmstrip, recording, radio program, or book is the follow-up. This provides the teacher with an opportunity to summarize and to clarify any discernible misconceptions pupils may have acquired. It provides an opportunity for pupils to ask questions and to learn by discussing issues or problems raised during the presentation period. The value of the follow-up period is emphasized in the statement which follows.

What do you do after the film has been shown? When people leave a movie theater they turn from the entertainment experience to some other interest—the film is "over." With an educational film, however, the logical next step takes the form of discussing "what the film said." Were the expected answers clear-cut? Do we agree with them? Does the information conflict with what we learned from other sources, including other films? Possibly entirely new questions arise in the minds of students—some new insights that call for new experiences. Learning, we must remember, is intended to develop new problems as well as to help solve old ones. It is a continuing process in which new questions grow out of present answers.[6]

Evaluation.   Both teacher and pupils should make continuing evaluations of the learning materials they use. Each of the following statements was made by a different student teacher, and each statement reveals an implied effort to evaluate an instructional resource.

"I wonder how much real value these workbooks are to the children."

"Television and radio have increased their vocabulary."

"It was really an exciting experience to have the class respond enthusiastically when I used the tape recorder to supplement the lesson."

The following list of questions is suggested for evaluating audio-visual materials.

Is the material appropriate for the age, intelligence, and experience of the learners?

Do the materials give a true picture of the ideas they present?

Do they contribute meaningful content to the topic under study?

Is the physical condition of the materials satisfactory?

Is there a teacher's guide available to provide help in the effective use of the materials?

Do they make students better thinkers, critical-minded?

Do they tend to improve human relations?

Is the material worth the time, expense, and effort involved? [7]

Printed Materials

Printed materials continue to constitute the largest and most widely used category of instructional aids available.

---

[6] Edgar Dale, *Audio-Visual Methods in Teaching*, rev. (New York: Holt, Rinehart and Winston, Inc., 1954), p. 77.

[7] *Ibid.*, p. 83.

Textbooks.   The textbook has long been the most widely used instructional resource. Although many resourceful and imaginative teachers supplement the textbook with numerous other instructional materials and aids and some have discontinued its use, a large number of teachers follow the textbook. Some rely almost completely on it as the chief instructional resource.

The place of the textbook in the instruction of pupils has been a subject of considerable controversy. There can be little doubt that following the textbook is the easiest, though not the best, way for the teacher to instruct pupils. It requires much less effort to assign "the next five or ten pages" in a textbook each day than to develop resource units and teaching units which include suggestions for enrichment through the extensive use of a wide variety of instructional media. This is undoubtedly the reason why many teachers persist in their great dependence on the textbook. Some of the limitations of relying on a single textbook are set forth in the statements which follow.

1. It is deadly to the good student to follow textbook reading with a discussion in which no new material is introduced.

2. It is impossible to find a single text suited to the interests and abilities of all the students in a group.

3. It does not encourage the development of initiative and self-direction to assign students three or four pages in a textbook.

4. It limits the scope of the course and does not encourage students to work up to their maximum ability.

5. It encourages belief in the infallibility of the printed page and reliance upon a single authority.

6. It provides little opportunity for students to compare and evaluate different points of view and develop critical-mindedness.

7. It encourages bad reading habits in students and rote memorization.

8. It tends to routinize procedure—so many pages to read, followed by recitation and a quiz on what was read.[8]

It is easy to understand how the shortcomings mentioned above result when teachers and pupils follow a textbook. In some

[8] From Dorothy G. Petersen, *The Elementary Teacher* (New York: Appleton-Century-Crofts, 1964), p. 413, and from *Education for Social Competence,* by I. James Quillen and Lavone A. Hanna. Copyright 1948, 1961 by Scott, Foresman and Company, Chicago, p. 227.

situations the word "follow" may be interpreted literally. Pupils can easily form the habit of following what is printed in the textbook without being stimulated to search for and enjoy an infinitely wider fund of knowledge available to them through other instructional media.

Although there has been marked improvement in both the format and content of textbooks they remain, as the name suggests, "*text* books." The circuit-riding minister of American frontier days carried in his pocket a small book containing numerous short statements from the Bible, each of which might be selected as the *text* for a sermon. As he would ride on horseback between his parishes or parishoners, he was unable to write but could meditate upon the *text* he had selected for a sermon. When later he had an opportunity to sit at a desk, he would put his thoughts into writing and complete preparation for a sermon. In a similar manner the teacher can use the modern textbook as a *starting point* and, with the use of other instructional media, extend the thinking and experiences of his pupils to an extent which would be impossible if he used the textbook alone.

The fact that today's textbooks are greatly improved over those available some years ago is well stated by Petersen, who says:

In the first place, their physical format is infinitely improved. In general, children's textbooks are attractively and colorfully illustrated; the type is clear and easy to read; they are of a convenient size; and they have attractive and durable covers. Secondly, considerable effort has been directed in recent years toward improving the content of textbooks. Great emphasis is placed upon accuracy of material, clarity of expression, suitable vocabulary, and interesting writing style. Then too, the inclusion of many excellent study guide questions and suggestions for pupil activities and supplementary exercises makes the textbook a valuable teaching tool for the teacher.[9]

The proper use of the textbook can contribute much to the sound education of youth. When wisely used it can:

1. Provide a reference point from which pupils may start in exploring a topic, concept, or problem.

[9] Petersen, *op. cit.*, p. 412.

2. Introduce pupils to an authority in a field of knowledge.

3. Become an instrument for motivation of further study.

4. Be used as an outline to unify the thinking of pupils in dealing with a topic, problem, subject area, or field of knowledge.

5. Facilitate the development of work-study skills such as use of the index and table of contents; ability to skim, outline, summarize, and find the central idea; and improvement of the rate and comprehension of what is read.

Many elements in the teaching-learning situation influence the ways a textbook may be used most effectively. In some situations, considerable reliance on the textbook may be necessary and desirable. In other instances, where there is careful planning and a wide range of instructional media is available, the designation of a specific textbook may not be essential. In still others, a textbook in combination with many instructional materials and aids may be the most appropriate plan.

A useful arrangement which has worked well includes the following:

1. A curriculum guide prepared cooperatively by teachers, principals, and the instructional staff is provided by the central office of the school system. This curriculum guide contains a clear statement of policy on the role of the textbook and on the development and use of a wide variety of instructional materials and aids.

2. Textbooks are used in most subjects or subject areas.

3. Access is provided to several textbooks and many supplementary references.

4. Resource units are prepared cooperatively by committees composed of members of the instructional staff. These resource units contain suggestions for the development of teaching units and include lists of specific references, audio-visual materials, and other teaching aids.

Other printed materials. A wide variety of printed material is available to schools which possess the human and financial resources necessary to obtain them. The student teacher or intern is likely to be confronted with the problem of selecting from many possibilities those printed materials that are most likely to help him achieve his goals. They include dictionaries, encyclopedias, almanacs, atlases, pamphlets, newspapers, and magazines.

Audio-Visual Aids

There is an old Chinese proverb to the effect that "one picture is worth a thousand words." In recognition of the value of sight and sound in reinforcing the effectiveness of the spoken word and printed page, the value of audio-visual aids to learning has increased considerably in recent years.

Films.   The sound motion picture is used extensively by teachers of children of all ages and variations in ability. Some of the reasons for this wide acceptance are summarized by Dale who says:

Motion pictures can
   1. Present certain meanings involving motion,
   2. Compel attention,
   3. Heighten reality,
   4. Speed up or slow down time,
   5. Bring the distant past and the present into the classroom,
   6. Provide an easily produced record of an event,
   7. Enlarge or reduce the actual size of objects,
   8. Present physical processes invisible to the naked eye,
   9. Build a common denominator of experience,
   10. Influence and even change attitudes,
   11. Promote an understanding of abstract relationship,
   12. Offer a satisfying esthetic experience.[10]

In large school systems some films are produced by the system itself, although in most instances they will be obtained from other sources. Films may be borrowed from state departments of education, universities and colleges, state and municipal libraries, and commercial agencies. These film-distributing agencies prepare and distribute catalogues which usually contain classified

[10] Dale, *op. cit.*, pp. 218–219.

lists of films suitable for use with various units, subjects, or topics, and for pupils of varying abilities and interests.

As a means of facilitating the selection, ordering, distribution, and use of audio-visual materials and equipment most school systems employ a director of audio-visual education or designate a person with some similar title. It is the practice in many school districts for a person within each individual school to serve as school or building coordinator of audio-visual aids. This procedure makes it possible for the individual teacher, including the student teacher or intern, to use these aids with minimum effort and maximum effectiveness.

The prospective teacher needs to develop skill in using audio-visual equipment. Although operators of equipment are sometimes provided, in the majority of situations the teacher will need to operate projection equipment. As a beginning teacher he should learn about equipment and its operation. This will help him acquire knowledge and self-confidence, increase the satisfaction and enjoyment he receives from his work, and improve his teaching.

Filmstrips and slides. The filmstrip, sometimes called slide film because it is really a series of pictures taken on 35 mm film, is favored by many classroom teachers. The prospective teacher soon discovers this to be one of the most readily available and easy to use audio-visual aids of the projection type. Some of the advantages of filmstrips are:

1. They permit the user to regulate the speed of operation, thus permitting as much pupil participation, questions, and comments as desired.
2. They are inexpensive, averaging about six dollars. This means that most schools or school systems may maintain their own filmstrip library and do not have to depend solely on rentals.
3. They are available on a wide variety of topics, and maturity levels of pupils ranging from kindergarten through college.
4. They are contained in very small containers (about 1 inch) which makes them easy to store and transport.
5. They are available in many topics in either black and white or in color.

6. They require only a slightly darkened room and can thus be shown in most ordinary classrooms.
7. They present a subject in a fixed sequential order of frames, which means that individual frames can not be lost or misplaced.
8. The filmstrip projector is lightweight, portable, easy to operate, and relatively inexpensive. [11]

Frequently, printed narrative commentary accompanies a filmstrip. This can be a helpful aid for the teacher if it is used to supplement, rather than supplant, the teacher's preparation for the filmstrip presentation. Sometimes a filmstrip is produced with an accompanying synchronized recording. More often explanatory material is incorporated in the filmstrip itself as a part of each picture.

Slides are widely used in classrooms. Each slide consists of a separate picture or illustration. This feature makes it possible to show an individual picture in any order desired and thus avoids one of the limitations of the filmstrip where pictures or illustrations occur in a fixed sequence.

The 2 by 2 inch 35 mm transparencies are favored by many teachers. One reason for this is that an inexpensive camera in the hands of pupils or teacher can produce good results. These pictures can be developed into 2 by 2 inch black-and-white or color slides. It is thus possible to acquire a valuable and flexible instructional aid at relatively little expense.

The 3¼ by 4 inch slide, like the smaller one, has a variety of classroom possibilities. Its larger size allows for more detail when it is projected. For the same reason it is easier for pupils or teacher to produce drawings, diagrams, charts, and similar material when school-made slides are to be used. Glass, cellophane, and plastic materials are used in making slides of both dimensions, though the use of glass is declining and there is increased use of the 2 by 2 inch slide as compared with the larger size.

Flat pictures. For many teaching purposes flat pictures such as photographs, illustrations of various kinds, paintings, and pictures which appear in various publications are a valuable teach-

[11] Petersen, *op. cit.*, pp. 419–420.

ing resource. They can be used effectively with learners of any age or level of ability, and they are applicable to any subject area or field of knowledge. Following are some examples of their use.

1. A teacher of a group of third-grade pupils, through the use of photographs, found it possible to correct the erroneous impressions of many of her pupils about how a bunch of bananas is attached to the tree.

2. Sixth-grade pupils acquired a better understanding of the development of transportation by obtaining pictures from magazines and travel folders which showed modes of transportation from primitive times to the jet age. The children looked at the pictures individually, and then they were mounted and shown to the total group with the use of the opaque projector.

3. By using a series of photographs and drawings, a junior high school music teacher in a small school helped his pupils obtain a better idea of the construction and use of the lyre which they had read about in their study of early musical instruments.

4. A high school science teacher helped those in his class prepare for a field trip to an oil refinery by showing them a series of photographs and diagrams of similar refineries.

Pupils and teachers often take pictures for granted. They are so common in everyday life that their educational value is frequently overlooked. Pictures are relatively inexpensive in comparison with other audio-visual aids. Many that are suitable for instructional use may be clipped from magazines, newspapers, brochures, and other printed materials. Many commercial firms follow a practice of lending or giving illustrative material to schools.

Learning opportunities when children make their own collection of pictures should not be overlooked. This practice should not be carried beyond the point of diminishing returns, but for some pupils, in some situations, it can be a useful form of motivation.

The problems of mounting, storing, and filing pictures so that they may be kept in good condition, correctly identified, and readily available for use can be met in various ways. Some teachers have made the mistake of collecting many more pictures than can be used effectively because they cannot be located at the time they are needed most. Ways of mounting, storing, and filing are discussed in references at the end of this chapter. Information may also be obtained from the director of audio-visual education in the school system with which the prospective teacher is affiliated.

Bulletin boards and flannel boards.   Classrooms today contain bulletin boards of two types. One, usually small, serves as a place for *posting notices and announcements* the teacher, principal, or other person connected with the school believes should be called to the attention of pupils and/or teachers. Another type, sometimes called a tackboard, is larger and is used as an *instructional aid*. It serves the dual purposes of (1) enabling the teacher to convey information to pupils by posting materials of a visual nature and (2) providing for pupils a means by which they may display and share some of the results of their learning. The comments which follow relate to bulletin boards used for instructional purposes.

The importance of the bulletin board as an instructional aid is indicated by the fact that in new school buildings an increased amount of space is provided for this purpose. That bulletin boards can be used purposefully is illustrated by the statement of a sixth-grade student teacher whose pupils were working on a social studies unit: "Although I have three bulletin boards filled with informative material and pictures, the students are still bringing in things that are useful and different."

The following are sound suggestions for the use of the bulletin board:

1. The subject matter should relate to current instruction; it should be interesting and appropriate to the ability of pupils.

2. Motivation is facilitated through involvement. Pupils can participate in determining criteria for wise bulletin board use.

They can participate in the selection of material and assume some responsibility for keeping it attractive, timely, and interesting.

3. The material displayed should be changed as needed to synchronize with changes in the instructional program.

4. Monotony can be avoided by changes in the arrangement, organization, and techniques for mounting material displayed. At the same time pupils can be encouraged to learn sound principles of artistic display.

The flannel board or felt board is a versatile instructional aid. It may be purchased or made by the teacher. One intern made his own inexpensive flannel board by stretching and gluing flannel cloth over a piece of waste plywood obtained from the school shop. The same material in various colors was used to make some of the designs, letters, and figures used for display on the flannel board. This device can be used effectively in many teaching situations, e.g., in mathematics where numbers are used, in language arts with words or letters, in chemistry with symbols, or in most any subject or area where pictures or designs are helpful.

This same principle is applied in another type of adhering board. This is the commercially produced magnetic board which involves the use of magnetic materials. It has more limited applications than the flannel board, but is useful for the manipulation of small objects, figures, numbers, or letters.

Auditory aids—radio and recordings. The radio is a useful instructional tool. In some situations only live radio can provide the pupil with on-the-spot information and insight into significant happenings. The fact that important and unusual radio programs may be recorded and used at times when they will be most effective adds to radio's value as an instructional aid.

Some commercially produced radio programs are suitable for school use. Another excellent source of radio programs is the educational broadcast sponsored by a school system, university, or other educational agency. Many of these programs are prepared for a specific audience, for example, music for the lower elementary grades, science for the junior high school, or a social studies program for twelfth-grade pupils. Commercial as well as educational broadcasting stations frequently transcribe the programs they produce and make them available to schools through sale or loan. This procedure makes the transcription usable over a much wider geographical area than the original program.

Another type of recording now in general use in the classroom is that made with tapes. Tapes have the advantages of being economical, permanent, and easy to handle, transport, and store. Most schools now have one or more tape recorders, and there is much to be said for having one in each classroom. The tape recorder may be used in a number of ways to help the imaginative teacher achieve his instructional goals. For example: motivation is facilitated when a group of elementary children know their demonstration, culminating event, or program is to be recorded and heard by others; self-evaluation is encouraged when high school pupils in a speech class hear their own voices; and the student teacher or intern can benefit by hearing his own voice as he instructs his pupils.

Other audio-visual aids. In addition to the instructional aids considered thus far and those in the following discussion of innovations, there are others which deserve mention here. *Concrete materials* such as collections, models, objects, and living things can play a very important part in helping the teacher and his pupils attain goals they have set. *Exhibits,* prepared by the teacher, by pupils, or by a commercial firm, represent another useful audio-visual aid. The *demonstration,* by either the teacher or the pupils, should not be overlooked. The *field trip* is also a valuable aid to instruction.

Beginning teachers sometimes overlook the value of the *chalkboard* in facilitating learning. Before the appearance of the numerous audio-visual aids now in use, it was the only visual aid available for instructional purposes. There are correct and incorrect ways to use the chalkboard effectively. References at the end of this chapter contain specific and useful suggestions.

TAKING ADVANTAGE OF INNOVATIONS

Many far-seeing teachers and teacher-educators believe that the contemporary student teacher or intern is entering the profession during one of the most revolutionary periods in the history of education. Four important conditions relating to the future of education, mentioned in Chapter 1, support this view, namely: (1) there are more pupils to be instructed than ever before, (2) there is a growing demand for more and better education for each individual, (3) the world's fund of knowledge has increased tremendously in recent years and this trend is continuing at an accelerated rate, and (4) advances in technology have made and are continuing to make available media which offer great promise of bringing changes and improvements in the instruction of children and youth.

In order to work as an effective teacher in this changing environment the prospective teacher needs to:

1. Become skillful in working with instructional media now in general use.

2. Be aware of the degree of acceptance of the new media by teachers and administrators.

3. Endeavor to become informed about, and develop skill in, the use of the new media as rapidly as possible.

4. Acquire an attitude toward change which will make it possible for him to work harmoniously with both opponents and proponents of change as he endeavors to improve instruction through the use of all media.

Educational Television

There has been considerable controversy about the value of television as an instructional aid. It has had staunch supporters and vigorous opponents. Television is being used extensively and successfully at all levels—in elementary schools, secondary schools, colleges and universities. There is little doubt that it will be used even more widely in the future and that new and better ways of using it will be found.

What are the advantages of television as an aid to instruction? They have been listed by Petersen as:

1. Providing a high quality of instruction for children. Instruction by television may be superior in many ways to ordinary classroom instruction for two good reasons. In the first place, only the highly-skilled, exceptionally capable teacher is chosen as the television teacher. Secondly, the television teacher has much more time to plan, and many more facilities to draw upon, to perfect a single lesson than does the classroom teacher who teaches a full day's schedule.

2. Distributing superior quality of instruction to a large number of schools. This is an especially important consideration for those under-privileged or rural schools that cannot otherwise afford the equipment, visual materials, laboratories, and expert teachers televised instruction may offer them.

3. Improving the quality of instruction. Television may help to improve the instructional procedures of those teachers who teach on television as well as those who view the televised lesson. By means of kinescopes the television teacher may view and evaluate his own performance, which should provide a strong means of professional growth. Then too, the classroom teacher has the opportunity of watching a master teacher at work, an opportunity denied to him under ordinary circumstances. Such an opportunity should certainly help to strengthen his teaching performance.

4. Offering unique educational experiences. The television camera can do things a live classroom teacher simply cannot do. It can enable all children in the group to look through a microscope at the same time. It can give children an intimate close-up view of any process or object. It can combine the teacher's presentation with films, filmstrips, and other visuals to an extent and with an ease just not possible in the ordinary classroom situation.

5. Offering possibilities for patterns of instruction different from the traditional one teacher per class type. Television makes it possible to teach larger groups when this is educationally desirable. It makes it possible to differentiate instruction according to the needs of several groups. It may make it possible for the classroom teacher to spend more time with certain individuals or small groups.[12]

There can be little doubt that the foregoing list of advantages is impressive. What are the objections to television instruction?

[12] Petersen, *op. cit.*, pp. 433–434.

One is that it does not permit direct, face-to-face give and take between teacher and pupil. Another is that television instruction tends to determine the curriculum and, thus, does not allow the classroom teacher or the local school autonomy in determining content. It may be argued that these are not really limitations of the television medium as an instructional tool but, rather, faults in the way the tool is used.

What are the pertinent points relating to instructional television to which the prospective teacher should give consideration? As a classroom teacher using educational television he should:

1. Recognize that educational television is here to stay. Although it lacks the seasoning of older instructional aids, experimentation and research have shown it to be a useful tool.

2. Take advantage of opportunities to use instructional television effectively.

3. Understand the objectives of the television teacher and the total program which pupils view and make the necessary preparation for each telecast.

4. Help pupils who view the telecast to develop an attitude of acceptance toward instructional television and the television teacher, and help them to make the necessary preparation for each telecast.

5. Bridge the gap between the television teacher and the pupil which is caused by the absence of a face-to-face relationship between them. This can be done in such ways as: (a) knowing each pupil as an individual; (b) working with individuals, small groups, or the total group as necessary; (c) using procedures and/or instructional materials most likely to achieve the objectives intended by the television teacher.

6. Serve as an understanding guide or counselor of each learner in the group. The classroom teacher needs to know the ability, home background, interests, and anxieties of each pupil in the group so that he may help the learner benefit by having viewed a television program.

7. Consider educational television as one of many instructional aids, each augmenting the other.

The Instructional Team

The student teacher or intern who participates in team teaching should find this experience valuable in his later work with pupils. One who has not had this experience should assume responsibility for becoming informed about the possibilities of team teaching so that he may be a constructive participant when the opportunity arises.

The term *instructional team* is used in this discussion in recognition of the fact that individuals other than teachers, such as the "teacher aide" and "clerical aide," are frequently included as members of the instructional team and can add much to its effectiveness. It is assumed that pooling the competencies of each team member in a cooperative and coordinated effort will result in greater benefit to the pupil than when teachers work separately.

It must be recognized that the terms "team teaching" and "instructional team" have been used loosely and that there are many types of team organization. Following is a helpful list of general characteristics of the instructional team:

1. A teaching team consists of from three to seven or more teachers jointly responsible for the instruction of 75–225 or more pupils in one or more grade or age levels.

2. Teams may have teachers assigned to different levels of responsibility, depending on their ability and experience, with higher salaries and higher status given to the senior teachers and the team leader.

3. . . . most team teaching programs permit supervision of the junior members of a team by the senior or leadership personnel. The schedule also permits less experienced personnel to observe the outstanding teacher adjusting his program as the teaching-learning situation develops.

4. Team teaching programs emphasize the team, rather than the individual teacher, in the planning, teaching, and evaluating cycle.

5. In the classroom situation, however, teaching teams protect the professional autonomy of each teacher and stress the use of his unique abilities in the instruction of children.

6. In many team teaching programs, each member of the team specializes in a different curriculum area and helps all members of the team plan, teach, and evaluate in the area of his specialty.

7. All team teaching programs emphasize the effective utilization of the strengths of each member of the staff.

8. As team teaching promotes non-gradedness within the school, so does non-gradedness promote team teaching. The theory of continuous pupil progress is basic to most team teaching programs.

9. Team teaching programs emphasize varying class sizes and class lengths based upon instructional objectives, context, techniques, and pupil needs.

10. Class size and length of period are closely related to the flexible scheduling practices for pupils and teachers which are characteristic of many team teaching programs.

11. Many team teaching programs use aides for nonprofessional tasks.

12. Most team teachers make more effective use of mechanical and electronic equipment.[13]

School systems throughout the country have experimented with use of the instructional team. It has been used at all grade levels and with various subjects, and also where content is integrated and cuts across subject lines. The team has varied in size, organization, and in the kinds of responsibilities assumed by each team member. The organization of one instructional team and some of its characteristics can be understood by a study of Figure 3.[14]

Two terms which are used in the accompanying figure need to be clarified. The commonly accepted definition of the terms "teacher aide" and "clerical aide" is given by Shaplin and Olds as follows:

Teacher aide. A person who enjoys direct contact with children. A teacher aide does not qualify as a teacher but can supervise or work with pupils in noninstructional situations: e.g., supervise bus arrivals and departures, recess and lunch periods; operate mechanical aids to instruction; do housekeeping tasks; correct objective tests. Specific tasks are defined by the particular demands of each team.

Clerical aide. A person for whom no professional preparation is necessary. This person assists with the routine, nontechnical aspects of team operation: typing, duplicating, filing, and recording attendance.[15]

[13] Medill Bair and Richard G. Woodward, *Team Teaching in Action* (Boston: Houghton Mifflin Company, 1964), pp. 28–33.
[14] Judson T. Shaplin and Henry F. Olds, Jr., *Team Teaching* (New York: Harper & Row, 1964), p. 195.
[15] *Ibid.*, p. 196.

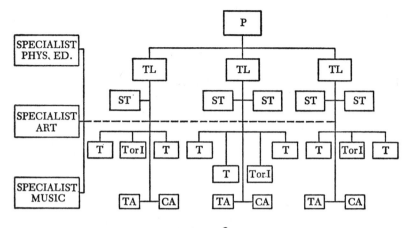

FIGURE 3.

The Lexington Team Structure. P: Principal; TL: Team Leader; ST: Senior Teacher; T: Teacher; I: Intern; TA: Teacher Aide; CA: Clerical Aide.

Programmed Instruction

The teacher in this age of advanced technology needs to be informed about technological advances in his own field. Programmed instruction is the subject of much discussion and controversy among teachers and the lay public. Today's young teacher begins his career in a field in which teaching aids of all kinds, including those of a technological nature, will be used increasingly. He needs to become informed about programmed instruction, which is already widely used.

"Programmed instruction" refers to the use of materials and procedures designed to provide self-instruction. How this may be done is described by Schramm.

By programed instruction I mean the kind of learning experience in which a "program" takes the place of a tutor for the student, and leads him through a set of specified behaviors designed and sequenced to make it more probable that he will behave in a given desired way in the future—in other words, that he will learn what the program is designed to teach him. Sometimes the program is housed in a "teaching machine" or in a "programed textbook." If so, the machine or the book is little more than a case to hold the program. The *program* is the important thing about programed instruction. It is usually a series of items, questions, or statements to each of which, in order, the student is asked to make a response. His response may be to fill in a word left blank, to answer a question, to select one of a series of multiple-choice answers, to indicate agreement or disagreement, or to solve a problem and record the answer. As soon as he has responded to the item, he is permitted to see the correct response so that he can tell immediately whether his response has been the right one. But the items are so skillfully written and the steps are so small between them that the student practices mostly correct responses, rather than errors, and the sequence of items is skillfully arranged to take the student from responses he already knows, through new responses he is able to make because of the other responses he knows, to the final responses, the new knowledge, it is intended that he should command.[16]

Advantages claimed for programmed instruction include:

1. The learner can set his own pace.
2. Material presented the learner is carefully selected and well organized.
3. The learner is given immediate knowledge of success or failure.
4. The learner is an active participant in the learning process.
5. The machine is impersonal. It does not interfere with learning as is sometimes true when teacher and pupil do not work well together.

The following disadvantages in programmed learning are among those most often mentioned:

1. Programming is difficult, time-consuming, and costly. If programming is to be good it must be done by those who possess special knowledge of the content to be taught, of principles of learning and teaching, and of programming techniques.
2. The programmed material determines the content which the pupil is offered. This restricts the teacher and the school in determining the curriculum.

[16] Wilbur Schramm, *Programed Instruction: Today and Tomorrow* (New York: Fund for the Advancement of Education, 1962), pp. 1–2.

3. Programmed devices do not make adequate provision for individual differences. Although the pupil may proceed at his own rate, every pupil must take specific and detailed steps identical with those every other learner takes; this prevents individualization.

4. Desirable interaction between teacher and pupil is restricted when programmed materials are used.

A great deal of investigation and experimentation is being carried on to determine the effectiveness of programmed instruction. In the meantime, both programmed textbooks and teaching machines are being produced, distributed, and used extensively. The prospective teacher must keep informed about the results of research in this area.

Other Innovations

It is not to be expected that every teacher should become proficient in the utilization of each new development which shows promise of improving instruction. It is not unreasonable to expect, however, that he will become informed about each innovation and that he should be receptive to its use if and when the opportunity is presented. The beginning teacher will find it profitable to learn about such other innovations as are mentioned in the following paragraphs.

The electronic laboratory, commonly termed the "language laboratory," is an innovation that has been tested and widely accepted. This is revealed in the following:

Electronic laboratories have been used by many school systems to improve their teaching of foreign languages. To date, some 6,000 language laboratories have been installed in the nation's public schools. There were 46 in 1957.[17]

Simulation is another innovation in teaching which its supporters believe shows prospects of becoming a helpful teaching tool. In simulation learning is encouraged by simulating circumstances,

[17] Austin J. McCaffrey, "Instructional Materials for Today's Schools," *The Instructor*, 73 (March 1964), p. 69.

situations, or events which have occurred or might have occurred. For example, a social studies group might learn about the functioning of the United Nations by simulating situations which have come before it, or about the operation of a political nominating convention by simulating one. Considerable research is in progress to discover the value and ways of using simulation.[18]

Flexible buildings, though not strictly defined as instructional aids, are nevertheless an innovation which can facilitate good instruction. Many buildings which make possible flexible scheduling and efficient use of the innovations discussed in this chapter are now in use throughout the country and many more are in the process of construction. Possibilities are mentioned by Trump as he writes about the high school of the future:

> Because class groups will vary in size, the school plant of the future must provide rooms for groups of 10, 20, 50, 100, or possibly more students. A variety of instructional and resource areas will replace the present series of standard, stacked classroom cubicles, each designed to contain 30 students and one teacher. Study halls as they are now known will not exist. Instead there will be study-resource rooms where students may read, listen to and view tapes, observe films and slides, work on self-teaching and self-appraisal machines, use science and other equipment, think, write, and participate in other more or less individual study activities. . . . Because of the variety of methods of instruction and the variety in group sizes in the school of tomorrow, flexibility of space, furniture, and equipment will be necessary. Larger rooms will be divided into smaller seminar rooms for small-group discussions. Auditoriums will be divided into several large-group areas so that they will be used for most of the day rather than for the 10 percent of the school day for which they are now used.
>
> Educational facilities of the future will be functional, flexible, pleasant, and utilitarian. Buildings will have improved acoustics, better light and ventilation control, and readily movable partitions. Architects, engineers, scientists, and educators will work together to design better equipment and supplies and better structures to house them.[19]

[18] For illustrations of the use of simulation the following are helpful:
Cleo Cherryholmes, "Developments in Simulation of International Relations in High School Teaching," *Phi Delta Kappan*, 46, (January 1965), 227–231.
Bert Y. Kersh, "Simulation in Teacher Education," *Programmed Instruction*, 2:4 (April 1963).
[19] J. Lloyd Trump, *Images of the Future* (Washington, D.C.: National Association of Secondary School Principals, 1959), pp. 28–30.

SUMMARY

An instructional material has been defined as any medium of communication used by pupil and teacher to advance learning. Today's teacher may select from an imposing array of instructional materials those which are most likely to achieve desired results.

Sound pedagogy makes it imperative that instructional materials be selected in terms of goals sought rather than indiscriminately. Sources of instructional materials within the school system include the classroom, school office, library, and teaching materials center. Among sources from outside the school are the teacher education institution, public library, state traveling library, community, commercial organizations, and professional organizations for teachers. Best results are obtained when those involved in the educational process work together in selecting instructional media. The supervising teacher is likely to be of most assistance to the prospective teacher, but other school personnel will also be helpful to the student teacher or intern who has the ability and willingness to work with others. Pupils can assist in obtaining instructional materials of various kinds.

Preparation, presentation, summarization, clarification, reflection, and evaluation are essential steps in the effective use of instructional media.

The quantity of printed materials available for instructional purposes continues to increase, and the teacher who uses sound criteria in selecting instructional materials will find the quality better than ever before. Textbooks have been improved in both format and content, but they remain *text* books and need to be supplemented with a variety of instructional materials.

The teacher needs to be aware of the numerous audio-visual aids which are available and to become skillful in using those which can improve instruction. These include films, filmstrips and slides, flat pictures, bulletin boards and flannel boards, and auditory aids such as radio and recordings.

In view of increasing numbers to be educated, demands for better education, and the growth in the world's fund of knowledge, it behooves the teacher to understand and use appropriate innovations which improved technology has made available. Educational television, the instructional team, programmed instruction, and other innovations need to be understood and used wherever possible as preparation for teaching in present and future teaching situations.

USEFUL REFERENCES

Association for Student Teaching. *The Student Teacher and Team Teaching*. Cedar Falls, Iowa: The Association, 1966.

Brown, James W., Richard B. Lewis, and Fred F. Harcleroad. *A-V Instruction: Materials and Methods*, 2d ed. New York: McGraw-Hill Book Company, 1964.

Clark, Leonard H., Raymond L. Klein, and John B. Burks. *The American Secondary School Curriculum*. New York: The Macmillan Co., 1965.

Dale, Edgar. *Audio-Visual Methods in Teaching*. New York: Dryden Press, 1954.

————. "Instructional Resources," in *The Changing American School*. Yearbook of the National Society for the Study of Education. Chicago: The Society, 1966, Part II, Chap. 4.

"Educational Technology," Special Feature, *NEA Journal*, 53 (April 1964), 24–34.

Finn, James D., and Donald G. Perrin. *Teaching Machines and Programmed Learning, 1962: A Survey of the Industry*. Washington, D.C.: National Education Association, 1962.

Fry, Edward. *Teaching Machines and Programmed Instruction*. New York: McGraw-Hill Book Company, Inc., 1963.

"Instructional Materials: Educational Media and Technology," *Review of Educational Research*, 32 (April 1962).

Lumsdaine, A. A., and Robert Glaser. *Teaching Materials and Programmed Learning*. Washington, D.C.: National Education Association, Department of Audio-Visual Instruction, 1960.

Lysaught, Jerome P. and Clarence M. Williams. *A Guide to Pro-*

grammed Instruction. New York: John Wiley and Sons, Inc., 1963.

Midwest Program on Airborne Television Instruction, *Using Television in the Classroom*. New York: McGraw-Hill Book Company, 1961.

Petersen, Dorothy G., *The Elementary Teacher*. New York: Appleton-Century-Crofts, 1964.

Shaplin, Judson T., and Henry F. Olds, Jr., *Team Teaching*. New York: Harper & Row, 1964.

Trump, J. Lloyd, and Dorsey Baynham. *Focus on Change—Guide to Better Schools*. Chicago: Rand McNally and Company, 1961.

Wittich, Walter Arno, and Charles Francis Schuller. *Audio-Visual Materials: Their Nature and Use*, 3d ed. New York: Harper & Row, 1962.

CHAPTER EIGHT
GUIDING PUPILS
TOWARD DESIRABLE
BEHAVIOR

Most prospective teachers are concerned about whether or not they can "maintain classroom control," "have good discipline," or "keep pupils quiet." One who has this feeling of anxiety should realize that this does not necessarily portend difficulties with pupils. In fact, successful, experienced classroom teachers at times experience behavior problems which may tax their resourcefulness.

It is wise, nevertheless, to make a study of pupil behavior in planning for teaching. Lack of desirable pupil behavior in the classroom is one of the chief reasons for a teacher's having an unsuccessful first year. On the other hand, many capable student teachers, interns, and experienced teachers have enjoyed the satisfaction that has resulted from helping children and youth—even the most undisciplined and apparently incorrigible individuals—grow in self-discipline, in self-esteem, and into responsible citizenship. It is the purpose of this chapter to aid the student teacher or intern in defining desirable behavior of pupils, in meeting difficult behavior problems arising in the classroom, and in finding ways to help pupils develop desirable behavior.

UNDERSTANDING THE MEANING OF DESIRABLE BEHAVIOR

In course work and through contacts with young people both in and out of the classroom, most prospective teachers have had opportunities to form opinions about what constitutes desirable and undesirable behavior of pupils. Efforts to crystallize one's thinking on this topic should result in better preparation for teaching.

Varying Opinions About Discipline

In thinking of ways to help pupils acquire good behavior, the prospective teacher would do well to consider how experienced teachers view behavior in the classroom. It is important to recognize that no classification is likely to be all inclusive. In the same classroom one might discover elements of each of the three types of classroom behavior discussed below. However, most groups may be classified as predominantly in one of the three following categories.

TEACHER DOMINANT—FEW PUPIL DECISIONS

Expected behavior is defined by the teacher. Rules are made and enforced by the teacher.

There is little noise in the room as pupils work on teacher-assigned tasks. The group is expected to be quiet.

Pupils seem to feel secure. With a fixed daily schedule and many directions from the teacher, they know just what to expect. However, there is limited evidence of independent thought or action.

PUPIL DOMINANT—SCANT TEACHER GUIDANCE

Expected behavior is not clearly defined. There are few rules, and those that are made are apt to be enforced in an inconsistent manner. Sometimes undesirable behavior is ignored by the teacher. At other times, pupils are punished for the same type of misbehavior.

There is considerable noise and confusion, much of it because pupils are not sure of assignments. Pupils seem to demonstrate a feeling of insecurity. Noise and lack of direction contribute to their frustration.

There is little responsible independent action. Pupils exhibit much irresponsible independent action such as aimless moving—even running—about the room.

PUPIL–TEACHER COOPERATION—MUCH TEACHER GUIDANCE

Expected behavior is defined by teacher and pupils. There are few rules, and those are made by pupils with teacher guidance. They are administered by the teacher, though often with the assistance of pupils. Emphasis is placed on pupil understanding.

There are various sounds associated with work activities. The room is neither "noisy" nor "quiet." Many of the activities being carried on are the results of pupil–teacher planning.

Pupils seem to feel secure, though puzzled at times about next steps. They have learned that solutions to problems need to be sought and that through a pooling of individual and group effort they will be found.

There is considerable evidence of independent thought and action.

Perhaps most prospective teachers can see themselves in one of the above classroom categories. Whether or not a student teacher or intern is able to identify himself in this classification at this stage of his growth is really not important. It *is* important that he take steps which will help him become skillful in establishing the kind of classroom environment that will contribute to the desirable development of pupils.

Classroom Living and Good Citizenship

It would appear that a teacher in the first category listed above, "Teacher Dominant," is interested primarily in maintaining a quiet room. A teacher in the second group, "Pupil Dominant," is probably most concerned about permitting freedom among pupils. A teacher in the third group, "Pupil–Teacher Cooperation," is likely to be interested in encouraging self-control and responsible independent thought and action. Each teacher can profit by formulating his own viewpoint about the behavior of pupils in the classroom. In doing so it is helpful to consider the goals to be set for and with pupils. How can these goals be determined?

The point of view presented here is that the classroom teacher has both an opportunity and a responsibility for helping children and youth live as useful citizens in a democratic society. A good citizen in our society needs to obey laws and regulations, to make decisions, to assume responsibility in individual and group situations, and to work toward the improvement of the society in which he lives. Teachers who accept this view have a basis for formulating guides to action. This concept will be composed of such elements as the following:

1. Each individual in the group is different from every other individual.

2. Each individual is, or has potentialities for becoming, a constructive member of the classroom group and of society.

3. Each individual brings to the group his own background of experience and interest. These can be tapped by the teacher to facilitate that individual's development.

4. Each individual needs to acquire controls of conduct which will aid him in his total growth. This necessitates an optimum amount of self-discipline.

5. Each individual is capable of assuming responsibility and needs to learn to be responsible for his own acts.

6. Each individual will profit from guidance and leadership by an understanding and capable teacher.

Growth Toward Good Behavior

The good teacher accepts the learner as he is and attempts to help him make progress. Individuals and groups show wide variation in their development toward self-discipline, just as they do in their development toward mastering skills or acquiring knowledge. We do not expect an individual to solve a difficult problem in higher mathematics until he has mastered the appropriate mathematical concepts; by the same token, we should not expect a pupil in the classroom to exhibit self-discipline under extremely trying situations until he has passed through the stages in his own development toward emotional maturity which make self-discipline possible for him in such a situation.

ESTABLISHING A POSITIVE PROGRAM

Beginning teachers frequently expect to have discipline problems. They apparently believe it is the job of the teacher to deal with problems after they have arisen, rather than to devote time and energy from the very beginning to the development of a program of instruction designed to prevent problems.

Skillful Teaching and Pupil Behavior

The teacher who selects appropriate subject matter, plans carefully, motivates pupils adequately, and conducts a sound, lively, and interesting program is fostering the development of desirable behavior of pupils. A student teacher in a lower grade emphasized the importance of a good educational program in the following statement.

The children at my school learn courtesy, good discipline, self-control, and cooperation early in the term. They help solve their problems in an atmosphere of mutual understanding and cooperation. Mrs.———— gives each child individual guidance and praises each child to give him a feeling of success. The children are in a social climate that is conducive to wholesome living. I have observed that ideas flow freely and that ideas accompany problems. Mrs.————is a guide to, and a source of, further knowledge.

The following statement of a young intern working with high school pupils reveals evidence of good teaching and the resulting desirable behavior of his pupils.

Like most beginners I thought I probably would have many discipline problems, but much to my surprise students seem to obey me quite well. I actually feel that these students do respect me. I have not been overly friendly with them, but have tried to be reserved and professional. However, I have not carried this behavior to such an extreme that my students feel it is just an act, and not really me.

Observing Classroom Teaching of the Supervising Teacher

An opportunity to watch another individual teach can be a valuable learning experience for the thoughtful observer. Observing the supervising teacher at work with pupils can be of special benefit if one has encountered a problem involving the behavior of one or more individuals in the group. If the prospective teacher takes note of such problems while he is observing, and if a conference with the supervising teacher is held soon after the observation, he can learn much that will be of real value to him.

A prospective high school teacher wrote the following after observing her supervising teacher:

In observing Mrs.————I find that she expects good behavior from her students. She is fair and the students understand the reasons for rules, but there is no foolishness.

Another student teacher working with elementary children obtained greater insight into ways of working with children by observing her supervising teacher. She said:

It is important to learn to observe the entire room while you are helping a reading group. Those at their desks must have enough to keep them profitably busy so that they will not disturb others.

DISCIPLINE AND PUNISHMENT

The term "discipline" has been used sparingly in this chapter. It would be a mistake, however, to assume that its infrequent use implies that it is not a respectable word to be used in a discussion of pupil behavior.

Discipline and Self-Discipline

What does the word "discipline" mean to teachers? To many it means something the teacher accomplishes with, or does to, pupils in the classroom. If the group is reasonably quiet and pupils are well behaved and are going about their tasks in a systematic fashion, a teacher is said to have *good* discipline. If, on the other hand, the group is noisy, pupils are misbehaving, there is much confusion, and pupils are unable or unwilling to study or work, a teacher is said to have *poor* discipline.

What does the word "self-discipline" mean? Referring again to usage by teachers, it frequently means to them something which the pupil brings about within himself.

In recognition of this common usage of the terms "discipline" and "self-discipline," we emphasize here that prospective teachers need to encourage the development of self-discipline in pupils as a means of fostering in them the development of desirable behavior.

It is doubtful if self-discipline among individuals in a classroom can occur until "good" discipline, as it has just been defined, has been achieved. Self-discipline is usually the second step in the process of growth toward desirable behavior. Many teachers never get their pupils beyond the first stage of "good" discipline, and unfortunately some teachers do not succeed in leading their pupils beyond the "poor" discipline stage. It is perhaps unfortunate, but nevertheless true, that the best teaching, the kind which brings about desirable change in pupils, is more difficult than poor or mediocre teaching. It is more difficult to help a pupil acquire self-discipline than to be the external disciplining agent who *tells* him what his behavior should be. When the latter procedure is followed, the pupil comes to rely on the teacher rather than on himself. Because of this difficulty, many teachers stop short of helping pupils achieve self-discipline. This fact should challenge every teacher as he works toward the goal of becoming a superior teacher.

Punishment

Emphasis throughout this chapter has been placed on encouraging desirable behavior rather than on ways of dealing with misbehavior. Teachers who carry on a good instructional program adapted to differences in individual pupils are likely to encounter relatively few behavior problems. Yet it is unrealistic to assume that problems will not occur.

It is sometimes assumed that the term "punishment" refers solely to the application of force in some form to the person of a pupil. Punishments, however, vary; force is only one example. Physical punishment has little place in a positive program for the development of desirable behavior. This is a question one should discuss with the supervising teacher. It is important to understand his viewpoint and to obtain from him information about the policy of the school and about practices in other schools.

More subtle, more effective, and perhaps more humane forms of punishment are available to the teacher when they are needed. A specific act or procedure intended as punishment may not be interpreted as such by the pupil to whom it is directed. What one pupil considers severe punishment may not be interpreted as such by another. A high school pupil, for instance, who is extroverted and much interested in sports might consider withdrawal of the privilege of participating in an intramural sports event harsh treatment, while an introvert who cares little for athletics might view such treatment as no penalty at all. One child in the primary grades might interpret a disapproving glance from the teacher as reproof, whereas another individual in the same group might be unaffected. The key to success in the use of nonphysical forms of punishment as a means of developing desirable behavior, as in most other aspects of good teaching, is knowledge about each person in the group as an individual personality.

When undesirable behavior requires punishment to be determined and administered by the teacher, such punishment should be related to the specific act of behavior or misbehavior and should occur as soon as possible after the undesirable act. It is essential that the pupil understand clearly the nature of the misbehavior and the reason a specific type of punishment is administered. For example, a pupil who wishes to continue as a group chairman is told that he is relieved of this privilege by the members of the group because he did not perform in accordance with rules previously formulated.

DEALING WITH BEHAVIOR PROBLEMS

It is to be expected that teachers will be confronted from time to time with problems in the area of pupil behavior. There are many possible solutions for the same or similar types of problems, depending upon the many variables involved and the creativity and imagination of the teacher. The two situations described here illustrate ways to help pupils acquire desirable behavior.

The Individual Pupil with Problems

Jack was a tenth-grade pupil in a four-year high school of 1200. He was considered by his past and current teachers as a disruptive force in most of his classes. He annoyed his neighbors by hitting them, by tripping them when he could, and by throwing objects at them. He would talk in an undertone during class discussions and would argue at length with his teachers. He had been sent to the principal's office by several different teachers. Although his peers were much annoyed with his frequent disruptions, he was well liked by them.

Henry Williams was the young student teacher assigned to the biology class in which Jack was enrolled. Toward the end of the semester prior to his student teaching assignment Henry spent a day visiting the school in which he would be working. While he was observing in the biology class, Jack exhibited his usual disruptive behavior. Henry discussed the situation with Mrs. Smith, his supervising teacher, and volunteered to make a special study of Jack and his problems along with his other duties as a student teacher. Under the direction of Mrs. Smith and with her complete cooperation, he spent part of several days working on the situation before his student teaching semester began. He read everything that was to be found in the cumulative record about Jack. He talked with the principal, the guidance counselor, and several of Jack's former teachers. In the early days of his student teaching period Henry observed Jack very closely and, as a participant in the work of the classroom, had occasion to work with him directly on several small assignments. He talked with Jack informally in the corridors, in the library, during homeroom period, and in the lunchroom.

Henry discovered that Jack was very intelligent, that he was an only child, and that his father was a busy corporation executive nearing retirement age. Both parents seemed to be very fond of their son, but both were busy people. Also, because of wide age differences, parents and son had few similar interests. The family spent very little time together. Henry discovered that Jack had received only average marks, that he had participated in no co-curricular activities, and that some of his teachers considered him lazy.

The first time Henry had responsibility for the class Jack took issue with a statement he had made and persisted in arguing the point. Henry acknowledged that Jack might be right and asked him to investigate and report to the class. Jack made an exhaustive study and in a remarkably short time, considering the work involved, reported his findings in elaborate and exacting detail, showing conclusively that he had been correct. Henry complimented Jack and commented to the class that he hoped all members of the group would approach everything they study in a similar critical and thorough manner. Henry took this action because contacts with Jack, study of his school record, knowledge of his school history, and knowledge of his home situation had convinced him that Jack was a capable boy who needed to be motivated to work up to capacity. Henry was also convinced that Jack wanted and needed recognition and that he did not have to exert himself at home to get what he wanted. At school he followed the same behavior pattern. It was more work for Jack to participate in school activities than not to participate. It was more difficult to study than not to study, and, after all, he was receiving passing marks.

Henry showed Jack that he respected Jack's studied opinions and sought ways to help him extend his thinking in academic fields and his participation in the life of the school. Through casual suggestions and direct mention Jack was encouraged to find answers to many of his own searching questions. He was encouraged to read numerous books and scientific magazines. Through the motivation of his student teacher, Jack was encouraged to investigate the development of molds. He prepared an exhibit on molds and entered it in the city high school science exhibit. This same interest led to membership in the science club where he became an interested and dependable member.

The class continued to be annoyed at times by Jack's interference, and he still argued with his teachers, although both irregularities became less frequent and less disruptive. During all this time Henry worked very closely with Mrs. Smith, who made many constructive suggestions which proved helpful to both pupil and student teacher.

Except for a few temporary lapses, Jack made steady progress in his relationships with his peers, with his student teacher, and with his regular teacher. Teachers of other courses in which Jack was enrolled commented on his improvement, and so did Jack. Henry and Mrs. Smith helped Jack understand the reasons for his improvement. As the semester ended Jack, Henry Williams, and Mrs. Smith were very much pleased with what had been accomplished.

The Group that Needs Direction

Nancy was a capable and attractive young college student who discovered during the fourth week of her semester of full-time student teaching that she was having difficulties managing her group of better-than-average fourth-grade pupils. She was disturbed and disappointed because she had enjoyed working with children of this age in informal situations during her high school days and in her college work prior to student teaching. Children had enjoyed working with her, and she had always wanted to be a teacher.

The group responded well to Mrs. White, her supervising teacher, a very capable and highly regarded member of the faculty. In fact, the group had warmly welcomed Nancy, and they seemed much pleased to have her working with them as a student teacher. Everything had gone well at first, but later she found that children worked well at assigned tasks for a short time and then seemed to lose interest in what they were doing. They asked directions repeatedly, classroom noise increased, there was much needless moving around the room and much purposeless activity. During discussion periods it became apparent that many of the children were not learning, and in their written work an increasing number of pupils showed carelessness about checking on facts.

Mrs. White, who was very capable in working with student teachers, made helpful suggestions, but they did not seem to work and Nancy became more discouraged. Mrs. White suggested that Nancy prepare a brief statement of her problems,

make a list of the factors which she believed contributed to her
difficult situation, and suggest things she might do to improve.
Mrs. White agreed to do the same things. After this had been
done, Nancy and Mrs. White spent considerable time discussing
the situation and in preparing a plan of action. Here are some of
the things they agreed upon.

1. Nancy had greatly underestimated the ability of the group.
The members of the group needed to be challenged with work
more nearly in line with their capacity to achieve. More interesting and more difficult assignments were needed.

2. The class had been viewed as a group rather than as made
up of individuals. A wider range of activities and experiences
needed to be provided. Plans needed to provide for individuals or
small groups to work as segments of the larger group.

3. Nancy had little knowledge of the personal and scholastic
background of each child. As much pertinent information as possible should be obtained about each pupil. Every possible means
of securing this information should be employed, including study
of cumulative records, talks with previous teachers, observation
of individuals, and informal contacts.

4. Teaching had not been viewed by Nancy as real work. As
she observed Mrs. White and other teachers at work, Nancy had
not realized that much detailed preparation had been made prior
to the teaching observed. Nancy had not prepared adequately for
her work with pupils.

Nancy should study carefully all material to be assigned. She
should locate pertinent material in addition to that assigned the
group so that each individual or small group would be kept
profitably busy as the need would arise. She should have specific
suggestions to help individuals locate needed references and materials.

5. Nancy's desire to obtain the good will of pupils had led to a
chumminess that had caused children to view the student teacher
as a peer rather than as a helpful, friendly leader and teacher.

A friendly but firm and businesslike attitude should be shown toward pupils. A feeling of self-confidence on the part of Nancy and constant direction of pupils toward self-improvement should aid in gaining the respect of pupils.

Belatedly, Nancy realized that Mrs. White had since the first time they met been emphasizing each of the five points mentioned in the foregoing analysis. She was now aware of the fact it was going to be much more difficult to complete her student teaching successfully than it would have been if she had planned and worked more thoroughly from the beginning. But Nancy was intelligent, she was not afraid of work, she knew that Mrs. White would always be ready to help her whenever help was needed, and she was determined to succeed. She was glad that she had not waited longer to ask for help and that there was still time to correct her mistakes.

She worked diligently on the program that had been outlined, she conferred frequently with Mrs. White, she kept in very close touch with the progress of each individual as well as of the total group, and she took steps to evaluate the work of the group and her own effectiveness as a teacher. Progress was slow at first. Nancy learned that good work habits and good behavior of pupils can deteriorate more rapidly than they can be rebuilt. But improvement did come gradually, and in a few weeks she found that her hard work was showing results. Children were more interested in their work, they understood what was expected of them, and they were discovering the satisfaction that results from success in work well done. Pupils learned that with two teachers in their room they were receiving help that would not have been possible with one and they showed respect for Nancy, who helped them in many ways, both individually and as a group.

The Prevention of Problems

One learns much from experience. This well-known fact has special meaning for student teachers or interns who have had discipline problems because they did not use appropriate procedures in their initial teaching. They have discovered that incorporating the following ideas in their teaching can help to prevent behavior problems.

1. Order in the classroom must take precedence over individual liberty. In the classroom conditions must be such that constructive work is possible. Little learning can take place when noise, distractions, and confusion prevail.

2. The teacher has a responsibility for fostering the welfare of each individual pupil and that of the total classroom group. There are times when a teacher may need to aid the development of a pupil by encouraging considerable recognition of him by the total group. It might be against the best interests of the group, however, if such recognition continued to the point where he became egotistic or domineering in his relationship with others. On the other hand, the teacher needs to prevent the development of a situation where the group might for some reason do harm to, or deal unjustly with, an individual member of the group.

3. The teacher must provide continuous leadership from the very first time he assumes responsibility for a classroom group. He must be active, not passive. If he fails to assume an active leadership role, pupils will take the initiative with the result that they, rather than the teacher, are in command of the situation.

4. Pupils will "test the limits" of authority. They will do this in every situation—with parents, with the Scout leader, sometimes with civic officials, and certainly with the teacher in the classroom. These limits are preferably determined cooperatively by teacher and pupils, but they must be understood.

5. Getting started right with a group of pupils is important. The first day in the classroom is a crucial one. Pupils need to know that their teacher is firm, wholesomely aggressive, active, businesslike, and systematic. It is better to be judged by pupils as a bit on the stern side than to have one's efforts to be friendly mistaken for chumminess. It is much easier for the teacher and better for pupils to become less stern gradually than to start by being chummy with pupils and later attempt to regain respect.

6. Long-range and daily planning and preparation are essen-

tial. The teacher who is well prepared and knows "what to do next" is in a position to be self-confident and, thus, to encourage the respect and esteem of pupils. This respect for the teacher, in turn, can contribute to a favorable attitude toward learning.

7. Pupils must be motivated so that they will be kept busy with wholesome and worthwhile learning activities. This places a tremendous responsibility on the teacher. The best motivation is the kind that makes each pupil assume a maximum amount of responsibility for keeping busy at worthwhile tasks which he believes are of value for him.

The greatest source of strength in the prevention of behavior problems is the teacher's individual strategy. This strategy can be strengthened if he will ask himself the questions which follow, answer them honestly, and act on the resultant thinking.

Have I made careful long-range and daily plans?

Am I well prepared for each school day and for each class?

Do I know each individual as well as I should? Have I studied all pertinent information in the cumulative record? Do I know the problems and interests of each pupil? Do I know the home situation.?

Am I well enough acquainted with the community and the school neighborhood to understand the conditions that are peculiar to the group?

Do I like the pupils with whom I work, or do I merely tolerate them?

Do my voice, appearance, and attitude contribute to desirable behavior or produce the opposite reaction?

Do I give each pupil the consideration and respect he should receive from me?

Do I employ teaching procedures which foster good behavior?

Using Sound Procedures

The teacher's efforts should be expended in the direction of a positive program in which emphasis is on the prevention of behavior problems. In most classrooms, however, problem situations develop from time to time. Prospective teachers frequently seek help in coping with these situations by raising such points as those below.

Sending a pupil out of the classroom. Sending pupils from the classroom as a means of punishment is open to question for several reasons. In the first place, when this is done the teacher admits to himself and to members of the group that he is unwilling or unable to deal with the problem in the classroom. Second, this action is not likely to result in a good learning situation for the pupil. If the pupil is to sit in the corridor or alone in a vacant room, he is without supervision; under such circumstances, he may either cause harm to others or be harmed himself. In most instances, it might be better to ignore the offense temporarily and confer with the pupil after the class is dismissed or seek ways to involve the individual in beneficial constructive activities.

Sending a pupil to the principal's office. It is understandable that principals expect the classroom teacher to deal effectively with discipline problems which arise during their teaching. The principal will usually assist in ways he deems helpful to the teacher such as observing the classroom situation, providing information about individual pupils and parents, and conferring with the teacher. If, after careful study of the abilities, performance, and personality of a pupil, the evidence is clear that the individual and the group would profit by withdrawal of the child from the group, this action might be requested.

Detention of a pupil. When a pupil is kept in the classroom during a recess period or during some other period when the group engages in regularly scheduled activities, the detained individual is denied the benefits those activities were designed to provide. The pupil is also denied the benefits that may result from association with his peers.

If a pupil is held in the classroom after school, plans he and his parents may have made are disrupted and his welfare may be jeopardized in his return to his home on a schedule that is different from the usual one. If the pupil rides on a school bus or with others who maintain a fixed schedule, detention may cause inconvenience to a number of people. For these and other reasons detention as a means of punishment is not recommended. Other forms of punishment which are appropriate to the act of misbehavior—those which do not conflict with the educational objectives of the school program—should be employed.

Group behavior.   It is often desirable to establish standards of behavior for the classroom group. These standards should be developed by the group with the leadership of the teacher. This makes it possible to remind individuals and the group when necessary that it is the standards of the group which are being violated.

It is wise to maintain a middle-of-the-road position between making an issue of each minor infraction of good behavior on the one hand and ignoring them on the other. It is important to avoid continuously challenging the behavior of an individual or the group, but it is very important to detect and deter even minor incidents which may lead to major problems. The teacher should avoid punishing the group for the misbehavior of one or two individuals.

Dealing with Unusually Difficult Situations

Ours is rapidly becoming an urban society. This trend has resulted in crowded cities where living conditions for children and youth are frequently undesirable. Children in some sections come to school from an environment where food, clothing, and shelter are inadequate; where supervision both in and out of the home scarcely exists; and where hope for a brighter future seems only a dream. Frequently these young people are in and out of schools because parents are forced to move from place to place. In many instances they are enrolled in schools where buildings are inadequate, classes are larger than desirable, and teachers are overworked. Such schools are sometimes termed "slum" schools.

The student teacher or intern in a school of this kind is faced with both a challenge and an opportunity. He may be challenged immediately to "keep order," "maintain discipline," "stop fights," and "show them who's boss." He has an opportunity to help each pupil experience success in school. How can he be successful in a slum school? No prescription can be written which will solve each specific set of problems. Here, however, are points to keep in mind which other student teachers and interns have found useful.

1. The primary goal in teaching is to help the pupil learn and become a self-respecting and useful citizen.

2. The supervising teacher is available to assist when needed. In the early stages of the assignment, and perhaps throughout the assignment period, it may be desirable to engage in a great deal of cooperative teaching. The combined efforts of two adults in the classroom may be needed most of the time.

3. The school principal, someone from his office, or other appropriate school personnel will usually be available to assist the student teacher or intern when needed.

4. If bedlam is to be avoided, teacher and pupils must understand that order in the classroom must take precedence over unrestricted freedom on the part of individual pupils. Pupils usually can be led to understand that they ultimately benefit by the application of this principle.

5. Each pupil needs to acquire self-discipline. The individual progresses from control imposed by the teacher to self-control at his own rate. For some this will be slow. Perhaps for some there will be no progress. One should use those techniques and procedures which are necessary to aid each individual's maximum growth in the shortest time possible. Some pupils will come to school with an unusual respect for the authority of the teacher. Others will come with no respect for authority of any kind, including that of the neighborhood police. The prospective teacher is usually committed to the sound theory that physical force should never be used with pupils. He may find it disconcerting to observe a school official or teacher remove a knife or gun from a

child or youth—or to do it himself. He may need to realize that this can be the first step in helping the pupil down the long road from teacher control to self-control.

6. While the student teacher or intern must use a firm hand to control individuals and the classroom group as members develop self-control, he also must help pupils know of his interest in each individual. He must continuously convey to pupils the idea that it is the undesirable behavior and not the personality that is unacceptable to the teacher. The developing teacher must always keep in mind that it is his goal to facilitate growth by providing an interesting, varied, and rich instructional program.[1]

TEACHER COOPERATION AND PUPIL BEHAVIOR

Good communication and a clear understanding of school policy as it relates to pupil behavior are essential to a well-coordinated school program.

Two Teachers in the Classroom

There are unusual opportunities to learn from a superior teacher about ways of solving problems related to pupil behavior. However, this close association between prospective teacher and supervising teacher can result in misunderstandings which may contribute to the undesirable behavior of pupils. The prospective teacher has a very heavy responsibility for coordinating all of his plans directly involving pupils with the plans of the supervising teacher. The supervising teacher is very much interested in helping his younger colleague do a superior job of working with pupils, but it is impossible for him to anticipate how another person will proceed unless there is close communication between the two. Here are some of the things one should do to facilitate good communication.

---

[1] For additional help in dealing with difficult behavior problems see Dorothy M. McGeoch, *Learning to Teach in Urban Schools* (New York: Teachers College Press, Teachers College, Columbia University, 1965).

1. Understand the viewpoint of the supervising teacher in the area of pupil behavior. If viewpoints differ be sure they are discussed with a view to resolving them.

2. Prepare a usable checklist of all the things the supervising teacher does to encourage desirable pupil behavior.

3. Discuss with the supervising teacher in advance any changes that are to be made from established procedures or from instructions previously given pupils.

4. Be sure that major changes involving procedures or instructions are clear to pupils.

5. Become acquainted with all school-wide and classroom regulations involving pupils.

6. Avoid granting requests or issuing directions which are not clear to both student and supervising teacher. If in doubt, check with the supervising teacher or other appropriate person.

7. Use every possible opportunity to demonstrate to pupils that the prospective teacher and the supervising teacher are partners who work in close cooperation.

Resolving Conflicting Viewpoints

Persons who are beginning their work in the classroom frequently are puzzled by the discovery that there is wide variation in the way faculty members view the behavior of children and youth. These conflicting points of view are sometimes revealed in comments one may hear teachers make such as: "I wish I could find some way to bring Joan out of her shell," "These adolescents are so irresponsible they've got to be told off," or, "It's easier to let them make the rules." Pupils sometimes comment about a teacher with such expressions as "that old battle-axe," "Mister Milktoast," or "she really helps you."

Sometimes staff members will offer advice—probably conflicting advice—about how one should "control" pupils. There may be staff members in the school who are characteristic of the "teacher dominant," "pupil dominant," or "pupil-teacher cooperation" groups previously mentioned.

How can one synthesize his thinking and the expressed opinions of others to formulate a workable philosophy? This is not an easy task. Some experienced teachers have never achieved it. One will be a better teacher and at the same time work in harmony with other faculty members if he can find an answer which will satisfy himself. These are some usable ideas.

1. There is no one best formula for the development of desirable behavior in pupils. There are excellent teachers to be found in each of the categories previously given.

2. It is helpful to glean ideas from others, but the individual teacher alone can determine a philosophy that will work best for him.

3. Avoid becoming a carbon copy of the supervising teacher. He will undoubtedly be the best single source of help, but he will expect his counselee to use only those ideas or procedures which are suitable in the individual situation.

4. Maintain a flexible viewpoint, one that can be modified as experience is gained and as one grows in knowledge and teaching skill.

5. Continue to search for ways which modify and strengthen a philosophy as it relates to the development of desirable behavior.

SUMMARY

It has been the purpose of this chapter to help the prospective teacher guide pupils toward desirable behavior. It should be the goal of the teacher to help young people live as useful citizens in a democratic society.

Suggestions for building a positive program included obtaining help from the supervising teacher and helping pupils feel responsibility for their own learning.

Attention was given to the distinction between discipline and self-discipline and to the viewpoint that it should be the goal of teachers to help pupils develop self-discipline. Physical punishment has little place in a positive program for the development of desirable behavior. An understanding of human behavior and extensive knowledge about each individual are essential in using nonphysical forms of punishment effectively.

A student teacher or intern has unusual opportunities to discover ways to help pupils develop good behavior. Suggestions were made to help him crystallize his thinking about pupil behavior as he works with teachers who hold differing views on this subject.

USEFUL REFERENCES

Association for Supervision and Curriculum Development. *Perceiving, Behaving, Becoming.* Washington, D.C.: The Association, 1962. Chapter V, "The Positive View of Self."

Cutts, Norma E., and Nicholas Moseley. *Teaching the Disorderly Pupil.* New York: Longmans, Green and Company, Inc., 1957.

Hymes, James L. *Behavior and Misbehavior.* Engelwood Cliffs, N.J.: Prentice-Hall, Inc., 1964.

Jensen, Janet, and Norman Jensen. *The Student Teacher: Managing An Elementary Classroom.* Cedar Falls, Iowa: Association for Student Teaching, Bulletin No. 23, 1964.

McGeoch, Dorothy. *Learning to Teach in Urban Schools.* New York: Bureau of Publications, Teachers College, Columbia University, 1965.

Muuss, Rolf E. *First-Aid for Classroom Discipline Problems.* New York: Holt, Rinehart and Winston, Inc., 1962.

National Education Association. "Special Feature on Discipline," *NEA Journal* 52 (September 1963), 8–22.

———. *Student Behavior in Secondary Schools.* Research Division Report. Washington, D.C.: The Association, 1964.

National Society for the Study of Education. *Social Deviancy Among Youth.* Yearbook, Part I. Chicago: The Society, 1966.

Peck, Robert F., and James V. Mitchell, Jr. *Mental Health* (What Research Says to the Teacher, No. 24.) Washington, D.C.: National Education Association, 1962. 33 pp.

Petersen, Dorothy G. *The Elementary School Teacher.* New York: Appleton-Century-Crofts, 1964.

CHAPTER NINE
WORKING IN THE
TOTAL SCHOOL
PROGRAM

A school is a complex enterprise, and the teacher is called upon to engage in a variety of activities—some recognizable as being professional, others merely duty assignments. Yet many of these so-called "nonteaching" assignments are essential and are more closely related to teaching than at first they may appear. To be a teacher, one must know all of the jobs that need to be performed in connection with the school program.

UNDERSTANDING THE SCHOOL SITUATION

The teacher's effectiveness is increased when he views the school as a unit, is knowledgeable about the school system as a whole, and knows how the school system is organized.

Structure and Organization of Schools

It frequently happens that the student teacher or intern becomes so deeply involved in planning for teaching and in the responsibilities of the classroom that he does not take the time or have the inclination to acquire an understanding of the larger setting in which he is working. A teacher needs to gain this broader perspective.

The school district.   School districts vary in size from the small rural school with a few pupils to the large urban district such as the New York City school system. The trend in recent years has been toward fewer but larger districts. The decline in the number of districts is revealed in the results of a nation-wide research study: "In 1940, there were 116,999 school districts in the country; in 1950, there were 83,614. In 1962–63, the number reached an all-time low of 32,891." [1]

Some school district boundaries are coterminous with those of a unit of government such as a township, city, or county; others are not. The governing board in some school districts is identical to the governing body of a civil governmental unit or is appointed by it. In other situations it is independent of the board responsible for the administration of a unit of civil government.

The prospective teacher who can answer questions such as the following about the school district is likely to improve his understanding of the community and of the people with whom he works both in and out of school: How large is the district? What are the boundaries? Who are the members of the board of education? Are they appointed or elected? If appointed, by whom? How many pupils are enrolled? How many teachers are employed?

It will be helpful to learn as much as possible about the administration of the school system. What are the responsibilities of the superintendent of schools? How is the central office structured and organized? It is desirable to become informed about the responsibilities of the assistant superintendents, the number and responsibilities of consultants or supervisors, and the work and organization of the staff in charge of research. Information about the number of schools at the elementary and secondary levels and the way they are staffed will be helpful. This information can usually be obtained from the school handbook. If no handbook is available, such information can be obtained from the supervising teacher or principal.

School organization, vertical and horizontal. The kind of work the teacher does and in some instances the success with which it can be done are, in part at least, determined by the way the school is organized.

Some school districts offer work in the elementary grades only,

[1] *NEA Research Bulletin,* 41: No. 1 (February 1963), p. 6.

or in high school only, but the majority of school districts in the United States offer instruction from kindergarten or grade one through grade twelve. A variety of plans for organizing schools has developed. Some of the widely used plans include 8–4, 6–3–3, and 6–6. There is a trend toward a 6–4–4 plan in communities which provide a public junior college program. All of these plans are found in combination with the kindergarten.

One who is working in a school district comprising both elementary grades and high school should become informed about the organization of the total school. This knowledge will help him to confer in an intelligent manner with professional colleagues at all grade levels and with laymen in the community. It is important that pupils progress through the school from kindergarten to the termination of their formal schooling without abrupt interruptions and difficult periods of adjustment. Many pupils need assistance in preparing for a different level of the school system and in adjusting to it. A pupil in a school district where the K–6–3–3 plan of organization exists will be aided in his transition if his teachers help him prepare for, and become adapted to, his entry into the elementary school, the junior high school, and the senior high school.

Ordinarily the student teacher or intern will work in either a *departmentalized* situation or in a *self-contained classroom*. Although a number of variations exist, these continue to be the most common plans for organizing individual grade or class groups. One who teaches in a junior or senior high school will very likely work in a departmentalized program. The prospective teacher in this situation can profit by obtaining answers to such questions as the following:

1. What are the responsibilities of the department head? If there is no department head, how is the work of the department or subject area coordinated?

2. If there is a department of instruction in the central office, how is it coordinated with the department or departments in

which one works? What is the role of the subject-matter special-ist?

3. How is the work of the department or subject area synchro-nized with the principal's responsibility for instruction?

4. How do teachers within a department or subject area work together? Do staff members work as an instructional team?

5. What steps are being taken to help pupils discover relation-ships between subjects? Are core programs or other similar plans being used or under consideration?

The prospective teacher who works in the kindergarten or pri-mary grades of an elementary school will usually be teaching in a self-contained classroom. One who is teaching in the intermediate or upper grades of an elementary school may be working in either a departmentalized or a self-contained classroom situation or in both.

The elementary student teacher or intern will profit by obtain-ing information about the points which follow.

1. Is there the traditional grade-level organization, or is there some other plan of organization, e.g., an upper and a lower divi-sion without the usual grade levels?

2. Is there a uniform plan for self-contained classrooms throughout the elementary grades, or are some of the grades de-partmentalized? If there is departmentalization, in which grades is this plan followed? How is departmentalization administered?

3. What procedures are employed for focusing attention on the individual pupil in departmentalized situations?

4. Are the special subjects such as art, music, and physical edu-cation taught by special teachers, by the regular classroom teach-er, or is this teaching a joint responsibility of specialist and room teacher?

5. How is the work of the department of instruction in the cen-tral office coordinated with that of the elementary teacher? What are the roles of consultants or supervisors?

6. How does the principal work in coordination with teachers and the department of instruction in the central office?

School Policies and Regulations

Every well-administered organization is guided by certain principles, policies, and regulations which experience has demonstrated to be helpful in the successful functioning of the enterprise. Each school district and each individual school has its own special guides to help professional personnel, other school employees, pupils, and parents to work together effectively. Some of these are regulations established by the board of education, and thus apply to the entire school system. Others have been developed by the faculty of a specific school and will be applicable only to that school. Usually, most of these guides for action will be in written form, though in some schools they are unwritten. Many schools prepare a handbook which provides information of this kind for the guidance of school personnel.

COOPERATING WITH COLLEAGUES

In much the same way as a prospective medical doctor has an opportunity to observe and learn from a number of experienced doctors at work in a clinical situation, the prospective teacher in his clinical setting has an unusual opportunity to learn from experienced teachers. He can discover the kinds of situations in which school personnel work together and can obtain first-hand experience by working in cooperation with staff members in some of these situations.

Working with the School Principal

The student learning to teach should explore with his supervising teacher ways of understanding how the principal's office functions in the administration of the school program. In some instances, especially where there are several student teachers or interns in a school, the principal or someone from his office meets with prospective teachers to accomplish this purpose. In other situations the student teacher spends some time as an assistant in the office of the principal. There he has an opportunity to learn about school records and how they are kept and used, how the principal works with teachers and other school personnel, how instructional materials and supplies are obtained and issued, and how parent contacts and public relations are maintained.

Participating in Faculty Meetings

The intern will be expected to attend meetings of the faculty. The student teacher will need to check with his supervising teacher about attendance at these meetings. The trend is toward including student teachers in professional meetings. There is wide variation in the way faculty meetings are conducted. In some instances they are used primarily for announcements and routine administrative matters, whereas in other situations professional considerations and the improvement of instruction are the chief items of concern. There is wide variation, also, in the time, frequency, and length of meetings.

One should learn from the supervising teacher how to prepare for these meetings and how to contribute to their success. It is wise to do everything possible to learn from these meetings, to earn the respect of faculty members, and to synchronize one's functioning in the school with policies, decisions, and procedures which may be determined in meetings of the faculty. One future teacher, after attending a faculty meeting in his school, commented:

. . . another thing which has contributed greatly to this feeling of acceptance and appreciation is the action of the principal and teachers. . . . Such an atmosphere of free exchange of ideas and opinions among all teachers would seem to be vitally important to successful teaching in any school system.

Working with the Custodial Staff

Elsewhere in this book emphasis has been placed on the importance of a good physical and emotional climate in facilitating desirable learning and behavior in the classroom. Members of the custodial staff are important people in the life of the school and can make a positive contribution to wholesome school living. The modern custodian in an up-to-date school is an intelligent worker who is interested in doing his job well and in contributing to the well-being of teachers and pupils. He has a right to expect good treatment, cooperation, and respect from a professional person. The prospective teacher should respond to his efforts to aid teachers and children by cooperating with him and encouraging pupils to do the same.

In many instances a custodian will have been in his position for some time and will be well acquainted with parents, children, and faculty. He may believe he can help a young newcomer by sharing his knowledge of individuals. The prospective teacher should keep in mind the fact that he has the education of a professional person, whereas the custodian does not. It is not ethical to discuss with him professional matters of a confidential nature, certainly not those which relate to individual parents, children, or school employees.

ENGAGING IN CO-CURRICULAR ACTIVITIES

Although the major responsibilities of most teachers occur within the classroom, most teachers also have other responsibilities which demand time and attention. Typically, the secondary school teacher finds more of his time occupied with co-curricular activities than does the individual working in an elementary school, but some of these responsibilities are also a part of elementary teaching.

Guiding Learning Both In and Out of the Classroom

In good schools desirable learning is not confined to the classroom. The capable teacher strives to motivate the learning of pupils in whatever setting he works with them. For example, it may be discovered that pupils need to develop the kind of poise and self-confidence that can result from appearing before large groups. This may lead the teacher to volunteer to work on a committee which has responsibility for planning school assembly programs and, perhaps, for working with pupils in preparing and presenting programs. A teacher can motivate and facilitate the learning of his pupils if he becomes informed about the various out-of-class activities in which they engage and if he works in cooperation with the person in charge of each such activity. The fact that a classroom teacher shows interest in, and provides encouragement for, individual participation in worthwhile activities may mean the difference between success and failure on the part of pupils. Churchill and Rothman emphasize the value of these activities in the following statement:

Extraclass activities are among the most valuable experiences at the command of education for fostering integrating behavior on the part of students, for they help to bridge the gap between the more formal elements of education, the daily life of students, and that of the community. Because this is so, such experiences provide a stage on which students can relate formal educational experiences to everything else they do and feel.[2]

Directing Learning in a Variety of Situations

When pupils participate in co-curricular activities they can obtain experience which will be of value to them in their present and future living. A teacher does not ordinarily have major responsibility for directing more than one co-curricular activity. These are points to keep in mind as one becomes informed about co-curricular activities in schools and looks ahead to a career in teaching. During the clinical assignment period the prospective teacher is likely to have opportunities to work in such co-curricular activities as the following.

School government. Most high schools and many elementary schools have established some system designed to give pupils an opportunity to formulate some of the policies which affect them. There are many values in such an arrangement, including that of learning to assume responsibility. The student council is the most

[2] Ruth Churchill and Philip Rothman, "Extraclass Experiences," in *The Integration of Educational Experiences* (Chicago: The National Society for the Study of Education. Yearbook, Part III, 1958), p. 140.

common means of providing pupil participation in school government. The prospective teacher will profit by reading its constitution and by-laws. He might also talk with the sponsor about how
the council works and perhaps attend one or more of its meetings.
Pupils should be helped to understand its purposes and functioning and should be encouraged to develop respect for it.

Recreational activities.   Teachers and school officials have long
been conscious of the important contributions that wholesome
recreation can make to good living, both in and out of school.
The increasing amount of leisure time available to many people
in various segments of our modern society increases the need for
a school program designed to help the individual use this leisure
time in ways that will be beneficial, and schools are responding to
this need. Recreational opportunities are being provided through
social events, music activities, scheduled physical education
classes, intramural athletics, and supervised play in the elementary school.

Publications.   School publications in elementary and secondary schools can be used to encourage creative writing among pupils. They also serve as a vehicle for helping pupils learn to work
cooperatively. They can help the community understand its
school. Publications include the newspaper, the yearbook, the
school magazine, and others designed to achieve specific goals.

The student teacher or intern should become informed
about the publications that exist in the school and should learn
how faculty members and pupils cooperate in their preparation.
If he is working in an elementary school, he may want to explore
with his supervising teacher the possibility of working with pupils
in preparation of a classroom newspaper or magazine. The prospective teacher in the secondary school may find it possible to
become identified with a publication related to his field of interest.

Clubs.   Some pupils find the school club program most helpful. Some schools encourage each pupil to belong to a club, indicating that the school also considers clubs important in the education of the individual. The administration of a comprehensive

club program requires the assistance and cooperation of a number of staff members. This situation provides an opportunity for the student teacher or intern to study the club program in his school and perhaps to participate in the activities of a club. He should observe how a comprehensive club program is organized, how an optimum amount of pupil participation is provided, and how faculty responsibility for clubs is coordinated.

USING ENERGY CONSTRUCTIVELY

The capable and professional-minded person will undoubtedly attempt to view the school in its entirety. As a conscientious person he will very likely wish to carry his share of duties which extend beyond the classroom. The alert and energetic individual may become interested and involved in a number of activities which make heavy demands on his time and energy. He will need to survey the total school situation, consider his own interests and resources, and then decide in which activities he should participate to contribute most to the welfare of pupils. He will need to avoid becoming so heavily involved in activities outside the classroom that he cannot do a good job of directing the learning of his pupils. He should discover and maintain a balanced load which will make it possible for both him and his pupils to find their work together satisfying and profitable.

SUMMARY

The need to view the school as a whole has been emphasized in this chapter.

Teachers need to understand the structure and organization of the school district, as well as that of the specific school in which they work. If the student teacher or intern is to understand why things are done as they are and if he is to avoid the embarrassment that might result from conflicts with established practices, he must become informed about established policies and regulations in the school.

The prospective teacher will be in a better position to work in close cooperation with school personnel if he becomes informed about the duties of the principal, attends meetings of the faculty, and understands the role and contributions of the custodial staff.

When co-curricular activities are well organized they can contribute much to the attainment of desirable goals of education, and teachers have the responsibility for directing these activities. The student teacher or intern can obtain valuable experience by assisting with such activities.

The importance of understanding the total school and participating in various activities was emphasized, but the prospective teacher was cautioned against overparticipation which might result in doing an ineffective job as a classroom teacher.

USEFUL REFERENCES

Chandler, B. J. *Education and the Teacher*. New York: Dodd, Mead and Company, 1961.

Dahl, John A., Marvin Laser, Robert S. Cathcart, and Fred H. Marcus. *Student, School, and Society. Cross-currents in Secondary Education*. San Francisco: Chandler Publishing Company, 1964.

Edwards, Helen E. *Building Good Relationships: A Major Role of the College Supervisor*. Cedar Falls, Iowa: The Association for Student Teaching, 1964.

Goodlad, John I. *School Curriculum Reform in the United States*. New York: The Fund for the Advancement of Education, 1964.

Hartford, Ellis Ford. *Education in These United States*. New York: The Macmillan Company, 1964.

Knight, Douglas M., Charles A. Quattlebaum, James McCormack, Vincent A. Fulmer, John A. Perkins, and Daniel W. Wood. *The Federal Government and Higher Education*. Englewood Cliffs, N.J.: Prentice-Hall, Inc., 1960.

National Society for the Study of Education. *Vocational Education*. Chicago: The Society, Yearbook, Part I, 1965.

Neubauer, Helen. "Helping the Student Teacher," *National Elementary Principal*, XLII (1963), 53–55.

CHAPTER TEN

EVALUATING
GROWTH IN
TEACHING SKILL

Who is a good teacher? This question is answered in different ways. The layman's answer is likely to be influenced by his own school experience or by the way he views the teachers of his children. The answer of the experienced teacher will no doubt be influenced by many factors, including the type of pupils and parents with whom he works. The sections which follow can aid the prospective teacher in his efforts to recognize and evaluate teaching skill.

SOUND PRINCIPLES OF EVALUATION

As the student teacher or intern studies the components of good teaching and attempts to evaluate his growth in teaching skill, he will find it helpful to refer to certain guideposts or basic principles of evaluation. The following list is useful for this purpose.

The fundamental purpose of evaluation is to promote growth.
Evaluation involves appraisal of agreed upon values and goals.
Evaluation is an integral and important part of the learning process and should be continuous.
Evaluation should be based upon both quantitative and qualitative evidence and employ a variety of techniques for recording and interpreting behavior.
Evaluation is a cooperative process in which the learner and all those concerned with his growth should participate.
Evaluation takes into account both the ability of the learner and the

215

standards and competence generally required in the situations in which the individual will be engaged.[1]

It should be observed that the foregoing principles are similar to those considered in Chapter 6, "Evaluating Pupil Progress." It is appropriate to emphasize three of these principles.

The fundamental purpose of evaluation is to promote growth. It is not enough to assess one's progress from time to time just for the sake of knowing how well one is doing in some phase of his teaching. Growth results when the student teacher takes the next step and initiates appropriate action. For example, he might discover through introspection or through a conference with his supervising teacher that he needs to use a variety of instructional materials rather than to rely on exclusive use of the textbook. He may act on this knowledge and form the habit of planning for the use of a variety of appropriate instructional aids. If he does so, evaluation can result in his increased competence as a teacher.

Evaluation is an integral and important part of the learning process and should be continuous. A simple illustration of evaluation as an aid to learning occurred when a student teacher was told by his supervising teacher that his exclusive use of the lecture in conducting a junior high school class was hampering effective communication with pupils. The two teachers discussed the situation and together decided upon several alternative procedures. As a result of the evaluation and its follow-up the student teacher learned to use questioning effectively, to motivate his pupils better, to ask pertinent questions, and to listen to his pupils discuss issues while at the same time guiding the discussion into productive channels. The student teacher or intern also needs to keep in mind that *continuous* self-evaluation is just as essential to his development as a teacher as it is to the growth of the pupils he teaches. He will profit by engaging in self-evaluation following the completion of each aspect of the work in which he engages. He will anticipate—even solicit—suggestions from his supervising teacher which will lead to improvement of his teaching. Although

[1] Florence B. Stratemeyer and Margaret Lindsey, *Working with Student Teachers* (New York: Bureau of Publications, Teachers College, Columbia University, 1958), p. 431.

the prospective teacher and his supervising teacher may wish to establish certain chronological check points for evaluation, for example, each week, each month, mid-semester, or the end of the semester, there should be provision for continuous daily evaluation.

Evaluation is a cooperative process in which the learner and all those concerned with his growth should participate. The primary purpose of the student teacher is *to learn how to teach.* He can learn much through cooperative evaluation with his supervising teacher and college supervisor. In some instances the principal, department head, or another teacher will also work closely with him. He should welcome opportunities to work in cooperation with these members of the staff and to obtain their assistance in helping him grow in teaching skill.

EVALUATION IN TERMS OF GOALS

The first step in the evaluation of teaching skill is determination of the goals to be achieved. These goals are frequently stated in terms of teaching competencies. One authority groups these competencies under six major headings as follows:

I. Director of Learning
  Adapts principles of child growth and development to planning of learning activities
  Plans teaching-learning situations in accord with acceptable principles of learning
  Demonstrates effective instructional procedures
  Utilizes adequate evaluation procedures
  Maintains an effective balance of freedom and security in the classroom
II. Counselor and Guidance Worker
  Utilizes effective procedures for collecting information about each pupil
  Uses diagnostic and remedial procedures effectively
  Helps the pupil to understand himself
  Works effectively with the specialized counseling services
III. Mediator of the Culture
  Draws on a scholarly background to enrich cultural growth of pupils

Directs individuals and groups to appropriate significant life application of classroom learning

Designs classroom activities to develop pupil ability and motivation for finding democratic solutions to current social problems, recognizing and identifying key problems, understanding their inter-relationships and defining the issues

Directs pupils in learning to use those materials from which they will continue to learn after leaving school

Develops pupil-attitudes and skills necessary for effective participation in a changing democratic society

Helps his students acquire the values realized as ideals of democracy

IV. Link with the Community

Utilizes available education resources of community in classroom procedures

Secures cooperation of parents in school activities

Assists lay groups in understanding modern education

Participates in definition and solution of community problems relating to education

V. Member of the Staff

Contributes to the definition of the over-all aims of the school

Contributes to the development of a school program to achieve its objectives

Contributes to the effectiveness of over-all school activities

Cooperates effectively in the evaluation of the school program

VI. A Member of the Profession

Demonstrates an appreciation of the social importance of the profession

Contributes to the development of professional standards

Contributes to the profession through its organizations

Takes a personal responsibility for his own professional growth

Acts on a systematic philosophy, critically adopted and consistently applied [2]

The difficulties involved in defining good teaching and determining teacher effectiveness are recognized by researchers in these fields. Biddle emphasizes the problem in his discussion of "A Seven-Variable Model for Teacher Effectiveness." His seven variables consist of five "main sequence variables": *formative experiences, teacher properties, teacher behaviors, immediate effects, long-term consequences,* and two "contextual variables";

[2] From *Six Areas of Teacher Competence* (San Francisco: Commission on Teacher Education, California Teachers Association, 1964).

classroom situations, and *school and community contexts.*[3]

The complexities involved in defining and evaluating teacher effectiveness compel one to recognize that agreement on a definition of good teaching has not yet been reached. It follows that consensus on ways of evaluating teaching will not be achieved until there is agreement on what is to be evaluated. From a practical viewpoint, however, it is quite obvious to the parent, the school board member, the superintendent of schools, the principal, the supervising teacher, and the prospective teacher that an individual may be known as an "excellent" teacher, a "good" teacher, or an "average" teacher. Most school systems attempt to select competent teachers and to help each teacher improve his effectiveness through a program of in-service education. Similarly, the supervising teacher and college supervisor attempt to help the prospective teacher discover ways of becoming a good teacher and of increasing his effectiveness.

This assistance is provided by various means. One of the most common tools is an evaluation form. Other means of aiding the prospective teacher to develop teaching skill include conferences and the use of anecdotal records, diaries, notebooks, checklists, time sheets, recordings, and telecasts or kinescopes. A number of these will be mentioned in this chapter.

EVALUATION WITH MEMBERS OF THE TEAM

The student teacher or intern works more closely with the supervising teacher and the college supervisor than with others. It is pertinent to consider how this close association can facilitate the evaluation of his growth in teaching competence.

The Supervising Teacher

As we have said before, rapport between the student teacher or intern and his supervising teacher is essential if growth is to result

[3] Bruce J. Biddle and William J. Ellena, eds., *Contemporary Research on Teacher Effectiveness* (New York: Holt, Rinehart and Winston, 1964). For a complete discussion of Biddle's seven variables see Chapter 1. A discussion of scholarly attempts to define and evaluate teacher effectiveness through recent research appears in the other chapters of this book.

through evaluation. This condition is facilitated when the developing teacher assumes an attitude of objectivity and genuinely welcomes constructive suggestions. It is difficult, if not impossible, for a capable supervising teacher to contribute to the professional growth of one who is overly sensitive to criticism, lacks forthrightness, is fearful of the marks he may receive if he admits he is seeking help, and is generally uncooperative. This point deserves emphasis because in some instances the prospective teacher has not assumed his share of the responsibility for developing good working relationships.

Conferences. "My conferences with my supervising teacher have been informal and very helpful to me." This statement was made by a student teacher after a conference in which his teaching had been discussed. The following are suggestions for making the planned conference between the prospective teacher and his supervising teacher successful.

1. Each person should make adequate preparation for the conference.

2. Each person has responsibility for clarifying the purposes of the conference.

3. Each person should accept responsibility for promptness.

4. Each person should bring pertinent materials to the conference.

5. Each person should be willing to confer freely and openly.

6. Each person should accept responsibility for the wise use of time.

7. Each person should record suggestions, agreements, and responsibilities growing out of the conference.

8. Each person should leave the conference with a resolution to act.

9. Each conference should reflect continuity with previous conferences. Each should contribute to the improvement of teacher effectiveness.

Using the evaluation form. The student teacher or intern should assume responsibility for understanding the evaluation form used by his college or university. He can gain this understanding by conferring with his supervising teacher and college supervisor and by studying the evaluation form prior to or at the beginning of the clinical assignment. The accompanying form, along with instructions for its use illustrates this device.[4] In using this or any other evaluation form, the prospective teacher's involvement should not be limited to the mechanical exercise of checking each item in what appears to be the most appropriate space. It is important to be able to understand and justify the response to each item and to support each with concrete evidence and specific illustrations. Other points to be kept in mind in using the evaluation form effectively include the following:

1. Use the evaluation form frequently rather than at irregular intervals or just prior to an evaluation conference. Evaluation for all learners and especially for the prospective teacher should be continuous.

2. View evaluation and the use of the evaluation form as a cooperative endeavor. The supervising teacher recognizes his responsibility to be helpful. The student teacher or intern must also assume responsibility for successful evaluation procedures.

3. Take the initiative in asking for assistance through an evaluation when it is needed. The supervising teacher may not recognize the concern the prospective teacher feels about his development in a specific area or at a specific time.

4. Be specific about questions which need to be answered, e.g., voice, appropriateness of dress, knowledge of subject, adequacy of plans.

5. Use some systematic means of retaining pertinent data which will be needed later when considering items mentioned on the evaluation form. This may be done in various ways, including the use of a diary, notebook, anecdotal record, or time sheet.

The College Supervisor

The wide contacts and relationships of the college supervisor provide him with a background and overview which make his contributions valuable. An understanding of certain facts (pp. 223–4) can aid the student teacher or intern in obtaining help from the college supervisor.

[4] A more comprehensive evaluation form appears in the Appendix.

SUGGESTIONS FOR PERIODIC EVALUATION OF
ELEMENTARY STUDENT TEACHING

Marks are not used in student teaching. At the end of the student teaching period "credit" or "no credit" will be reported by the supervising teacher. This plan of procedure makes it possible to concentrate on the development of competency in teaching. Continuous evaluation, especially self-evaluation, is needed to facilitate this growth. An evaluation instrument, "Periodic Evaluation of Student Teaching—Elementary," has been developed as a means of helping student teachers grow in professional competency.

It is suggested that this blank be used twice during the student teaching period—perhaps at the end of the first month of student teaching and again at the end of the second month. At the *end* of the student teaching period the supervising teacher will use "Evaluation of Supervised Teaching Experience."

The "periodic evaluation" blank should be filled out by supervising teachers, by the college representatives, and by the student teacher (a self-evaluation).

Each supervising teacher and student teacher will keep his own blanks rather than forward them to the college. However, inasmuch as this "periodic evaluation" blank is primarily a learning device, all people concerned with those forms should confer with each other regarding their evaluations. (1) Supervising teachers and student teachers should discuss their evaluations with each other. Supervising teachers and student teachers may also separately confer with the college representative. (2) The college representative will discuss his own evaluation with the supervising teacher and also with the student teacher. These conferences will be held as the college representative makes his visits to the classroom.

The blank forms for the periodic evaluation of student teachers are distributed to student teachers (with copies for their supervisors) at the seminar. They may also be distributed to supervising teachers directly by the college representative.

It is believed that, if used in the manner outlined here, this instrument will serve as a learning device in improving the work of the student teacher. Suggestions regarding these evaluations will be welcomed by the staff of the Division of Teaching. These suggestions might relate to the *structure* or *use* of the blank.

INDIANA STATE UNIVERSITY
DIVISION OF TEACHING
PERIODIC EVALUATION OF STUDENT TEACHING—ELEMENTARY

NAME	Outstanding	Above Average	Average	Below Average	Please use descriptive statements after each of these categories whenever possible.
SCHOOL					
DATE					
Appearance					
Voice					
Poise					
Emotional stability					
Use of English					
Expresses ideas effectively					
Reacts favorably to criticism					
Has a good educational background					
Comprehends subject matter					
Assumes responsibility and shows interest					
Plans carefully—daily and long-range					
Selects and organizes a variety of materials					
Makes good use of facilities					
Keeps adequate records and reports					
Exhibits skill in directing learning activities					
Exhibits professional ethics					
Works well with children and adults					
Understands children and how they learn					
Provides for individual differences					
Fosters development of desirable pupil behavior					
Helps students feel secure and useful					
Helps students learn to assume responsibility					

Check appropriate column

*Indicate estimate of present status as compared with an average beginning teacher.

Signed _____

1. *Observation by the college supervisor* provides much first-hand information necessary for evaluating the teaching of the student learning to teach.

2. *Two-way conferences between prospective teacher and college supervisor* make it possible for the student teacher or intern to raise questions and for the college supervisor to make specific

suggestions. They provide an opportunity for the use of the evaluation form if that seems to be in order. If a log, diary, notebook, or collection of anecdotes is used by the prospective teacher, each can provide pertinent information to facilitate effective evaluation.

3. *Three-way conferences between prospective teacher, supervising teacher, and college supervisor* make it possible for the developing teacher to obtain help when clarification or other kinds of assistance may be needed from both individuals. In some teacher education programs it is customary for these three individuals to use the evaluation form as a basis for a joint evaluation.

4. *Group meetings of the college supervisor with the prospective teacher and his peers* provide opportunities for informal evaluation. The individual who may be experiencing difficulty in motivating the group he is teaching may receive help by learning how another has met a similar problem. In some instances arrangements are made for a prospective teacher to observe the teaching of a colleague, with the result that both benefit through the mutual evaluation which results.

EVALUATION WITH OTHERS

In some situations, though certainly not in every situation, the principal, pupils, or parents may make a useful contribution to one's effectiveness as a teacher. Directly or indirectly they may offer constructive suggestions for improvement.

The Principal

In some schools, most frequently in the smaller schools, though often in larger schools as well, the principal takes a personal and direct interest in the professional growth of the student teacher or intern. Because he views the prospective teacher as a potential member of his staff or for other reasons, the principal sometimes visits him at work in the classroom. Some principals hold individual or group conferences with prospective teachers. In some instances the principal will use the college evaluation form and/

or that of the school system in evaluating the work of the young teacher.

Pupils

Pupils are continually evaluating those who teach them, and skillful teachers are sensitive to the reactions of their pupils. There are conflicting viewpoints about pupil evaluation of a student teacher or intern. It is most useful when pupils have learned to think objectively and where there is rapport between pupils and the student teacher or intern. One recent study reveals that: "Reactions from approximately 115 student teachers and 60 supervising teachers to these observational and pupil rating techniques have been excellent." [5]

Because the prospective teacher seeks the cooperation of pupils, he is likely to court their good will. Sometimes he does this, either consciously or unconsciously, in ways he will not employ later as an experienced teacher. If a problem has arisen because pupils have taken advantage of his friendliness, pupil evaluation should be delayed until the undesirable condition has been corrected.

It is possible to discover the kinds of evaluations pupils make of their teachers through the use of informal techniques without employing a specific evaluation instrument. For example, it is reasonable to assume that pupils believe they have a good teacher when they make the following kinds of responses:

Begin an assigned task promptly without repeated requests for clarification.

Complete assigned work in a reasonable time rather than dawdling over it.

Expend effort to suggest ideas and locate materials instead of displaying an attitude of boredom.

Display a friendly rather than a hostile attitude toward the teacher.

[5] Virginia B. Morrison and W. Robert Dixon in *The College Supervisor, Conflict and Challenge* (Cedar Falls, Iowa: Association for Student Teaching, Yearbook, 1964), p. 106.

Show respect but not undue friendliness in relations with the teacher.

Make comments which imply that they are being helped to learn useful facts, acquire knowledge, and develop desirable attitudes.

The supervising teacher is in an excellent position to observe the kind of evaluation pupils are making of the student learning to teach. When both the supervising teacher and the prospective teacher are alert to pupils' reactions and communication between these two individuals is good, pupil evaluation can be effective. The student teacher or intern might request the supervising teacher to react to such questions as the following:

How do pupils view me as a person—appearance, voice, poise, educational background, enthusiasm, emotional stability?

How do pupils view me as a teacher—planning, instructional techniques, understanding of pupils, maintenance of discipline, fairness, helpfulness, evaluation of their work?

SELF-EVALUATION

Self-evaluation can be a valuable learning experience in the quest for teaching competency. This fact is emphasized in the following statement:

Evaluation is an essential part of the student's learning. It is important that he build attitudes toward, and habits of, evaluation that help him to become his own best critic. Often he may be the only person to commend or to criticize his action in a particular situation. To be able to evaluate one's present status, to know how to appraise one's needs, to be able to propose next steps, are important aspects of growth.[6]

Like his pupils, the student teacher or intern is most likely to learn what he accepts as truthful and useful to him. Honest self-evaluation can help him crystallize his own beliefs and discover useful teaching procedures.

[6] American Association of Colleges for Teacher Education, *Teacher Education for a Free People* (Oneonta, New York: The Association, 1956), p. 303.

Aids to Self-Evaluation

The form provided by the institution with which the prospective teacher is affiliated, or those mentioned in this chapter, will be useful for *self*-evaluation. There are other appropriate aids which should be used whenever possible.

The checklist. The checklist can be useful for obtaining experience in most of the activities in which teachers engage. The teacher education institution may provide a list of this kind; if not, one can be devised with the help of the supervising teacher or college supervisor. The following checklist is adapted from one used by prospective elementary teachers in one university.

CHECKLIST FOR PROSPECTIVE TEACHERS

Have I:

1. Used a motion picture in my teaching?
2. Planned a bulletin board?
3. Provided independent seatwork activities?
4. Made a field trip?
5. Taken charge of an activity period?
6. Used the tape recorder?
7. Used a radio or television program?
8. Taken charge of the lunch period?
9. Kept attendance records?
10. Planned a culminating activity?
11. Read some professional articles?
12. Had an interview with a pupil?
13. Consulted children's files for information?
14. Introduced myself to visiting parents?
15. Taken part in a parent conference?
16. Attended a PTA meeting?
17. Experimented with my own ideas?
18. Attended community functions?
19. Encouraged the development of pupil self-discipline?
20. Made evaluations based on available information including standardized tests?

The recorder. The following comments were made by student teachers who used the recorder as they attempted to evaluate the effectiveness of their own teaching.

"I played it back (a recording of a teacher and pupils in an English class) and listened for points on which I should improve. I was amazed at the sound of my own voice."

"I used the recorder during my spelling class and my reading class to determine the atmosphere of the class during my teaching, to discover the conduct and response of class members, and to evaluate my voice and presentation of material."

"I want to tape a unit lesson that I teach in order to criticize myself and detect the areas in which I need to improve."

The increasing availability of recording devices makes their use possible. Recordings at regular intervals during the student teaching or internship period can greatly facilitate the process of self-evaluation.

The motion picture and television recorder. With motion picture and television records the prospective teacher can both view himself and hear his voice after teaching a class. This can be done in an increasing number of teacher education institutions through the cooperation of the college supervisor and the audio-visual center of the college or university. One procedure is simultaneous use of the motion picture camera and the recorder. Another is the use of the videotape recorder. Opportunities for self-evaluation are greatly increased when one can view a motion picture or telecast of himself and at the same time hear his own voice as he has taught his pupils. He can see himself as others see him in the classroom. He can observe the performance and needs of the class group and of specific individuals as he teaches them. He can detect the reactions of the group and of individuals toward him. He can discover how effectively he is communicating with pupils.

Communication between the prospective teacher and the supervising teacher can be increased when both have the opportunity to view a film or telecast of the young teacher at work. For example, it may be difficult for a student teacher to comprehend fully what is meant when he is told by his supervising teacher that he needs to develop poise before the class or that pupils seem bored with the overuse of the lecture. However, when both see and hear him the reason for such constructive criticism becomes apparent.

Observing others teach. The thoughtful and discerning person can increase his effectiveness as an evaluator of his own teaching by observing others teach and by comparing his teaching with that observed. Those he might observe include his supervising teacher, other teachers in the school, and other prospective teachers. As he observes he will find it helpful to refer to the evaluation form he and his supervising teacher use in evaluating his work. In addition to direct observation of the individuals mentioned above, the prospective teacher should not overlook opportunities for observation of excellent teachers at work in commercial and noncommercial films and telecasts that are available from the local school, the teacher education institution, and various other agencies mentioned in Chapter 7.

Other aids to self-evaluation. It would be difficult to make a complete list of the aids to self-evaluation which might be used by a creative student of teaching. Additional ones include the anecdotal record of critical incidents, the diary, the log, the notebook, and the time sheet.

Self-Evaluation in Action

Prospective teachers can profit from the experiences of those who have been in situations similar to their own. The following comments were gleaned from papers written as a part of the preparation for participation in a seminar for prospective teachers. Each statement was written by a different individual.

"I became fully aware of the importance of including in a unit experiences which are purposeful, stimulate problem solving, provide for individual and group activity, and call for a variety of instructional materials."

"I have found that motivation gives zest to learning, direction to study, and order to the classroom."

"Each day I have gone home from student teaching I have tried to evaluate the experiences of that day. I pick out the most profitable experiences and draw conclusions as to why they were profitable. With the less beneficial experiences I try to determine why they were as they were and how they could be improved."

"Teaching in many areas becomes more meaningful and purposeful when it is conceived as productive of the bases for independent action."

"Interest in children, ability to work with others, and teaching skill are just three things out of many that we need to consider as prospective teachers, but my experiences in student teaching have made me become more aware of them. I now realize how important they are to success in the teaching profession."

"I believe the time has come when individual needs are going to have to be met more effectively and more practically than they have been in the past."

"Self-evaluation is an important phase of my learning to be a teacher."

"The pupils responded to me better than I had ever hoped. The only trouble I have had so far is running out of time before we complete everything I want to accomplish."

"Prospective and experienced teachers need knowledge about pupils' needs. I have come to realize how important it is for the teacher to know the physical, social, intellectual, and emotional needs of pupils."

"I am aware of these children [who do not participate in discussion] but I seem to get so engrossed in my own teaching that certain awarenesses slip my mind."

"I am able to plan ahead now and make effective, unique, and practical lesson plans. This is something I was woefully poor at doing in September."

"This initial experience gave me an increasing amount of self-confidence. I am glad to know that I have what it takes to plan, teach, and evaluate a lesson."

"During student teaching I have become aware of my use of language."

"As I look back over this past week, it has been most profitable to me. I have seen the many sides to teaching—the joys, the disappointments, and the ups and downs."

"When I have planned carefully beforehand, things run smoothly and I have no trouble whatsoever. My only problems result when I am not too sure of what I am trying to do."

SUMMARY

It is the purpose of this chapter to aid the prospective teacher in his efforts to recognize and evaluate teaching skill. Emphasis has been placed on self-evaluation. The importance to good teaching of evaluation in terms of sound principles was mentioned and specific principles were stated.

The evaluation of teaching skill should be in terms of the goals one hopes to achieve. Worthwhile goals are frequently stated in terms of teaching competencies. A list of six generally accepted teaching competencies, with appropriate subheadings under each, was mentioned.

Researchers have not reached agreement in defining good teaching, with the result that consensus on ways of evaluating teaching has not been achieved. Nevertheless, employing officials, school administrators, supervising teachers, and prospective teachers all must attempt to develop and encourage what is conceived to be good teaching and to evaluate it in terms of this conception. Evaluation is commonly facilitated through the use of various types of evaluation forms which list personal and professional traits, characteristics, and behaviors believed to be associated with good teaching.

Evaluation of the prospective teacher with other members of the teachingteam, the supervising teacher, and the college supervisor, was discussed. Evaluation with the principal and pupils was also considered.

Capable teachers understand the importance of self-evaluation in facilitating their growth in teaching competence. It is a valuable learning experience for the prospective teacher. Aids to self-evaluation include the evaluation form, checklist, recorder, motion picture and television recorder, and observation of other teachers. Other aids are the anecdotal record of critical incidents, diary, log, notebook, and time sheet.

The chapter ended with several brief statements by prospective teachers which can help the student teacher or intern who is attempting self-evaluation of his own growth in teaching skill.

USEFUL REFERENCES

Allen, Dwight W. and Richard E. Gross. "Microteaching—a New Beginning for Beginners," *NEA Journal* 55 (December 1965), 25–26.

Amidon, Edmund J., and Ned A. Flanders. *The Role of the Teacher in the Classroom*. Minneapolis: Paul S. Amidon and Associates, Inc., 1963.

Association For Student Teaching, *Evaluating Student Teaching*. Yearbook. Cedar Falls, Iowa: The Association, 1960.

California Teachers Association, *Teacher Competence: Its Nature and Scope*. Burlingame, California: The Association, 1955.

Educational Leadership. Issue devoted to "What Is Teaching?" 19 (December 1961), 146–200.

Gage, N. L., ed. *Handbook of Research on Teaching*. Chicago: Rand McNally and Company, 1963.

Kinney, L. B. "Self-Evaluation: The Mark of a Profession," *Educational Leadership* 15 (1958), 228–231.

Mitzel, H. E. *A Behavioral Approach to the Assessment of Teacher Effectiveness*. New York: Office of Research and Evaluation, Division of Teacher Education, College of the City of New York, 1957.

Ryans, David G. *Characteristics of Teachers: Their Description, Comparison, and Appraisal, a Research Study*. Washington, D.C.: American Council on Education, 1960.

Schueler, Herbert and Milton J. Gold. "Video Recordings of Student Teachers—A Report of the Hunter College Research Project Evaluating the Use of Kinescopes in Preparing Student Teachers," *Journal of Teacher Education* 15 (December 1964), 358–364.

Smith, B. O. "A Concept of Teaching," *Teachers College Record* 61 (1960), 229–241.

PART THREE

PLANNING FOR A CAREER IN TEACHING

CHAPTER ELEVEN

WORKING TOWARD
A SUCCESSFUL
FIRST YEAR

A good start in teaching is more than a matter of luck. The probabilities of success are increased when the student teacher or intern makes careful plans for his first year as a regular teacher. This chapter is intended to help him achieve that goal.

OBTAINING A SUITABLE POSITION

The first year as a regularly employed teacher can be a pleasant one which will increase knowledge of teaching and enthusiasm for the teaching profession. If circumstances are such that it is not stimulating and satisfying, interest in and enthusiasm for teaching may be lost or diminished and may be difficult to recover.

Establishing Criteria for Selecting a Position

Occasionally a prospective teacher follows a lackadaisical attitude in locating a position and accepts whatever offer happens to come his way. He may overemphasize the merits of his home community as a place in which to teach, without investigating opportunities elsewhere. He may decide to teach in a school system because a friend has located there, or he may make a decision solely on the basis of the salary offered him. The thoughtful individual who takes a more mature view of teaching and is interested in a place where he can both give and receive an optimum amount of professional assistance will give attention to the apparent opportunities and limitations of each position considered.

What are some of the factors which should receive attention in exploration of the possibilities in a teaching position?

Community. The prospective teacher's marital status and family situation will influence his choice of location. The unmarried person can move about more easily than one who is married and has a family; many will consider taking a position in the home community. Our's is rapidly becoming an urban society so that most persons who have prepared for teaching will ultimately teach in a city. However, to the extent a choice is possible, the teacher candidate needs to choose between an urban and less urban community.[1]

Nature of the instructional program.   Some schools are known to be conservative and traditional in their approach to learning and in the administration of the curriculum. Others maintain an attitude of experimentation and flexibility. Still others have a reputation for assuming a middle-of-the-road position. These differences in viewpoint should be considered so that upon accepting a position the teacher can work with his colleagues without conflict in philosophies. Viewpoints are frequently revealed in the kind and quantity of instructional materials available for teachers and children and in the extent to which the acceptance of promising innovations in teaching is in evidence.

Professional assistance.   Some school systems provide an excellent orientation program for new teachers; others do not. For example, the new teacher in a small school where there is a teaching principal and no supervisory staff from the central office is likely to receive much less professional help than the teacher in a school system where a supervising principal, an assistant principal, and consultants from the central office are charged with responsibility for assisting beginning teachers. There are also wide differences in opportunities for in-service education of teachers.

Financial considerations.   Communities differ in their ability and willingness to provide financial support for a good educational program. These differences are reflected in the adequacy of

---

[1] Reference to "Study of Pertinent Community Information" in Chapter 2 should prove helpful.

buildings and equipment, amount and quality of instructional materials and aids, and compensation of teachers. Although salary should not be the major consideration in selecting a position, it is an important one. Attention should be given not only to the beginning salary, but also to salary increments and the maximum salary. Various fringe benefits such as group insurance, sick leave, and hospitalization should be understood. It is wise to ask if professional improvement of teachers is encouraged by financial remuneration for the expense of in-service education or by provision for sabbatical leaves. The nature and functioning of the retirement program should be understood.

Differences in the cost of living should not be overlooked. The effect of a high salary in a "boom" town or in an exclusive suburban community may be more than offset by such factors as high rent, high taxes, or inflated costs of food and clothing. It should be noted that both salaries and living costs vary considerably between communities, states, and sections of the country.

Personal satisfaction. Most individuals perform better if they work in an environment which is pleasant and satisfying to them. Conditions which make this possible include opportunities to meet friends of one's own age; recreational facilities; cultural advantages; opportunities for reading and study; presence of others of the same race, religion, or nationality; and the kind and amount of restriction upon personal living.

Using Placement Services Effectively

Most teacher education institutions maintain a placement bureau to assist prospective and experienced teachers in locating a position. Some institutions make enrollment with the bureau a requirement for all individuals who plan to graduate on a teaching curriculum. Registration usually involves filling out and filing a series of forms and an interview with a placement official. Some individuals, especially those who have the promise of employment without utilizing the services of the bureau, have questioned the necessity for this requirement. A complete file of this kind is a permanent record which can be updated at intervals and can be useful for both the teacher and employing officials over a long period of time. The conference with a placement bureau official can be a very important factor in the placement of the student teacher or intern in a position that will be most satisfactory to both employee and employer. During the conference the prospective teacher can obtain information about policies of the bureau, placement opportunities in a geographical area or specific school system, salaries, and working conditions. The placement official can discover the preferences of the prospective teacher as they relate to such items as geographical area, subject or grade level, salary, working conditions, and long-range plans for the future. He can also obtain information about the prospective teacher's personal qualities, attitudes, and personal and professional philosophy.

Prospective teachers often are not aware of the fact that there are commercial placement agencies which assist teachers in locating a position. These agencies exist to make a profit, but they also render a service to teachers. They ordinarily charge a small registration fee for assembling credentials and making them available to employing officials and a commission, often 5 per cent of the first year's salary, when a position is obtained through the efforts of the agency.

The question often arises about whether or not one should utilize the services of a commercial agency. In most instances, especially during times when demand exceeds supply, most teachers can obtain a position without paying a commission to a commercial agency. There are two types of situations in which commercial agencies can be useful. One is when the teacher wishes to be placed in a state or location at considerable distance from the campus and which is not ordinarily served by the institutional placement bureau. Commercial agencies frequently have offices in various parts of the country and thus serve a larger geographical area than many institutional bureaus. A commercial agency can also be helpful when a prospective teacher's field of preparation is one for which his institutional placement bureau receives few calls or in which the supply exceeds the demand. One who plans to use the services of a commercial placement agency should make certain that he registers with an agency of good reputation. The National Association of Teachers Agencies each year publishes a list of agencies affiliated with that association and which it considers reliable. This list and the address of the organization may be obtained from any institutional placement bureau.

In some states a placement bureau is operated by agencies other than those mentioned above. The state department of education or the state teachers' association may maintain a placement bureau for the teachers in the state. In some instances where there is a shortage of teachers these agencies may be used by out-of-state teachers as a means of encouraging teachers to locate within a state. Although a charge is made for this service it is considerably less than the amount the teacher would be asked to pay to a commercial placement agency.

When a teacher utilizes the services of an institutional, commercial, or other placement bureau, he should give it his complete cooperation. He should reply promptly to all notices of openings and should inform the bureau of all steps taken toward obtaining employment, including acceptance of a position.

Employing Effective Placement Procedures

In addition to determining criteria for a position and working with a placement bureau, the teacher can follow other procedures which can facilitate successful placement.

The letter of application. The letter of application is not as widely used now as it was in the past, primarily because the increasing number of institutional placement bureaus has made it unnecessary in many instances. It is a common practice for a placement bureau official to send credentials to an employing official and arrange for an interview without a written communication from the candidate. There are, however, frequent instances when a letter of application is necessary and important. For example, an individual may wish to locate in a school system at some distance from the campus or in one which does not contact the institutional placement office.

The application letter should be typed or handwritten in black ink on one side of standard 8½ by 11 inch paper. The letter should be brief, direct, and the content clearly stated. The standard form for a well-written business letter should be used. The letter which follows is illustrative of the kind one might use.

10 Maple Avenue
Eastlawn, Iowa
March 25, 1965

Mr. William Asbury
Director, Personnel Services
Templeton Public Schools
Templeton, Utah

Dear Mr. Asbury:

The Placement Bureau at Sweetbriar University has informed me of a vacancy in Junior High School mathematics in your school system for next year. I should like to be considered for that position. I have traveled in Utah and the West and would like to locate in your area of the state.

I will graduate from Sweetbriar University in June with a Bachelor of Arts degree. My major field is mathematics. I completed my student teaching last semester when I taught mathematics in Highland Junior High School in the Wasatch school system, Wasatch, Iowa.

If you are interested in receiving my credentials, the Placement Bureau at Sweetbriar University will send them to you promptly at your request. I shall be glad to fill out an application form should you wish to send one to me. I will supply additional information you request and will answer questions you may wish to ask about my personal or professional qualifications.

If you are interested in my application I will be glad to arrange for a personal interview at your convenience. I would prefer a Friday, Saturday, or Monday.

Sincerely yours,

James Andrews

The application form. Most school administrators ask all applicants for a teaching position to fill out an application form. Students frequently ask why this should be necessary when they have supplied detailed information to the institutional placement bureau which in turn makes this information available to employing officials. The application form is of value to both employer and candidate. From the viewpoint of the employing official it provides a source of permanent information about a teacher. It makes basic information about the teacher easily available. Placement bureau forms are not standardized and are often difficult to read. If the candidate is employed and credentials are returned to the placement bureau, the application information is still available for reference. If the teacher is not employed but might be hired later, it can serve as a reference for contacting potential staff members at some future time. Even when credentials are available, the application form provides an outline of basic information about a teacher without study of the credentials in detail. When a candidate accepts a position and the application form is kept on file, the fact that this information is available when needed makes it unnecessary for the teacher to supply it repeatedly.

The interview.   Most school officials require an interview as a condition of employment. It may take place on the campus or in the office of the superintendent of schools or of someone designated by him, frequently the director of personnel services. It is common practice for school administrators to conduct interviews in the placement office on the campus and to invite certain individuals interviewed to the school for a visit and a second conference. When this is done other key persons from the school, including the principal, may hold an interview with the candidate. This procedure is advantageous for the teacher. In fact it is wise to visit the school in which one may be working before accepting a position.

The best interests of both the candidate and the school are served when there is free and forthright discussion between both participants in the employment interview. The following suggestions should be of value in insuring a profitable employment interview.

PREPARATION FOR THE INTERVIEW

1. Become as well informed as possible about the community and school system under consideration.

2. Make a list of questions which need to be answered.

3. Be prepared to answer questions, both personal and professional.

4. Be prepared to give a brief history of personal and professional accomplishments.

5. Re-think experiences in general education, academic subjects, and professional education, thus making it possible to give a forthright statement of your beliefs about learning and teaching. Be prepared to describe benefits received from your student teaching or internship.

6. Dress for the occasion. Employing officials who work with experienced teachers and stable community citizens are not likely to be favorably impressed by the latest campus styles in clothes, facial make-up, or hair arrangement.

SUGGESTIONS FOR PARTICIPATION IN THE INTERVIEW

1. Be prompt.

2. Be courteous, polite, and friendly.

3. Be yourself. It is important that one present an honest picture of oneself. The experienced interviewer is quick to detect pretense.

4. Let the employing official take the lead and set the pace of the interview.

5. Respond frankly and honestly to questions.

6. Do not assume an antagonistic attitude or argue with the interviewer.

7. Obtain as many answers to pertinent questions as the situation permits. The interviewer usually encourages the candidate to ask questions. If he does not, questions might be raised near the end of the interview. Answers to questions in such areas as the following should be useful:

   a. *Community.* Attitude toward schools and teachers, financial support of schools, living arrangements available, living costs.

   b. *Nature of the instructional program.* How organized; prevailing viewpoints about learning and teaching; quantity, quality, and availability of instructional materials.

   c. *Professional assistance to teachers.* Orientation program for new teachers, help from consultants, opportunities for in-service growth.

   d. *Financial considerations.* Nature of salary schedule, if any; beginning salary; fringe benefits; retirement program.

e. Personal living. Opportunities to meet persons of a similar age; recreational facilities; presence of others of same race, religion, or nationality; restrictions on activities of teachers.

8. If you are interested, ask the employing official if he thinks a visit to his school is warranted. If so, arrange a time for the visit.

9. Indicate appreciation for consideration as a candidate and for the privilege of being interviewed.

No two interviews are identical. However, all interviews have certain common elements. Employing officials frequently seek the kinds of information implied in the following questions.

INFORMATION SOUGHT BY EMPLOYING OFFICIALS

1. Will you sketch briefly your personal history prior to entering college?

2. What has been your college history? point hour ratio? academic subject concentration? out-of-class activities?

3. What has been the nature of your student teaching and/or internship experience?

4. Why did you choose to prepare for teaching?

5. What are your plans for the future? Do you plan to make teaching a career?

6. What plans do you have for continuing your education?

7. What are your beliefs about meeting individual needs? organizing instruction? planning? developing desirable behavior of pupils?

8. What interest do you have in professional organizations for teachers?

9. Do you enjoy working with others or do you prefer to work alone?

10. What is your viewpoint about participation in community activities?

The person who conducts the interview will seek answers to such questions as the following: Does this prospective teacher

1. Present a pleasing appearance?
2. Seem to have serious physical, social, or intellectual handicaps?
3. Seem friendly, frank, communicative?
4. Possess initiative and enthusiasm?
5. Appear to be well informed and knowledgeable about current developments?
6. Show evidence of being genuinely interested in children and in teaching?

7. Demonstrate the kind of emotional, social, and professional maturity needed by a teacher?

8. Appear to be the kind of individual who will become a respected citizen of the community?

Understanding Contracts

The prospective teacher needs to be informed about the purpose and general nature of the teacher's contract. The laws governing the terms of the contract between the teacher and the school district vary somewhat from state to state. Although it will be helpful for the candidate to become informed about the laws in his own state, it is more important to understand the general nature of the contract and its implications.

1. The contract is an agreement between the teacher and the school system. It is a means of protecting the interests of each party.

2. The contract is between the Board of Education, the legally constituted body representing the school system, and the teacher. The superintendent of schools, as the chief executive officer of the board, recommends teachers to the Board of Education for appointment. He also recommends retention when appropriate and dismissal when that is deemed desirable.

3. When a teacher signs a contract, he agrees to abide by the rules of the Board of Education, even though they may not be specifically stated in the contract itself. It is important that the teacher knows these rules.

4. The contract may list specific conditions to be met and state conditions under which the contract may be terminated by either party.

5. The period of time to be covered by the contract may vary, but the first contract is usually for one year.

6. It is customary for a teacher to enter into a contract with a school system "subject to assignment." The superintendent is usually aware of the teacher's preference for school, grade, or subject and ordinarily attempts to place him according to any preference for which he is qualified. This is not always possible during the teacher's first year in a school system.

7. It is both illegal and unethical for either party to ignore the terms of a contract. It is unethical for a teacher to break a contract so that he may accept a position in another situation unless he is released from the contract by the Board of Education upon the recommendation of the superintendent.

It is desirable for a teacher to distinguish between what is legal and what is ethical in requesting that he be released from the terms of his contract. If he asks to be released within ten days from the date of request when the contract states sixty days' notice must be given and the board grants the request, this becomes a legal act. The question may be raised as to whether or not the teacher was ethical in requesting a release on such short notice. If the board had not granted the release, the teacher would be both legally and ethically bound to the terms of the contract. There is considerable variation among school boards in policy toward releasing teachers, though in general they are more than fair in this regard.

OBTAINING A TEACHING CERTIFICATE

Citizens, including members of the various professions, have discovered that certain procedures and regulations are necessary for protection from dishonest and unscrupulous persons. This is illustrated by the fact that doctors, dentists, lawyers, architects, and others must obtain licenses before they may become recognized practitioners and be entrusted to serve the public. Similarly a teacher must obtain a license or certificate before he can be permitted to obtain a teaching position and provide instruction for pupils.

Understanding Certification Requirements

Education is a function of the state, and the state has become the governmental unit which determines the basic requirements for the preparation and certification of teachers. Teaching certificates are issued through the office of the chief state school officer, frequently known as the state superintendent of public instruction. In actual practice this function is usually delegated to another agency in the state school office and administered by an individual who commonly bears the title of Director of Teacher Certification. He in turn is frequently responsible to, or advised by, a board or commission sometimes known as a Teacher Education and Licensing Commission. This board and its director have responsibility for determining requirements which must be met by both public and private institutions engaging in the preparation of teachers.

It is customary for each teacher education institution to designate some individual on the campus to serve as certification advisor for students on a teaching curriculum. This person is frequently a faculty member in the field of teacher education or an administrative official of the college or university.

The scholastic requirements for entering teaching, as for most other professions, have increased in recent years. In most states four years of preparation are required for the initial certificate, and the trend is in the direction of five years.[2] Often there are additional requirements such as good moral character, good health as certified by a physician, and a statement to uphold and support the Constitution of the United States.

It is usually necessary to teach for a period of time on an initial or "provisional" certificate before one is issued a "permanent" or "life" certificate. The initial period is commonly either three or five years. In an increasing number of states five years of preparation and the Masters degree are requirements for obtaining the second certificate.

Taking the Initiative in Meeting Requirements

Sometimes students enrolled in a teacher education curriculum believe they have met all the requirements for certification, only to discover that they cannot be certificated. In most instances this

---

[2] For a discussion of certification requirements in the various states see W. Earl Armstrong and T. M. Stinnett, *A Manual on Certification Requirements for School Personnel in the United States* (Washington, D.C.: National Commission on Teacher Education and Professional Standards—NEA, 1964).

situation could have been avoided if the person had made an effort to contact the certification official on his campus to check his progress toward meeting certification requirements. The following procedures should be helpful.

1. Consult the college or university catalog to be sure of graduation requirements for the appropriate curriculum and for any certification information which may be listed there.

2. Be alert to regular announcements appearing in the campus newspaper and those from such sources as the certification official, the chairman of the appropriate department, and college or university officials.

3. Consult with the person responsible for advising students on matters of curriculum.

4. Consult with the certification official. This should be done at intervals if one is in doubt about how well requirements are being met.

5. Fill out and return promptly forms designed to check courses completed and to report other work that has been done toward completing curriculum requirements.

6. Make it a point to meet any general requirements such as completing a physical examination and presenting a statement signed by a physician, presenting a receipt for taxes paid, and signing a statement to support the Constitution of the United States.

7. Send completed forms and certification fee to the state director of teacher certification when asked to do so.

8. Respond promptly to communications from the institutional and state certification officials and keep each informed about all matters which have a bearing on keeping the certificate in force.

PREPARING FOR LIVING AND TEACHING
IN A NEW SITUATION

After one has accepted a teaching position, he is faced with the task of preparing to live and work in ways which will be satisfying to him and helpful to the pupils he instructs. In past years it was common practice for the prospective teacher to complete his teaching curriculum in June and start teaching the following September. With an increased number of college and university students attending classes during the summer, many begin teaching a short time, sometimes only days, after completing the required program of preparation.

Rethinking One's Experiences as a Student Teacher or Intern

The experiences a student teacher or intern has had can be very helpful in his new situation if he will review them and study their implications for his new work. It can be helpful to recall things that worked well and note where change or improvement is needed. The following list includes topics previously discussed. Each might serve as a heading for appropriate notations: planning, directing learning, evaluating pupil progress, using instructional materials and aids, pupil behavior, working in the total school program.

In reflecting on the clinical experience, it is important to review what has been recorded, saved, or collected. The log, diary, notebook, lesson plans, unit plans, samples of pupils' work, and instructional materials acquired are useful in helping to crystallize one's thinking about those things which will be of value in future teaching.

Making Desirable Personal Arrangements

The new teacher will need to give thought not only to his readiness to function well professionally, but also to plans for his personal well-being.

Locating a place to live.   Many young people in their initial teaching position are for the first time compelled to manage their personal affairs alone. Some have either always lived at home or with relatives or in a college or university environment where food and housing, and perhaps other aspects of personal living, were to some extent arranged for them.

In some school systems administrative officials assist the new teacher in finding a suitable place to live. It is always desirable to discuss housing with school officials. Even if no list of places to live is available, one can obtain information about the most favorable or the undesirable sections in the area. One should ascertain whether teachers are required to live within the school district.

Factors to be considered in selecting living quarters include the following:

Location.   Distance from school, kind of transportation available, general desirability of the neighborhood.

Type.   Is house, apartment, hotel room, or room in a private dwelling preferred?

Physical conditions.   Provisions for heat, light, ventilation. Is there adequate space available? Are the quarters clean and easily maintained?

Cost.   It is easy to spend a disproportionate amount of one's income for housing. It is usually wise to seek a "middle-of-the-road" position between extravagance, on the one hand, and a feeling of apology for housing on the other. A related factor to be considered is the arrangement one makes for meals.

Atmosphere and privacy.   One who needs quiet surroundings should select a dwelling, apartment, or room accordingly. A single person needs to make a decision about living alone or with another person. There is much to be said for living alone during the first year of teaching or until one is well acquainted with the community.

Providing for other personal matters.   The beginning teacher should allow enough time before the opening of school to arrange for many of the details involved in his personal living. At least a week is needed to make oneself personally and professionally ready. It would be impossible to list all the items needing attention. However, the following suggestions can be useful in preparing for the first school year in a strange community:

Living quarters.   Put these in such condition that when school begins they will require a minimum amount of time and effort.

Personal services.   Locate and make arrangements for needed services such as the following: market, post office, bank, newspaper, laundry, dry cleaner, housekeeper, barber or beauty shop, garage, service station, utilities suppliers (telephone, electricity, gas, water).

Church.   If you are in the habit of attending services at a church or synagogue, the appropriate person may be contacted.

Planning for a Good Beginning

The individual who allows time to make adequate preparation for the opening days of school will be well rewarded for his time and effort when pupils arrive and the busy first days of school permit little time for anything but the most essential tasks.

Meeting with the principal.   In many instances the beginning teacher will not have had an opportunity to meet with the principal at the time of signing a contract. Even though he may have visited the school system before accepting a position, his specific teaching assignment might not have been known at that time.

The principal is interested in being as helpful as possible and in the success of each teacher in the school. He can be most helpful if the beginning teacher has a list of questions which relate to his own duties. The principal will acquaint the new teacher with the building and the quarters in which he and his pupils will work. He will provide the newcomer with much helpful duplicated material prepared to provide information about the school, community, and the teacher's responsibilities.

Preparing for the opening of school.   One needs to assume responsibility for identifying as many as possible of the tasks which need attention during the early days of school and for making preparation to perform them successfully.

It is important to become acquainted with the kinds of instructional materials available, both those in the classroom and those available from the various sources outside the classroom within the school and community. A visit to the instructional materials center, the library, and the audio-visual center will be helpful. In some school systems one is expected to request in advance materials and aids which will be needed during the first semester such as textbooks, reference books, supplementary books, films, filmstrips, and other audio-visual aids.

As soon as possible a list of names of pupils with whom one is to work should be obtained from the principal. A study of the cumulative record of each pupil will provide much helpful information about the ability, academic progress, and family background of the individual. Additional information about groups and individuals with whom one will be working may be obtained through a conference with the principal and with teachers who have recently worked with these pupils.

Pre-school orientation and faculty meetings. An increasing number of school systems provide an orientation period for beginning teachers prior to the opening of school. This is frequently combined with a workshop and/or orientation period for experienced teachers. The trend is for school districts to include this period in an extended school year so that teachers are paid while making preparation for the ensuing year. These pre-school meetings are organized and function in different ways depending upon purpose, length, and local conditions. Some are inspirational in nature, others are concerned with curriculum development, and still others combine these two functions.

It is customary in the pre-school orientation period to make provision for two types of meetings. One involves all school personnel, including both elementary and secondary teachers. In this meeting matters of policy, regulations, curricular developments, administrative matters, and announcements of concern to the entire staff are considered. A second type of meeting is one in which the principal and teachers of a specific school meet together. This meeting makes it possible to discuss developments of the previous general meetings and to plan the details of the opening days. It is common practice for the teacher to have a day or possibly several days following this meeting to prepare for the arrival of pupils and the opening of school.

Making a readiness check list. The following are some of the things that planning for a good beginning, including meeting the principal and attending orientation meetings, can call to the attention of the teacher. Those previously mentioned are not included here.

1. Check with the secretary in the principal's office, locate mail box in the office, and obtain all duplicated materials for distribution to new teachers.

2. Visit the school library, the instructional materials center, and the audio-visual center to become informed about instructional materials and teaching aids.

3. Visit the public library and check other sources of information and materials which may be used in instructing pupils.

4. Check cumulative records and obtain all the information possible about record-keeping and individual pupils with whom one is to be working.

5. Obtain a copy of the school handbook and study its contents.

6. Obtain a copy of the curriculum guide, course of study, or available resource units and become informed of their contents.

7. Obtain a copy of the calendar of school events and record important dates in diary or date book.

8. Check to be sure that school policies, regulations, and announcements are understood and make plans to inform parents and pupils about those for which it is the teacher's duty to supply information.

9. Understand which extracurricular activities the teacher is responsible for and be ready to carry them out successfully.

10. Meet and become acquainted with as many new and experienced teachers as possible.

11. Make all necessary preparations for the first day of school, including those mentioned in the following section.

THE OPENING DAY

If one is well prepared, the first day of school can be an enjoyable even though a very busy one. The following are suggestions obtained from beginning teachers.

1. Be prepared. Suggestions made in previous sections of this chapter can be helpful.

2. Pay attention to personal appearance. Pupils respond more favorably to the teacher who is appropriately dressed, clean, and well groomed than to one who is careless about the image he presents to others.

3. Be sure the room in which pupils meet is as pleasant and attractive as possible. Attend to lighting, temperature, and ventilation. Color can be added to a drab room through the use of flowers, attractive bulletin boards, centers of interest, and colorful books.

4. Have instructional materials to be used during the day available where they can be obtained immediately when needed.

5. Have a schedule for the day, but be flexible and prepared to deviate from it when change is desirable to capture the interest of pupils and provide motivation. There should be no indecision which might lead pupils to believe that their teacher is unprepared or inadequate.

6. Be friendly, courteous, polite, and businesslike. Pupils consciously or unconsciously tend to emulate their teacher. Characteristics such as these on the part of both teacher and pupils make for a pleasant and productive classroom environment and encourage desirable learning.

7. Be pleasant to pupils yet firm and decisive. They need to know from the start that they can count on the security in the classroom which results when they have no doubt that their teacher is an intelligent and able person capable of controlling the classroom situation.

The student who has planned carefully for a career in teaching, for his first year, and for the first day in his own classroom should be ready to appreciate the words of Bel Kaufman, author of *Up the Down Staircase* when she says:

The rewards of the beginning teacher are many: when a child who has been silent all term raises a faltering hand; when a boy takes out a library card for the first time; when a student says, "You're my favorite subject"; and the most exciting moment of all—when a pupil says, "Oh, I get it!"

You beginning teachers have certain advantages: your first, fine, careless rapture has not yet faded; you have not yet become tired, nursing your grievances and varicose veins; you have not learned to coast along or to repeat a lesson. I urge you not to lose those advantages.[3]

LIVING AS A RESPONSIBLE CITIZEN IN THE COMMUNITY

The life of the teacher in the typical American community can be pleasant and satisfying. In most communities the teacher is treated much like any other citizen. He can live a much less restricted life than was possible for the teacher even a few decades ago. He has an opportunity to live a normal life, free from restrictions and taboos, and a responsibility to contribute a reasonable amount of time and effort to community enterprises and community improvement.

The beginning teacher should take advantage of opportunities to become acquainted with parents and other residents of the community. He should not expect to be accepted by parents and other community citizens without exhibiting a genuine spirit of friendliness and interest in people and community affairs. He will do well to act as though he intends to live his entire life in the community. It is entirely possible that this is what will happen; it has happened for many teachers.

SUMMARY

The kind of career one will have in teaching is affected by the nature of the first year. The success of the first year is determined to a considerable extent by the care with which plans are made for it.

It is desirable to establish criteria to aid one in obtaining a po-

---

[3] Bel Kaufman, "The Real World of the Beginning Teacher," *NEA Journal* 54:17–19, October 1965. *Up the Down Staircase* is a publication of Prentice-Hall, Inc.

sition. Points to be considered include community, the instructional program, professional assistance, financial considerations, and personal satisfaction. Institutional placement services, a commercial placement agency, or a bureau affiliated with a state department of education or teachers' association might be used to aid in locating a position. The letter of application, application form, and interview, when properly understood and used, are helpful to the prospective teacher and the employing official. It is important for the teacher to understand the teaching contract and to use it ethically.

The prospective teacher needs to understand certification requirements and to assume responsibility for meeting requirements and obtaining a certificate.

Preparing for living and teaching in a new situation should include rethinking one's experiences as a student teacher or intern; making desirable personal arrangements, including a place to live; and arranging for personal services of various kinds. A good beginning can be facilitated by meeting with the principal, attending orientation meetings, and making detailed plans for the first day. Specific suggestions were given.

Living as a responsible community citizen is both an opportunity and a responsibility for the teacher. The beginning teacher will be aided in obtaining community cooperation and support by acting as though he intended to live his life there.

USEFUL REFERENCES

Berlin, I. N. "Unrealities in Teacher Education," *Saturday Review* 47:51; (December 1964) pp. 56–58, 65.

Blair, Lois C. *The Student Teacher's Experiences in the Community.* Cedar Falls, Iowa: The Association For Student Teaching. Bulletin No. 21, 1964.

Eye, Glen, and Lane Willard. *The New Teacher Comes to School.* New York: Harper and Brothers, 1956.

Garrett, Henry E. *The Art of Good Teaching*. New York: David McKay Company, Inc., 1964.

Jensen, Janet, and Norman Jensen. *The Student Teacher: Managing an Elementary Classroom*. Cedar Falls, Iowa: The Association for Student Teaching. Bulletin No. 23, 1964.

McGeoch, Dorothy. *Learning to Teach in Urban Schools*. New York: Bureau of Publications, Teachers College, Columbia University, 1965.

National Education Association. *Selections from the NEA Journal for the Beginning Teacher*. (Pamphlet, no publication date indicated.) The Association.

Stout, Irving W. and Grace Langdon. *Parent-Teacher Relationships*. Washington, D.C.: National Education Association, 1958.

CHAPTER TWELVE
PLANNING FOR CONTINUED PROFESSIONAL GROWTH

When a young man or woman accepts a teaching position, he or she discovers that significant opportunities and responsibilities accompany membership in that profession. To become a capable teacher requires considerably more thought and effort than need be expended in completing a teacher education curriculum and locating a position. It is important to identify and explore these opportunities and responsibilities while working as a student teacher or intern.

DEVELOPING INCREASING COMPETENCY AS A TEACHER

Even the best program of teacher education, including student teaching and/or the internship, cannot fully prepare one to become a thoroughly competent teacher in a specific teaching situation. Continued preparation is essential to success in any profession and especially in teaching.

Continuing as a Student of Teaching

The professional teacher continues to search for more knowledge of his field, for more effective ways of understanding children and how to work with them, and for ways to improve his teaching procedures. The skillful and successful medical doctor, dentist, lawyer, or architect continues to refer to the textbooks, notebooks, laboratory results, and lecture notes of his college or university years and to study current professional literature. The teacher who would become increasingly competent in his profession must also continue as a student throughout his career. A continuous search for positive answers to the following questions should help in the achievement of this goal.

1. Am I improving my knowledge of the ways pupils learn? Am I using this knowledge effectively?

2. How well am I discovering and meeting individual needs?

3. How effectively do I motivate pupils to discover their own educational needs and help them meet those needs?

4. Am I increasing my understanding of children and youth? Am I applying this knowledge in ways which yield maximum results?

5. Am I increasing my ability to cope with behavior problems in the classroom, to eliminate problems through the use of preventive measures, and to help pupils acquire an increasing amount of self-discipline?

6. Do I employ methods of teaching which are in accord with those recommended and used by leading authorities in my teaching field?

7. Do I continue to reflect on what was learned during my student teaching and/or internship experience? Do I, without question, continue to employ procedures and practices similar to those used by my supervising teacher, or do I make use of only those which, after careful thought and study, seem to be in line with sound educational theory and best practice?

8. Do I confer with colleagues in the local school, my former college supervisor, supervising teacher, major professors, or other knowledgeable educators in a continuing effort to synchronize theory and practice in a manner which will increase my effectiveness as a teacher?

Fostering Professional Development

The following sections call attention to means of professional advancement which many teachers have found useful.

Utilizing research findings. Because he is occupied with daily teaching responsibilities, the classroom teacher is not likely to engage in extensive research activities. In the past many teachers have appeared to hold the view that knowledge of the results of educational research is a concern of specialists, not of classroom teachers. Some even become a bit frightened when the word "research" is mentioned. The professional capability of the teacher and the welfare of pupils are jeopardized when this attitude is held. The beginning teacher who accepts this view is missing the benefits that can come to the consumer of sound and useful research. Fortunately, progress has been made in reporting research findings in a manner suitable for use by teachers. It is essential to the long-range professional development of the new teacher that he form the habit of utilizing these results.

There are two ways one can keep reasonably well informed with the expenditure of a minimum amount of time and effort. A series of bulletins with the general title, *What Research Says to the Teacher,* has been prepared through the combined efforts of the Department of Classroom Teachers and the American Educational Research Association, both affiliates of the National Education Association. Each bulletin of approximately thirty pages contains helpful information "for teachers everywhere who want concise, accurate, and authoritative information about subject matter techniques and about human growth and development, learning processes, and organizing for instruction." [1] Each publication contains a summary of pertinent research on a specific topic of significance for teachers. A list of useful references is included in each bulletin.

A second source of information about research is professional magazines for teachers. The teacher who reads several such publications regularly, including at least one in his field of specialization, can learn much to help him become informed of new developments.

[1] Over thirty bulletins have been prepared to date. They currently sell for 25 cents per copy, with reduced prices for ten or more titles. Bulletins or a brochure containing a list of titles may be obtained from the National Education Association, 1201 Sixteenth Street, N.W., Washington, D.C.

One type of research deserves special mention. This is the continuing research on teaching competency. Although it is recognized by teachers, other educators, and researchers that consensus has not been reached on the components of "good" teaching, individuals in these groups need to be aware of the need for continuing study and experimentation with a view to defining more clearly what is meant by "good" teaching. The teacher who is interested in furthering his understanding of teaching and his skill as a director of learning in the classroom will profit from consistent study of research results in this area. Findings of studies by such researchers as Barr, Flanders, Hughes, Mitzel, Ryans, and Smith can be included in this category.[2]

Although most classroom teachers will ordinarily be consumers rather than producers of research, they should not overlook opportunities to become involved in experimentation. There are numerous opportunities, either individually or in cooperation with others, for the ambitious teacher to participate in research activities. There are wide variations in both the magnitude and the complexity of research projects. The elementary teacher who explores the use and effectiveness of the "Initial Teaching Alphabet" or the secondary school teacher who experiments with the

[2] For results of research by these individuals and others see:

A. S. Barr and Robert E. Jones, "The Measurement and Prediction of Teacher Efficiency," *Review of Educational Research,* 28 (June 1958), 256–264.

Bruce J. Biddle and William J. Ellena, *Contemporary Research on Teacher Effectiveness* (New York: Holt, Rinehart and Winston, 1964).

Ned A. Flanders, "Diagnosing and Utilizing Social Structures in Classroom Learning," in *The Dynamics of Instructional Groups.* 59th Yearbook Part II, National Society for the Study of Education. (Chicago: University of Chicago Press, 1960), Chapter 9.

Marie Hughes and associates, *A Research Report: Assessment of the Quality of Teaching in Elementary Schools* (Salt Lake City: University of Utah Press, 1959).

Harold E. Mitzel, *A Behaviorial Approach to the Assessment of Teacher Effectiveness.* Office of Research and Evaluation, Division of Teacher Education, College of the City of New York, 1957.

David G. Ryans, *Characteristics of Teachers: Their Description, Comparison, and Appraisal, A Research Study* (Washington, D.C.: American Council on Education, 1960).

B. O. Smith, "A Concept of Teaching," *Teachers College Record* 61 (1960), 229–241.

use of various techniques and instructional media in teaching the gifted engages in a type of research which can be very useful to himself and others. In fact, research of this kind may result in greater value to the individual teacher and his school than participation in a large and complex research venture in which the teacher is less actively involved. The individual who is interested in increasing his capability as an experimenter or investigator will find considerable information in the educational literature to aid him.[3]

Developing creativity in teaching.   Many who have studied the work of teachers and the results they achieve agree with the writers who state that:

. . . most teachers teach in a way reflecting the concept that education consists primarily of what we put into children rather than what we can get out of them. It is admittedly an exaggeration—but it may help us make our point—to say that more often than not children seem to be viewed as computers in whom we store information so that it can be recalled upon certain signals.[4]

Marie Hughes, a respected researcher and student of teaching, implies a need for a more creative approach in dealing with elementary children in the classroom:

The furniture in the classroom, the color on the walls, the illustration in books . . . have all changed, as has the appearance and grooming of the teacher. But the basic pattern of teacher-child relation has not changed.[5]

There have always been those who search for improved, ingenious, and productive ways of helping their pupils and encouraging creativity in them. However, the need for creative persons in our present complex society is well stated in the following:

[3] The following is one example of a useful reference: Fred P. Barnes, *Research for the Practitioner in Education* (Washington, D.C.: Department of Elementary School Principals, National Education Association, 1964).

[4] Seymour B. Sarason, Kenneth S. Davidson, and Burton Blatt, *The Preparation of Teachers: An Unstudied Problem in Education* (New York: John Wiley and Sons, Inc., 1962), p. xii.

[5] Marie Hughes, *op. cit.*, p. 186.

Now, more than ever before in our history, creativity and its ramifications are occupying our attention. The incredible advance in knowledge, both constructive and destructive, by the sciences of the Eastern and Western hemispheres has placed us in a position where creative approaches to physical realities as well as to the problems of complex human relations can mean the difference between survival or annihilation. Individuals, groups, and nations are faced with the choice of creating new ways of meeting these changes or of facing disaster.[6]

It seems quite obvious as one looks to the world in which present and future pupils will live as adults that creativity will become increasingly important. What are the components of teaching that are likely to encourage creativity in pupils and thus help them meet conditions they will encounter? The creative teacher is skillful in comprehending the uniqueness of the setting in which instruction is occurring at any given time. He will make full use of the learning opportunities inherent in each specific situation. He will identify the components or elements in each situation which might serve as points of departure for deepening understanding and developing concepts. The following points are suggested for consideration by the individual who wishes to become a creative teacher. He will:

1. Continue his quest for greater competency in teaching and engage in continuous self-evaluation and self-improvement.

2. Seek constantly and through every possible means to discover the potentialities and needs of each pupil he instructs.

3. Challenge each pupil to achieve the best results of which he is capable, communicate to each individual the fact that he is interested in him, and help each learner increase his own expectations of himself.

4. Endeavor to develop understanding as contrasted with memorization.

5. Encourage exploration and discovery on the part of the learner without usurping the pupil's role.

6. Introduce each new teaching-learning situation with enthu-

[6] Mary Lee Marksberry, *Foundation of Creativity* (New York: Harper & Row, Publishers, 1963), p. 3.

siasm and with a sufficient number of suggestions so that pupils are encouraged to begin the undertaking with interest. The creative teacher is a good motivator.

7. Utilize a variety of teaching procedures.

8. Use a variety of instructional materials, aids, and media, and be willing to investigate the use of promising innovations.

9. Help the learner discover relationships, obtain meanings, and integrate curriculum content as a means of aiding him to become an integrated personality.

10. Encourage an optimum amount of pupil participation and pupil-to-pupil interaction, as contrasted with teacher dominance of the classroom.

11. Respect the contributions and thinking of pupils, even when they are erroneous, as a step in the process of discovering the truth.

12. Involve pupils in decision making and lead them to assume responsibility for the decisions they make.

13. Place a minimum amount of emphasis on grades and encourage self-evaluation with a view to helping each pupil increase his own accomplishments.

Obtaining assistance from organizations for teachers. Every profession maintains one or more organizations for the benefit of its members. Such organizations as the American Medical Association which serves the members of the medical profession and the American Bar Association of the legal profession are well-known examples. There are numerous professional organizations for teachers. Several hundred are listed in the Education Directory of the U.S. Office of Education.[7] This number includes state, regional, and departmental subdivisions of the National Education Association and many unaffiliated organizations. Apparently there are many teachers who are poorly informed about the role or

[7] *Education Directory* is published at regular intervals. Part 4, "Education Associations," contains a list of: "National and Regional Associations"; "College Professional, Fraternal, Honor Societies, and Recognition Societies"; "State Education Associations"; "Foundations"; "Religious Education Associations"; and "International Education Associations."

264 PLANNING FOR A CAREER IN TEACHING

function of professional organizations; relationships between organizations; and ways the individual teacher may either contribute to, or receive help from, a specific organization.

Beginning teachers are sometimes confused by the number and variety of possible affiliations and need help in determining which will be of most benefit to them. The following brief outline should help the teacher to obtain information and reach a decision.

1. What are the names of some of the organizations that are likely to be most helpful?
2. For each organization under consideration:
    a. What are its main purposes?
    b. What is the size of the membership?
    c. What are its publications, if any?
    d. How much are the dues?
    e. What are the benefits of membership in the organization?
    f. What opportunities are available for working to improve the profession?
3. Which *specific* organizations will both meet needs for professional growth and provide opportunities for service to the profession of teaching?

After considerable study and discussion with the supervising teacher and other local school personnel, one group of prospective teachers working with college supervisors in a seminar agreed that membership in the following types of professional organizations should be suggested for consideration as a minimum list for a beginning teacher.

1. A national organization of a general nature—National Education Association.
2. A state organization of a general nature—State Teachers Association.
3. A local organization of a general nature—Classroom Teachers Organization.

4. The local organization for parents and teachers.

5. At least one organization in the teacher's area of specialization.

Some teachers may believe that the amount of money involved in the payment of dues for membership in organizations in the categories mentioned above is excessive. Most, however, are likely to realize that it is quite moderate when considered in terms of a percentage of current salaries for teachers. The large number of classroom teachers who belong to more organizations than recommended by the above group indicates that many teachers do consider it a minimum list. It is revealing to some teachers to discover that dues paid each year by those affiliated with a craft or other labor union often exceed by a considerable amount the expenditures required for affiliation with professional organizations. Beginning teachers and experienced teachers as well are often unaware that some teachers spend less for dues in professional organizations than for such personal items as tobacco, soft drinks, liquor, cosmetics, and numerous "luxury" items. The professional teacher, like the professional doctor, lawyer, or scientist, realizes that he can not keep up to date, maintain his skill, and thus be in demand by discriminating clients without membership in helpful professional organizations with the consequent expenditure of funds. Like the successful businessman or industrialist he will "plow profits back into the business" and allocate money for "research and development."

Prospective teachers sometimes ask the question, "Must I join a teachers' organization?" There is no legal requirement that teachers affiliate with any organization or group. It should be pointed out, however, that officials frequently employ only those persons who, as a means of furthering their own professional growth, have sought help through such affiliation or have initiated plans for taking such action. Many school administrators are aware of the fact that the individual who, while a student or first-year teacher, has taken advantage of the assistance provided by professional organizations is likely to be a person who will continue his growth in service. The individual who studies the possible benefits of affiliation with professional organizations for teachers will discover that the following kinds of assistance can be provided:

1. Publications in specific subject matter fields.

2. Results of recent research in subject fields and in the general aspects of a teacher's work.

3. Magazines, yearbooks, bulletins, other publications, conferences, and workshops to keep him informed of what other teachers are doing as an aid in improving his own performance.

4. Information about education in countries other than the United States.

5. Assistance in understanding the basic purposes of education under a democratic form of government. An illustration is the work of the Educational Policies Commission of the National Education Association and the American Association of School Administrators.

6. Assistance to teachers' groups in the development of salary schedules and in their efforts to obtain adequate salaries.

7. Aid to teachers through efforts to obtain needed legislation for the improvement of schools, for tenure and retirement laws, and for improved working conditions for teachers.

8. Assistance in defending individual teachers and groups of teachers when their rights as citizens or as members of the profession are jeopardized.

The National Education Association is the largest and most influential organization for teachers in the world.[8] It sponsors numerous projects and services of the kind mentioned above. It has state affiliates in each of the fifty states and maintains contact with local organizations in each state. It maintains over thirty strong departments to serve the needs of various groups. Examples are the National Council for the Social Studies, the Associa-

---

[8] According to a statement in the *NEA Reporter* of June 17, 1966 published by the National Education Association, the membership for the 1965–66 school year was 986,113.

tion for Supervision and Curriculum Development, and the National Association of Secondary-School Principals. The *NEA Journal*, the official publication of the National Education Association, is read throughout the world by teachers, other educators, and laymen. In addition, the organization publishes and distributes a wide variety of professional literature. Some idea of the wealth of material available from this source may be gained from the fact that the *Publications Catalog*, which lists and describes approximately 1000 items, comprises 36 pages.[9]

The American Federation of Teachers is an organization of the "teachers' union" type. The AFL-CIO (American Federation of Labor–Congress of Industrial Organizations) is the parent organization. The number of teachers belonging to this organization is small when compared to the National Education Association but it is nevertheless influential in certain areas of the country, especially in urban school systems. The *American Teacher* is the official publication of this organization. National headquarters are in Chicago, Illinois and informative publications about the goals and work of the American Federation of Teachers may be obtained from that source.[10] The organization places considerable emphasis on efforts to obtain improved working conditions for teachers. As an affiliate of a labor organization, it assumes the labor union view toward administrators. A statement in literature distributed from the national headquarters makes this position clear:

Superintendents or other administrative personnel who are in the position of hiring and firing are not eligible for membership. The AFT regards the position of Superintendent with highest respect but rightfully considers him to be an Agent of Management.[11]

[9] The current *NEA Handbook for Local, State, and National Associations* contains a list of state and local affiliated associations, also departments, commissions, committees, and other pertinent information. The current *Publications Catalog* may be obtained by writing the National Education Association, 1201 Sixteenth Street, N.W., Washington, D.C. 20036.

[10] American Federation of Teachers, 716 North Rush Street, Chicago, Illinois. According to figures presented in the *American Teacher* of June 1965, the membership at the end of the 1964–65 school year was 112,000.

[11] From a statement with the title "Who May Belong," available from AFT headquarters, Chicago, Illinois.

Demonstrating ethical behavior. The teacher who is serious about increasing his professional competency will understand and practice ethical behavior. As a student teacher or intern he has opportunities to work with school personnel who demonstrate a high type of personal and professional conduct. Every highly regarded profession has developed a code of ethics for the guidance of its members. The best known code of ethics for teachers is that prepared by a committee of the National Education Association and adopted by that organization. Careful study of, and frequent reference to, this code can be of real help in developing ethical behavior. It delineates the components of ethical behavior in detail. It consists of a "preamble" with appropriate guidelines listed under four main headings or "principles" as follows:

Principle I   Commitment to the Student
Principle II   Commitment to the Community
Principle III Commitment to the Profession
Principle IV   Commitment to Professional Employment Practices [12]

Additional aids to the development of competency. One of the most essential and most helpful means of increasing one's competency in teaching is through professional reading. It has always been necessary for the individual interested in in-service growth to keep informed about changes in both theory and practice. It is more necessary at this time than in the past. The changes that are taking place in the field of mathematics and in the sciences illustrate the need for keeping up to date.

The tremendous amount of professional literature published continually makes it necessary to select and discriminate. A reading program which will allocate time for study of publications which appear at regular intervals, such as magazines, and those

---

[12] NEA Committee on Professional Ethics, *The Code of Ethics of the Education Profession* (Adopted by the NEA Representative Assembly, Detroit, Michigan, July 1963). Printed with permission of the National Education Association, Washington, D.C. Copies of the code may be obtained from the NEA.

which appear at irregular intervals, such as significant books or research reports, is desirable.

Although money as well as time must be budgeted if one is to develop and maintain an adequate reading program, expense need not become burdensome. Professional magazines are included in the membership dues of many organizations for teachers. Most schools subscribe to certain professional magazines and maintain a professional library for the use of teachers. Many of the corporations which publish books and other instructional materials provide free bulletins to teachers, and these can be used to keep informed in certain areas. In some communities, especially in the larger cities, the public library contains books, magazines, and other valuable literature of a professional nature for teachers. Other sources from which professional reading materials may sometimes be obtained include the state office of public instruction, the state teachers association, a state traveling library, or the teaching materials center of a college or university.

There is no substitute for one's own personal library of professional books. The development and maintenance of an adequate collection of significant educational classics, current books, and magazines is essential to development of teaching competence.

Professional growth can be fostered by utilizing the resources of various colleges and universities. In most instances it will be desirable for the teacher to keep in touch with the teacher education institution from which he has graduated. Some institutions have developed a program and allocated staff which makes it possible to maintain close contact with, and provide a certain amount of assistance to, teachers in their first year or two in local schools. Even when this type of follow-up service is not provided as a part of a planned program, the former college supervisor or other teacher education personnel will usually be available for conferences on the campus or for an occasional visit to the school. Other help from the teacher education institution may be obtained from enrollment in summer sessions, workshops, Saturday or evening classes, and attendance at conferences.

WORKING FOR AN IMPROVED PROFESSION OF TEACHING

There are certain qualities, characteristics, and behavior which identify a truly professional person. This is emphasized by Margaret Lindsey who writes:

An individual who qualifies as a professional, regardless of the particular profession of which he is a part:

Is a liberally educated person.

Possesses a body of specialized skills and knowledge related to and essential for the performance of his function.

Is able to make rational judgments and to take appropriate action within the scope of his activities, and is responsible for the consequences of his judgments and action.

Places primary emphasis upon his service to society rather than upon his personal gain.

Actively participates with his colleagues in developing and enforcing standards fundamental to continuous improvement of his profession and abides by those standards in his own practice.

Practices his profession on a full-time basis.

Is engaged in a continuing search for new knowledge and skill.

The teaching profession should be no exception in requiring its members to qualify by these standards.[13]

Both opportunities and responsibilities for the individual entering the teaching profession are greater today than in past years. Certification requirements have been increased and teachers are better prepared now than they were some years ago. Instructional materials are of higher quality and are more abundant. School buildings which make possible the development and administration of improved curriculums are being planned and constructed. Working conditions and salaries for teachers are improving, and promising innovations are being introduced continually.

One would be naive to assume that all the difficult problems in teaching have been solved or that most teachers have arrived at the advanced state of professionalization mentioned above as

[13] Margaret Lindsey, ed., *New Horizons for the Teaching Profession* (Washington, D.C.: National Commission on Teacher Education and Professional Standards, National Education Association, 1961), p. 6.

highly desirable. There are still teachers with inadequate preparation, classrooms with antiquated and limited instructional materials, crowded and inadequate school buildings, and teachers who are hampered in their work by poor working conditions and low salaries. As teachers work individually and collectively to improve undesirable conditions in schools, they also contribute directly or indirectly to the building of an improved profession for teachers. This can be done in such ways as the following. The teacher can:

1. Engage "in a continuing search for new knowledge and skill." This must be done by the teacher who wishes to maintain his own professional integrity and receive the deserved esteem of his colleagues, his pupils, and the public.

2. Give financial support to professional organizations which are working for improved educational programs for children and youth. This can be done through membership in worthwhile organizations and by purchase of appropriate publications which will contribute to the teacher's effectiveness.

3. Work in close cooperation with other educators and with lay individuals and lay groups toward the improvement of schools and school conditions. Capable and vigorous young teachers need to realize that many people must contribute time, effort, and money to accomplish desirable results.

4. Abide by the code of ethics of his profession; support ethical behavior on the part of his colleagues and oppose unethical behavior wherever it exists; and assume responsibility for aiding others, especially those just entering teaching, to understand and observe ethical conduct.

5. Assume responsibility for informing intelligent, energetic, and capable young men and women about the opportunities in the teaching profession and for helping them to make wise decisions about whether or not they should enter it.

6. Aid young people in teacher education programs to become capable teachers by providing encouragement and guidance and by sharing with them the knowledge and skill one has acquired through education and experience. This can be done in such ways

as welcoming them as observers in the classroom, through individual conferences, by sharing ideas and materials, by serving as a consultant in seminars, and by serving as a supervising teacher.

7. Cooperate with administrative and supervisory personnel and with colleagues in the development of a continuing in-service program which will contribute to the professional growth of school personnel.

8. Serve as an effective public relations agent for schools and a skillful liaison person in his own and other communities in a manner which will facilitate good communication between school and community and contribute to better education for children and youth.

MAINTAINING CONDITIONS FOR WHOLESOME PERSONAL LIVING

Every person, regardless of vocation, needs to adapt his manner of living to his environment in order to be productive and effective. The teacher associates with youth each day and pupils frequently are influenced by his attitudes and behavior. This places a special responsibility on him to exemplify the kind of behavior that will command the respect of good citizens both in and out of the classroom.

Maintaining Good Physical and Mental Health

Working with active and energetic children and youth requires the expenditure of a sizable amount of physical and nervous energy. Thus, it is imperative that a teacher be in good physical health. There can be little argument with the following statement:

. . . one needs to be educated in order to develop and protect one's health, and one needs abundant health to make full use of one's education. It is a reciprocal—and actual—relationship.[14]

---

[14] Elena M. Sliepcevich, *School Health Education Study* (Washington, D.C.: School Health Education Study, 1201 Sixteenth Street, N.W., 1964). A statement preceding page 1.

The welfare of pupils and teacher is jeopardized when the teacher is not in good health. Pupils are not likely to receive the kind of instruction they need and deserve if their teacher functions with reduced enthusiasm and vigor because he does not feel well. Pupils are severely handicapped when a teacher is absent from the classroom, especially for an extended period. The teacher needs to maintain a daily schedule which will provide for adequate rest and relaxation and an optimum amount of exercise. A proper diet is essential.

Like good physical health, good mental health of the teacher is important to the welfare of both teacher and pupils. Teachers experience the same pressures, anxieties, and frustrations that are common to every individual and, in addition, those which are peculiar to people who work with children or youth. The elementary teacher who spends the entire day with young children, no matter how challenging and stimulating they may be, needs enough association with wholesome adults during out-of-school hours to maintain an adult view of life. The secondary school teacher who works continuously with typical, or even the most mature, adolescents needs frequent contacts with his own peer group. The teacher needs to make a deliberate effort to develop a variety of adult interests to compensate for his extensive association with young people. He needs also to make provision for wholesome social and recreational activities which will contribute to good mental health.

The emotional well-being of pupils is influenced by the teacher's state of emotional maturity. This is recognized by Ryans when he states:

Good mental health, or emotional maturity, generally is assumed to be a requisite for satisfactory teaching performance. Emotional instability and maladjustment are believed to be not only detrimental to the teacher's efficiency but also to be reflected in both the intellectual and emotional behavior of the teacher's pupils.[15]

[15] David G. Ryans, Chapter 3 in Bruce J. Biddle and William J. Ellena, *Contemporory Research on Teacher Effectiveness* (New York: Holt, Rinehart and Winston, 1964) p. 84.

Further evidence of relationship is indicated in the following:

The significance of the teacher's role in mental health is well documented by research evidence. Bills has indicated that the concept of self held by a teacher has a direct effect on the child, specifically with respect to the child's self-feeling and thus his reaction to others. He has also shown that teachers with negative feelings about self will produce negative feelings about self in a significantly large number of children in their classes.[16]

Employing officials are giving more careful attention now than in the past to the selection of teachers who show promise of possessing and maintaining good physical and mental health.

The teacher and the pupils with whom he works will be fortunate if the school requires a periodic physical examination. It is regrettable that many teachers working in school systems where a periodic examination is not mandatory rarely receive a complete physical checkup. The teacher is reminded that a physical examination and consultation with a competent medical doctor at regular intervals can do much to prevent the development of health problems.

Managing Personal Finances

A good many professional people, including teachers, have acquired a reputation for inability to manage personal finances wisely. It frequently happens that an individual who is competent in his field and devoted to his profession finds little time to think about how his income may be used most economically for the essentials of food, clothing, and shelter, or how his savings may be prudently invested. As contrasted with the individual engaged in business who is often of necessity a student of finance, the member of a profession is reputed to be less capable in the management of money. It is not unusual to find that a young teacher who as a college or university student looked forward to his first year's salary as quite adequate discovers after several years of teaching that he is unable to "make ends meet" or has acquired a debt of

[16] J. Clayton Lafferty, Donald Dennerll, and Peter Rittich, "A Creative School Mental Health Program," *The National Elementary Principal*, 43 (April 1964), 32–33.

considerable size. It must be recognized that, on the other hand, there are many young teachers who as adolescents, as prospective teachers, or in the initial year of teaching have acquired the ability to manage their personal finances successfully.

Prospective teachers and first-year teachers frequently feel a need for assistance in making the transition from one who as a student has relatively little responsibility for managing money, which may have been provided by others, to one who as a first-year teacher has full responsibility for managing money he has received. The following suggestions should be helpful.

1. *Keep a professional goal in mind and lend financial support to the achievement of that goal.* The wise member of a profession, like the wise businessman or industrialist, will support and augment his initial investment. Expenditures which will increase one's competency as a teacher should receive priority. These may include expenditures for such items as additions to a professional library, dues to professional organizations, and funds for continuing one's education.

2. *Make a budget.* Include in the budget estimated income, estimated expenditures, and an amount to be allocated to savings. Make plans to adhere to the budget except for reasonable divergence for unusual circumstances or emergencies. A simple but adequate personal accounting system will facilitate administration of a budget. The individual in his first years of teaching who considers it impossible to budget for savings until some later date when he hopes his income will be larger is reminded that the experience of others has demonstrated that one who finds it impossible to save on a small income is not likely to save as his income increases. Postponing the day when one will "make ends meet" tends to become habitual. If not done at the beginning of the earning period it is not likely to be achieved later.

3. *Establish a sound financial credit rating in the community.* This can be done by opening an account with a financial institution or reputable business establishment and by meeting promptly all financial obligations.

4. *Exercise discriminating judgment in making contributions and donations.* It is important to learn before accepting a position about the official policy of the board of education or administration relating to contributions by teachers to projects for community improvement. One should, of course, support worthwhile community projects. After careful consideration of all the requests for funds, one might very well include the appropriate allocations in his personal budget.

5. *Learn to deal tactfully and effectively with those who might exploit a young and inexperienced person with an income.* It is common and legitimate practice for salesmen and representatives of business to maintain a file of those new to the community. Through various news media and often from published lists of school employees names of new teachers are readily available and afford a potentially lucrative market for those who are skillful in convincing the newly salaried teacher that he needs their product or service. It would be difficult to estimate the number of teachers who continue to make payments on such items as an automobile, insurance policy, or set of books sold them early in their first year of teaching—including many purchases which might have been omitted or delayed had the contact been made somewhat later.

6. *Develop a sensitivity to the relative value of items for which one's income may be expended.* It is important to keep in mind one's own personal goals and needs in the expenditure of money. The professional teacher will probably wish to include such goals as improving professional competency, maintaining good physical and mental health, and contributing to worthy enterprises. Two examples will illustrate what is meant by a sensitivity to relative value in terms of goals. One first-year teacher upon receiving his first salary check obligated himself to make such large monthly payments on a new and expensive automobile that he considered it financially impossible to affiliate with as many professional organizations as he had originally planned. His expenditures for a professional library had to be eliminated. A more foresighted first-year teacher budgeted his income and expenditures in a manner

which made provision for dues to professional organizations, additions to a professional library, enrollment in a needed university course during the second semester, and enrollment in graduate courses the following summer.

Living as a Person and with a Sense of Well-Being

Throughout this book emphasis has been placed upon the development of competency as a professional person. This has been its major purpose. The assumption has been made that the capable teacher will also be a well-adjusted individual whose personal life is satisfying and characterized by a sense of well-being. It has been assumed also that all the facets of one's life are so closely intertwined that to function most effectively in the classroom, the teacher's life outside the school must of necessity be pleasant and rewarding. Perhaps few people in teaching or in any profession fully achieve such a happy balance in personal and professional living. This goal will not even be approximated, however, unless one makes plans to bring it about. The following suggestions have been obtained through observation of teachers and from comments they have made on this point.

1. Attempt to budget time to provide for meeting professional responsibilities and for other activities as well. Plan an honest day's work and hold home work within reasonable limits.

2. Make teaching and related responsibilities a full-time job. "Moonlighting" is not a suitable practice for those in the teaching profession.

3. Maintain a personal financial budget and a simple system of accounting for income and expenditures. The professional teacher cannot function at his best when he is burdened with financial worries.

4. Make a realistic commitment to community responsibilities, but give professional responsibilities priority over all others. Some teachers are so burdened with work in various service, religious, and other organizations that little time and energy remains for the performance of professional responsibilities or for relaxation.

5. Keep out-of-school activities with children and youth to a minimum. Working with youth groups out of school does not provide the kind of stimulation that is needed for one who works with them throughout each week.

6. Make provision for spending some time outside the community engaging in wholesome and stimulating activities and broadening experiences.

7. Develop constructive and enjoyable associations with persons outside the field of teaching. Such contacts broaden horizons and help one develop an increased appreciation of the advantages and limitations of employment in other fields of work.

8. Explore a variety of possible leisure-time activities with a view to engaging in several forms of enjoyable and wholesome recreation. One can live more richly and with greater zest and enthusiasm if he exerts a continuous effort to upgrade his tastes for leisure-time pursuits.

9. Develop at least one hobby which can help you to forget regular duties and direct thinking into channels unrelated to responsibilities in the classroom.

SUMMARY

Even the best teacher education program cannot fully prepare one to become a thoroughly competent teacher. Continued preparation is essential to success in any profession, including teaching. Suggestions have been made to aid the teacher to continue as a "student of teaching."

The individual with a genuine interest in fostering his professional development has many opportunities for achieving this goal. Although some may participate in research projects, all teachers can benefit by utilizing research results, and significant findings are available to teachers in publications prepared for their use. There is a crucial need for creative teachers. Attention was called to procedures which characterize creativity.

Organizations for teachers represent another source of help toward in-service growth. A brief outline was suggested for ob-

PLANNING FOR CONTINUED PROFESSIONAL GROWTH 279

taining information about various organizations and reaching a decision about those with which to affiliate. Growth in competency includes growth in understanding and practicing ethical conduct. A code of ethics for the teaching profession was described. Professional reading is essential to increased competency, and the teacher needs to make adequate provision for it both by developing his own library and by utilizing other sources of pertinent literature.

In addition to fostering his own professional growth the capable teacher will be concerned about the in-service growth of others and the improvement of the teaching profession. Specific ways in which he may become involved in bringing this about were mentioned.

Maintaining desirable conditions for wholesome personal living is essential for the most efficient functioning in the classroom. This necessitates good physical and mental health; wise management of personal finances; and provision for rest, relaxation, and the development of out-of-school contacts and interests.

USEFUL REFERENCES

Biddle, Bruce J., and William J. Ellena. *Contemporary Research on Teacher Effectiveness.* New York: Holt, Rinehart and Winston, 1964.

Lindsey, Margaret, ed. *New Horizons for the Teaching Profession.* Washington, D.C.: National Commission on Teacher Education and Professional Standards, National Education Association, 1961

Marksberry, Mary Lee. *Foundation of Creativity.* New York: Harper & Row, Publishers, 1963.

National Commission on Teacher Education and Professional Standards. *The Development of the Career Teacher: Professional Responsibility for Continuing Education.* Washington, D.C. The Commission, National Education Association, 1964.

NEA Journal. Special Feature on "The Beginning Teacher" 54 (October 1965), 16–31.

Ryans, David G. *Characteristics of Teachers: Their Description, Comparison, and Appraisal, A Research Study.* Washington, D. C.: American Council on Education, 1960.

Sarason, Seymour B., Kenneth S. Davidson, and Burton Blatt. *The Preparation of Teachers: An Unstudied Problem in Education.* New York: John Wiley and Sons, Inc., 1962.

Torrance, E. Paul. *Rewarding Creative Behavior: Experiments in Classroom Creativity.* Englewood Cliffs, N.J.: Prentice-Hall, Inc., 1965.

Zirbes, Laura. *Encouraging Creativity in Student Teaching.* Cedar Falls, Iowa: The Association for Student Teaching, 1956.

APPENDIX A

EVALUATION OF SUPERVISED TEACHING EXPERIENCE*

Student Teacher_____ Course No.(s)_____ Date _____

Subject _____ Grade Level _____ School _____ City _____.

A. Extent of contact with student teacher.

  1. The student teacher was under my supervision during the semester for: (Encircle) half day, full day, other _____

  2. I observed or supervised the student teacher in: (Encircle all that apply.) classroom, laboratory, shop, gymnasium, study hall, playground, auditorium, hall duty, cafeteria, extra-curricular activities, school party, faculty meetings, P.T.A., other _____

B. Evaluation based on contacts with student teacher: (Check each item in one column only).

	Outstanding	Above Average	Average	Below Average		Outstanding	Above Average	Average	Below Average
Appearance					Selects and organizes a variety of materials				
Voice					Makes good use of facilities				
Poise					Keeps adequate records and reports				
Emotional stability					Exhibits skill in directing learning activities				
Use of English					Exhibits professional ethics, interest, enthusiasm				
Expresses ideas effectively					Works well with children and adults				
Reacts favorably to criticism					Understands children and how they learn				
Has a good educational background					Provides for individual differences				
Comprehends subject matter					Fosters development of desirable pupil behavior				
Assumes responsibility					Helps students feel secure and useful				
Plans carefully—daily and long-range					Helps students learn to assume responsibility				
SUMMARY EVALUATION: In my judgment this student will become a teacher who is (Check in one column only)									

C. Outstanding strengths of student teacher:

D. Qualities or characteristics needing improvement:

E. Comments on the student's professional understanding, attitudes, philosophy, etc.:

Signed _____ Signed _____

        Supervising Teacher   Director of Supervised Teaching

Signed _____

             College Supervisor

* Form used at Indiana State University

281

APPENDIX B

REFERENCES FOR THE
SUPERVISING TEACHER
AND COLLEGE SUPERVISOR

I. Publications of the Association for Student Teaching.
These publications may be obtained from the Association for
Student Teaching, State College of Iowa, Cedar Falls, Iowa.

A. Bulletins (Bulletin Series)
   No. 1. *Guiding Student Teaching Experiences*
   No. 2. *Helping Student Teachers Through Evaluation*
   No. 3. *Helping Student Teachers Through Conferences*
   No. 4. *Helping Student Teachers Work with Parents*
   No. 5. *Helping the Student Teacher Assume Responsibility for His Own Growth*
   No. 6. *Encouraging Creativity in Student Teaching*
   No. 7. *Prospective Teachers Learn Through Their Experiences with Children*
   No. 8. *Achieving Quality in Off-Campus Professional Laboratory Experiences*
   No. 9. *The Purposes, Functions, and Uniqueness of the College-Controlled Laboratory School*
   No. 10. *Using Off-Campus Facilities for Student Teaching*
   No. 11. *Providing a Comprehensive Program of Professional Laboratory Experiences for Prospective Teachers*
   No. 12. *Preparation for Cooperative Decision Making*
   No. 13. *Student Teaching: A Mission of the Elementary and Secondary Schools*
   No. 14. *A Case Study of a Workshop*
   No. 15. *The Value Approach to Student Teaching*

No. 16. *Building Good Relationships: A Major Role of the College Supervisor*

No. 17. *The Relationship of Theory to Practice in Education*

No. 18. *Case Studies in Student Teaching*

No. 19. *The Student Teacher Evaluates Pupil Progress*

No. 20. *Research and Professional Experiences in Teacher Education*

No. 21. *The Student Teacher's Experiences in the Community*

No. 22. *New Developments, Research and Experimentation in Professional Laboratory Experiences*

No. 23. *The Student Teacher: Managing an Elementary Classroom*

No. 24. *Student Teaching: Two Years After*

No. 25. *The Student Teacher and Team Teaching*

B. Research Bulletins

No. 1. *Studies in Professional Laboratory Experiences in Teacher Education*

No. 2. *Admission Policies and Practices in Teacher Education*

No. 3. *Studies in Professional Laboratory Experiences in Teacher Education*

No. 4. *Leadership Through Research*

No. 5. *Research on Student Teaching 1950–1965*

C. Yearbooks Published since 1947. Yearbooks contain the most complete and up-to-date bibliography on teacher education available. Each yearbook contains an annotation of each article or publication appearing during the previous year.

1966 *Professional Growth Inservice of the Supervising Teacher*

1965 *Theoretical Bases for Professional Laboratory Experiences in Teacher Education*

1964 *The Role of the College Supervisor in Student Teaching*

1963 *Concern for the Individual in Student Teaching*

1962 *The Outlook in Student Teaching*

1961 *Teacher Education and the Public Schools*

1960 *Evaluating Student Teaching*
1959 *The Supervising Teacher*
1958 *Improvement of Instruction in Teacher Education*
1957 *Guidance in Teacher Education*
1956 *Four Went to Teach*
1955 *Functions of Laboratory Schools in Teacher Education*
1954 *Developing Facilities for Professional Laboratory Experiences in Teacher Education*
1953 *Curriculum Trends and Teacher Education*
1952 *Ways of Bringing About Desired Change in Teacher Education*
1951 *Off-Campus Student Teaching*
1950 *Audio-Visual Materials in Teacher Education*
1949 *The Evaluation of Student Teaching*
1948 *Professional Laboratory Experiences*

II. Other Selected Publications

Andrews, L. O., *Student Teaching*. New York: The Center for Applied Research in Education, Inc., 1964.

Bair, Medill, and Woodward, Richard G., *Team Teaching in Action*. Boston: Houghton Mifflin Company, 1964.

Bennie, William A., *Cooperation for Better Student Teaching*. Minneapolis: Burgess Publishing Company, 1966.

Brown, Thomas J., *Guiding a Student Teacher*. (Secondary) New York: Harper & Brothers, 1960.

Brown, Thomas J., and Banich, Serafina Fiore, *Guiding a Student Teacher*. (Elementary) New York: Harper & Brothers, 1962.

California Council on Teacher Education, *The Teaching Internship*. Sacramento, California: California State Department of Education, 1960.

Conant, James Bryant, *The Education of American Teachers*. New York: McGraw-Hill Book Company, Inc., 1963.

Corman, Bernard R., and Olmsted, Ann G., *The Internship in the Preparation of Elementary Teachers*. East Lansing, Michigan: Bureau of Educational Research, Michigan State University, 1964.

Cottrell, Donald P., ed., *Teacher Education for a Free People*.

Oneonta, New York: The American Association of Colleges for Teacher Education, 1956.

Curtis, Dwight K., and Andrews, Leonard O. *Guiding Your Student Teacher*. Englewood Cliffs, N. J.: Prentice-Hall, Inc., 1954.

Haines, Aleyne Clayton, *Guiding the Student Teaching Process in Elementary Education*. Chicago: Rand McNally and Company, 1960.

Hodenfeld, G. K., and Stinnett, T. M., *The Education of Teachers: Conflict and Consensus*. Englewood Cliffs, N. J.: Prentice-Hall, Inc., 1961.

Hunter, Elizabeth, *The Cooperating Teacher at Work: Case Studies of Critical Incidents*. New York: Bureau of Publications, Teachers College, Columbia University, 1962.

Lamb, Pose, *The Student Teaching Process in Elementary Schools*. Columbus, Ohio: Charles E. Merrill Books, Inc., 1965.

Lindsey, Margaret, ed., *New Horizons for the Teaching Profession*. Washington, D. C.: National Commission on Teacher Education and Professional Standards, National Education Association, 1961.

Milner, Ernest J., *You and Your Student Teacher*. New York: Bureau of Publications, Teachers College, Columbia University, 1954.

Myers, George R., and Walsh, William J. *Student Teaching and Internship in Today's Secondary Schools*. Columbus, Ohio: Charles E. Merrill Books, Inc., 1964.

Perrodin, Alex F., ed., *The Student Teacher's Reader*. Chicago: Rand McNally & Company, 1966.

Shaplin, Judson T., and Olds, Henry F., Jr., eds., *Team Teaching*. New York: Harper & Row, Publishers, 1964.

Shumsky, Abraham, *Creative Teaching in the Elementary School*. New York: Appleton-Century-Crofts, 1965.

Steeves, Frank L., *Issues in Student Teaching: A Casebook With Related Problems in Teacher Education*. New York: The Odyssey Press, Inc., 1963.

Stratemeyer, Florence B., and Lindsey, Margaret, *Working*

with Student Teachers. New York: Bureau of Publications, Teachers College, Columbia University, 1958.

Woodruff, Asahel D., *Student Teaching Today.* Washington, D. C.: The American Association of Colleges for Teacher Education, 1960.

INDEX

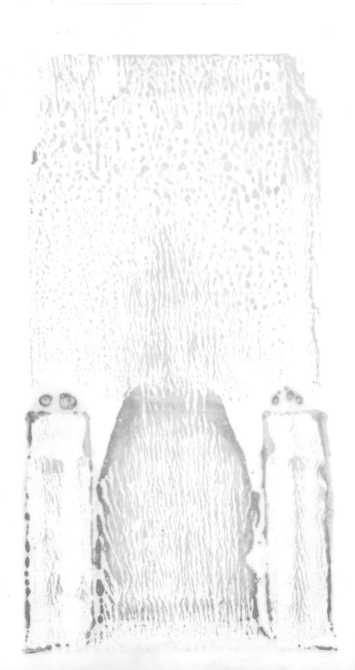